OFFICE ROMANCE

OFFICE ROMANCE

LOVE, POWER, AND SEX IN THE WORKPLACE

Lisa A. Mainiero, Ph.D.

RAWSON ASSOCIATES

NEW YORK

Rawson Associates
Macmillan Publishing Company
866 Third Avenue, New York, N.Y. 10022
Collier Macmillan Canada, Inc.

Library of Congress Cataloging in Publication Data

Mainiero, Lisa A.
  Office romance.

  Bibliography:
  Includes index.
  1. Sex in the workplace. I. Title.
HF5549.5.S45M35   1989   658.3'12   88-43096
ISBN: 978-1-5011-0967-6

Macmillan books are available at special discounts for bulk purchases for sales promotions, premiums, fund-raising, or educational use. For details, contact:

Special Sales Director
Macmillan Publishing Company
866 Third Avenue
New York, N.Y. 10022

Packaged by Rapid Transcript, a division of March Tenth, Inc.

Designed by Stanley S. Drate/Folio Graphics Co. Inc.

10 9 8 7 6 5 4 3 2 1

Printed in the United States of America

To David M. Mangini,
my husband and best friend

CONTENTS

PART TWO

Why Some Office Romances Work and Others Can Be Dangerous

7 THE SPECIAL CONCERNS OF WOMEN   116

PART FOUR

When Office Romance Involves a Power Game

8 LOVE BETWEEN UNEQUALS   129

PART FIVE

The Passion and the Pain: Who Gets Hurt?

PART SIX

What Management (and Couples) Should Know and Do

ACKNOWLEDGMENTS

The author would like gratefully to acknowledge the following people who helped in the process of putting together this book: Dennis N. T. Perkins, a former professor at Yale, who encouraged me not to be afraid of researching unusual topics; Cheryl L. Tromley, a Yale colleague who originally suggested the idea for this book; R. Keith Martin, Dean of the School of Business at Fairfield University, who provided research support; Paul Upham, senior vice-president at Donnelley Marketing, who reviewed many of the chapters on the management of office romance; Michael Mainiero, who provided many West Coast contacts for the research for this book; the library staff at Fairfield University, especially Nancy Haag and Rosemary Araneson, who helped with the reference material; Patricia Van der Leun, my friend and literary agent, who taught me about the world of trade publishing; and finally, Eleanor Rawson, who, after much kicking and screaming on my part, literally pulled this book out of me in the manner and style in which it is written.

"Office romance? You've got to be kidding!" said one academic colleague when I told him I was writing this book. "That's the fastest way to ruin your professional career. Don't do it!" he pleaded.

I thought about what he said for some time. Most academics in my field write popular books on leadership style or corporate strategies. Clearly a book on office romance would not fall into this category. But then I realized something that spurred me on. If this colleague believed I would suffer professional repercussions by simply writing about this controversial subject, there probably was an important story here that needed to be told.

Office romance represents a new wave of social change that is having a profound effect on corporate attitudes, values, beliefs, and philosophies. More and more, people are dating, meeting, and falling in love in the office. The management implications of this new phenomenon—and the consequences for office morale, productivity, ethics, and professional behavior—are far-reaching. Never before has such a subtle change sparked such confusion and concern.

In the pages that follow, you will find a number of stories about the people affected by this new phenomenon. Some have mismanaged their office affairs. Others have successfully negotiated an office relationship and, in the process, added a new dimension to the meaning of human resource management. Still others remain confused and bewildered about changes in social mores and corporate cultures.

I have written this book for those employees who are most affected by this change in corporate circumstance. This is a complex and highly interesting topic, one deserving of widespread research and attention.

Office romance involves much more than sex on the job. It has a major impact on workplace morale, satisfaction, and productivity. A new sexual revolution has taken place. We need to understand its consequences.

LISA A. MAINIERO, PH.D.
Fairfield, Connecticut
September, 1988

PART ONE

THE NEW SEXUAL
REVOLUTION:
LOVE IN THE OFFICE

1

LOVE IN THE WORKPLACE

There is no doubt about it. The workplace has changed. Love in the office is here to stay. In fact, for many workers, today's office is a very sexy place.

Sara, twenty-four, met the man of her dreams at her office. "Henry is everything I had hoped for in a man. We met in the duplicating room on our floor. He wanted to copy a letter he had written, but I was busy with several files. I made him wait, which really peeved him. A few weeks later, we had lunch together with friends at the company cafeteria. We have been dating ever since!"

Donna, twenty-eight, a telecommunications specialist, fell madly and passionately in love with her boss on her first day at work. "Dan mesmerized me from the start. I couldn't wait to get to the office on Monday mornings, and I spent my weekends doing overtime just to impress him. Talk about being motivated! I couldn't stop myself from working hard—even if I wanted to."

Barbara, thirty-three, met her husband at her office. After spending five years pursuing her career as a financial analyst while finishing her MBA at night, she was ready to settle down. "I had just about decided enough was enough. The bar scene was depressing. I am, and always have been, a homebody. But then Joe was hired into the company, and we were introduced by mutual friends. He's in engineering. . . . Once we met, we knew this was for real. We started dating, and a year later we were married."

More than ever before, the workplace has become a viable meeting ground for people to get to know one another, date, and establish a romantic relationship. Cupid is blowing kisses on company time. Many people believe that the modern-day workplace now serves as the contemporary equivalent to the dating game for today's busy professionals. A February 12, 1988, *New York Post* article headline read, "The Best Dating Service? Try the Workplace!"

Love is definitely blooming along the corporate corridors of America. Taboos against office romance are being openly violated. Colleagues routinely date, have flings, fall in and out of love, marry, and even divorce—and business goes on as usual. The lovers may be single or married, heterosexual or homosexual, open about their love or jealously protective of their privacy. They may be peers in the same department or colleagues in different divisions or subsidiaries. They may involve direct reporting relationships or cross hierarchical levels.

Just to give you an idea of how pervasive love in the office really is, a survey published in *Personnel* magazine in February 1986 by Carolyn Anderson and Phillip Hunsaker, professors of organizational behavior at the University of San Diego, showed the extent to which modern-day corporate romance is currently thriving. Over 86 percent of the employees whom they interviewed had been aware of, or had been involved in, an office romance. A survey of 444 readers of *Men's Health* magazine in fall 1987 showed even more surprising statistics: Over 50 percent of those surveyed had been sexually propositioned by someone at work; a quarter had sex in their place of work; and another 18 percent had sex with a coworker during work hours! Statistics like these make you wonder what you may be missing.

Current Trends Affecting Love in the Office

Why has romance in the office become so popular—and so widespread—so quickly? There are many reasons.

One reason concerns security, old-fashioned comfort, and safety. With the difficulties involved in meeting people of kindred spirit, and the rampant fear of sexually transmitted disease, we are more comfortable establishing relationships with those whom we already know well. We feel safer, more secure, and more knowledgeable about dating a coworker than, say, someone we meet at the local bar on a Saturday night.

One woman, a marketing executive who met her husband at work, said, "I don't know what I would have done if I hadn't met Jerry in the office. There is so much happening out there these days. . . . Jerry was someone with whom I worked on a series of projects. We got to know one another from our work together. I felt like I already knew him before we started dating officially. Now we're married, and we still work for the same firm."

Another reason is propinquity. The modern-day office has taken the place of church, neighborhood, and family networks in bringing people together. We choose employers today not only because we are challenged by a new and exciting job opportunity, but also because we genuinely will like the culture of the company and the people with whom we will work. In fact, in mobile America, it is probably more likely that we will develop friendships—and romantic relationships—with coworkers than in any other environment. The 1988 Bureau of National Affairs study, *Corporate Affairs: Nepotism, Office Romance, and Sexual Harassment,* quoting a Boston University study, reported, "It is now more likely that future spouses will meet at work than at school, social, or neighborhood settings. The work setting may be rapidly replacing the friendship network in the support system of employees."

Marian, thirty-five, a marketing representative, agrees. "At work, you become friends with your colleagues in a way that you may be unable to in other settings. You see their ups and downs, how it feels to lose a project. Somehow, working together makes you more vulnerable. There's a lot of support, mutual caring, and comfort."

Gloria, twenty-eight, an accountant in private practice, said, "It's just easier to get to know someone in the office. After all, you have been recruited to work for the firm on the basis of your fit with the corporate culture, so there are similar attitudes and values among the people with whom you work. You already have a built-in population of qualified romantic candidates."

In today's busy world, friendships are more likely to be formed in an office setting than anywhere else. Gone are the days of neighborhood socials, church associations, and lodge groups. Workaholism has overtaken more than half the American population. The quest for the American dream, while the cost of living rises, has made each of us more desperate for success.

A female lawyer said, "I have no time—free time—on my own to do the kinds of hobbies I used to. I'm always taking work home. That's why I met my fiance at the office. I had few opportunities to socialize elsewhere, and we already had a lot in common [with our work]."

This leads to a final reason—sheer practicality. One woman I met said, "The major benefit I see with office romances is that you know something about the guy before you start dating! At least you know whether he is married or not!"

"We only take one car to work," said Rosalie, forty-three, who met and married her husband at work. "It cuts down on our household expenses. Besides, the firm takes care of us as a team."

"Child care responsibilities are made easier because we both have the same schedule," said another.

A quiet sexual revolution is taking place. Love in the workplace has become so commonplace—and so natural—that few would deny that the implications are having a major impact on today's society.

The New Sexual Revolution

In my opinion, love in the workplace has become the new sexual revolution. Never before have sexual mores at work been so openly challenged.

Over the past two decades, sexual mores have become more flexible and open. Premarital sex and extramarital affairs have become more widely acknowledged and commonplace.

"Look, it's no big deal," said a female research scientist I interviewed for this book. "Sam and I had a lot in common, so we became involved in a physical relationship. We're from a different generation than some of the old fuddy-duddies who run this place. . . . We dealt with it, and that was that."

Those to whom she refers may be out of step with the times. Until recently, many corporations refused to allow married couples to work together. Love in the office never was openly acknowledged. But some corporations have opened their doors and embraced the new sexual mores. Some even believe it is good for business.

An executive in public relations at a well-known telecommunications firm said, "We believe . . . that there are a number of trends that suggest that developing policies for married couples working together is a good thing. . . . Our analysis of demographic trends shows more couples will be geographically restricted, and this may serve as a means to achieve staffing stability for the firm."

Changing corporate attitudes about the proper treatment and management of people also have contributed to the new sexual revolution. Recently, some corporations have undergone a subtle transformation from autocratic, "Theory X" management practices to participative, "Theory Y" management philosophies that value human resources. Those firms that now advocate a "Theory Y" approach are likely to espouse a more flexible attitude concerning married couples and workplace romance in general.

A woman who is a sales representative for a cosmetics firm that has undergone this transformation said, "I have worked for this firm for eighteen years, but I have seen more changes in corporate attitudes in the past five than in the previous thirteen. . . . Before, when I was first hired, we had no married couples here—if you met at work, one of you had to leave the firm. Now we have several married couples, and I'm thinking of suggesting my husband for a position that is now available."

But most dramatic and exciting is the change in women's roles that have altered workplace social mores. The influx of women into jobs that were formerly the sole province of men has made love in the office almost inevitable.

Under the prevailing norms of a generation ago, a corporate affair meant a semi-clandestine liaison between a male executive (married or unmarried) and a female secretary or low-level assistant. Doctors found wives in their nurses, bosses chased secretaries, and casting directors seduced young actresses desperate for a job. The office was a place where women who had not met and married a man in college could finally receive a "Mrs." degree.

In today's business environment, affairs are apt to involve coworkers of "equal ambition if not equal status," according to Susan Jacoby, writing in the _New York Times Magazine_ (November 29, 1987). It is now not unheard of for a woman to openly date one of her subordinates.

But women are moving ahead in more ways than one. Some are dating their bosses to get ahead. Others refuse to have anything to do with personal relationships at work, fearing that their professional reputations will be compromised.

"Women in the workplace now have an unfair advantage," said John, a thirty-year-old investment banker. "They can use sex to get ahead—even if it's just flirting—in ways that men can't. You can believe that the best salespeople are all women."

Karen, twenty-eight, disagrees. "I resent the notion that women are sleeping their way to the top. Most women that I know won't even consider a personal relationship at work."

But what corporate complications are created by an office romance? How has this quiet sexual revolution affected corporate behavior? Are women more likely to be compromised by love in the office than men? Are office romances really the answer to the dating dilemmas busy professionals face today? Or is a romance in the office likely to ruin your career?

Why I Wrote This Book

As a corporate consultant, professor, and researcher in the area of organizational behavior, I became interested in this new corporate trend while I was studying for my doctorate at Yale University. I realized that office romance was on the rise in many of the corporations for which I consulted. I also recognized that this new trend may not be without problems for workplace productivity, motivation, and corporate morale.

I first was alerted to the dilemmas of office romancing when I met Jennifer, age thirty, on a consulting assignment. I was part of a team brought in to design a new attitude survey for a well-known Fortune 500 corporation. Jennifer was a competent training and development specialist who had worked for this firm for five years. Having been coached to her present position by a powerful male mentor, she was respected for her credibility and expertise. When it was announced that Jennifer was heading up a new training program, people came running.

So imagine my surprise when, one day, I found Jennifer sitting in her office, looking depressed and despondent. I asked her what was wrong. She said, "Life is funny, isn't it?"

Taking the bait, I sat down. "Just hilarious," I responded. "Looks like you've had one of those days that gets you to thinking about things."

Jennifer said, "Here I am, this supposedly competent, professional woman, with my MBA behind me and a promising career in this department, and I may lose it all. For what? All because I fell in love with a man who works for this firm."

"Tell me what's going on," I said. "Maybe I can help."

Jennifer then began telling me about this man she was seeing. Not only was he married, but he was her boss's boss. The relationship had just been discovered by her own boss, who intimated he might take action against her.

"Jennifer," I naively said, "why would he have such a negative reaction to something that really is none of his business? After all, your personal life *is* your personal life."

Jennifer related several incidents in which her personal relationship had affected her business decisions, complicating the situation. Her amour had developed a habit of taking Jennifer along to a number of conventions out of state—conventions that her immediate boss really should have attended. In fact, her relationship had caused embarrassment for her boss on numerous occasions. In meetings when all three were present, Jennifer usually had access to important information that had not yet been told to her boss.

Jennifer said, "I feel like I'm walking on eggshells all the time. I'm glad he found out. Now it will all be out of the closet."

Jennifer wanted me to help her find a position in another

firm to resolve her dilemma. My initial reaction was that such a move might be too drastic. She was resolute, however, in her decision to leave the firm.

For weeks, I couldn't get Jennifer's dilemma out of my mind. On the one hand, I thought it was a waste of her talent to leave the firm. On the other hand, I understood the problems she was facing—that all three were facing—and how complicated the communication patterns among them had become. All my organizational behavior training told me it was a devastating situation for morale and productivity. But as a woman, I sympathized with her pain.

A few months later, on another consulting assignment, I met a very happy, equally talented woman who was in love with a colleague in her department. They had decided to get married, and the entire office was thrilled for them. In fact, on one of the days when I made an on-site visit, a "Jack and Jill" bridal shower was being orchestrated over lunch. Everyone wanted me to finish my business quickly so they could make the arrangements.

Curious about the positive reaction, I queried one of the workers, Vance, about the festivities. He said, "They really are a great couple. Jack has been a friend to all of us at one time or another, and Sally is a peach."

"No one in the ofice has been upset by their romance?" I ventured.

"Hell, no!" Vance said. "They've been great. We sort of pushed them together, because we all felt they would make a great team. Now that they're getting married, we couldn't be happier."

Melissa, another coworker who overheard my conversation, jumped in with her comments. "Not only are we pleased, but their romance really has improved morale in the office. With Jack and Sally together, we were able to resolve some of our previous conflicts and work things through in the spirit of compromise. Their relationship has had a decidedly positive effect."

A decidedly positive effect? How could this be? My natural curiosity as a researcher was aroused. Why did colleagues react so differently to both these romances? What had gone wrong with Jennifer's romance to cause her so much pain? What was so right with Sally and Jack that their coworkers openly supported their union?

I was drawn to the issue. When I accepted a position as an associate professor at Fairfield University, I decided to find out more about the topic. I wanted to know what effects office romances have on office morale, productivity, and motivation, what accounts for differences in coworker reactions, and under what conditions romances are likely to have positive and negative effects. In particular, I wanted to understand the impact of this new sexual revolution on women in the workplace. I also wanted to know how corporations were coping with the change.

About the Research for This Book

I began my research by reading everything that was written on the subject. I soon discovered that although much attention had been paid to this subject in the popular press, few serious academic researchers had tackled the topic. At the time I began my research, only two scholarly articles had appeared in the literature: a case study by Eliza Collins, then an editor of the *Harvard Business Review,* published in September 1983, and a survey by Robert Quinn, a professor of policy administration at the State University of New York—Albany, published in *Administrative Science Quarterly* in March 1977.

My second task was to gather data on the case histories of as many office romances as I could find. I talked to consulting contacts in the field, who regaled me with their stories. Friends, relatives, students, and acquaintances clued me in on romances they had seen and observed. When I heard an interesting case recounted, I interviewed participants or observed the subject in greater detail. After pursuing several leads, I gathered over thirty cases for my research.[1]

My third research task was to develop a survey of my own. I wanted to study a particular group—executive women—because I believed that the most polarized attitudes on this controversial subject would arise from women. I was granted the opportunity to survey 100 executive women in the Fairfield County area of Connecticut, drawn from a broad base of professional pursuits—

marketing, computer software/data processing, retail, medical/ legal, publishing, manufacturing, accounting, banking, media, insurance, education, and many other fields. Many of the women worked in Fortune 500 companies. Some had become entrepreneurs on their own. They told me of romances they had observed or in which they had participated. I analyzed their data and compared it to my previous case research for review.

To strengthen the survey results, I read a number of published reports of additional surveys and compared them against my own. The ones that appear frequently in this book are surveys by Carolyn Anderson and Philip Hunsaker, the professors at the University of San Diego who published the survey in *Personnel* magazine in February 1986; the original Quinn survey, published in *Administrative Science Quarterly* in 1977; and a survey of MBA student attitudes authored by Gary Powell, of the University of Connecticut, published in *Business Horizons* in July 1986. Other survey reports lent credibility as well: the 1988 Bureau of National Affairs report; an American Society for Personnel Administration survey on the management of office romance, published in *Personnel Administrator* in October 1987; and various newspaper and magazine articles appearing in publications such as *Business Week, Newsweek,* the *Wall Street Journal* and the *New York Times.*

I also spent a great deal of time discussing the issues with many colleagues, corporate contacts, and friends. I debated company strategies for handling office romances with my network of consulting contacts. I polled colleagues about attitudes toward office romance in the different industries where they worked. I contacted executives in forty different organizations to determine how they managed problematic office romances and to study their general attitudes and policies on this subject.

Finally, I wrote an academic article in October 1983 for the *Academy of Management Review,* a prominent management journal in my field, reviewing the relevant literature. Like Eliza Collins's article in *Harvard Business Review* and Robert Quinn's study in *Administrative Science Quarterly* before it, my article immediately caused a stir in the media. The press responded all over the globe—Australia, Brazil, Great Britain. In America, newspapers carried headlines about the research. I was approached by a literary agent to write a book.

Gathering the data for this book was simple. Whenever I mentioned this topic in conversation, a new story would surface. People willingly told me their anecdotes—at cocktail parties, on trains, in hallways, at the water cooler. I soon became absolutely convinced that the statistics on office romance are accurate.

As you read through the chapters that follow, you will find a number of case histories from three years of research that describe the joys, agonies, and dilemmas of those who have been involved in office romances. The names of case participants have been changed and company settings have been altered to further disguise personal identities. Some cases are composites drawn from multiple sources. Others are anecdotes used for purposes of illustration.

You also will find a number of quotes from the executive women I surveyed as part of the research for this book. Women mainly are quoted because my study primarily concerned the attitudes of women. However, the opinions of some male consulting contacts also are included for emphasis.

What This Book Will Reveal

What I learned from my contacts and survey research surprised me. A number of serious disadvantages should be considered in an office romance. But there also are some advantages.

It is true that *some* office romances spell trouble. Risks to career can pose a serious threat in some firms. The risks of gossip and sexual innuendo are real and should not be minimized. The widely publicized Bendix situation created a common myth that office romance is too complicated to be contemplated. Mary Cunningham, first hired as (then CEO of Bendix) William Agee's assistant and later promoted through a series of jobs to vice-president of strategic planning, was accused of sleeping her way to the top.

But office love does not always deserve such a widespread negative reputation. Although in some forms office relationships can be emotionally devastating for all concerned, office romance also has many surprising advantages. Love in the office, when handled properly and professionally, can energize the workplace.

In some cases, office love may improve worker morale, motivation, and productivity.

The benefits—and the risks—depend on the conditions, circumstances, and attitudes of the couple. This book will present the pros and cons, the conditions and circumstances, and the advantages and disadvantages of love in the workplace.

In my opinion, it should be everyone's responsibility to be aware of *all* the issues the new sexual revolution brings. By understanding both sides of the story, everyone who works in an office will be able to make an *educated* decision about corporate love—its benefits, risks, and far-reaching consequences for human resource management in the workplace.

2

WHY WE FALL IN LOVE
AT WORK

One day when I was looking for a chance to procrastinate before I began my afternoon activities, a colleague came to see me. I welcomed her interruption.

Maria poured a cup of coffee and sat down. "Guess what," she said. "Last night I finally went out with Jim, the new administrator who works on this floor."

I was all ears. This was the kind of conversation that could stretch out and allow me to procrastinate for a good hour. "Really?" I asked. "How was it?"

"Fantastic!" Maria smiled, filled with glee. "For months I have been watching him. I even dreamed about him once. Finally, last week we had lunch together, and last night we had an actual date. We had Chinese food and saw a movie."

"Sounds great," I said. "I'm glad you had a good time. What did you talk about?"

"University business, mostly at first," said Maria. "Then, later, we were able to just talk about ourselves. He told me how difficult the move here has been for him, and I told him all about my favorite topic—the problems of dating when you're a woman with a Ph.D."

Maria and I have had lengthy conversations on that particular topic a number of times. I decided to probe further. "What is it that attracted you to him in the first place?" I asked.

Maria sighed. "He's physically attractive, yes, but he has an air of assurance about him that I think really draws me to him. I watched him in an Academic Council meeting last semester, and I saw how he operates. I like his style." She paused. "I've been to all the bar scenes around here, and have had my share of jerks lately. I want to date someone at work whom I already know."

"Why at work?" I ventured.

"Because . . . at work you have a chance to observe the person, get to know him on a friendship basis first, and as a lover second. You can test the relationship a bit, and then determine how far you want to go. Besides, the best men around are the ones you work with. You have similar attitudes, beliefs, education; you basically can talk the same language. You already have something in common."

"You've dated men at the university before?" I asked.

"Oh, yes," Maria responded. "Not here, but elsewhere. I really feel it is the best situation."

Many people agree with Maria's perspective. Love is definitely blossoming on company time these days. If my survey results are any indication, you are probably aware of quite a few office romances like the one between Maria and Jim.

I cannot begin to tell you how many people have told me, "The office is the *only* place to meet people—I'm being worked so hard I never get a chance to meet anyone *but* coworkers!" Sixty-three percent of the women who responded to my survey said romance in the office is very common or becoming more and more commonplace. Seventy-nine percent also said they were aware of, or had been personally involved in, an office romance in their firm.[1]

The reasons my friend Maria gave for dating a man in the office have been echoed by a number of professional women. Working together allows a romantic friendship to develop naturally. And having work in common aids the unfolding of romance.

Debra, a thirty-eight-year-old former public relations executive now running her own entrepreneurial firm, said, "I have been involved in several office romances since becoming divorced. My job is in consulting to the not-for-profit sector—a high-pressure situation and quite difficult. Being with someone who understands the situation is a big comfort."

Sandra, forty-two, a secretary, said, "The men I meet in the office are much more interesting than those I meet in other settings. We already have a lot in common, so it makes everything else in the relationship easier."

In the office, we develop close friendships with coworkers. They become our family. We learn one another's hopes and dreams, strengths and limitations, hurts, joys, and expectations. This kind of closeness fosters a natural attraction.

According to Dr. Marcy Crary, an associate professor at Bentley College and author of an article reprinted in _Organizational Dynamics_ on this subject in Spring of 1986, the realities of office life are conducive to intimacy. Dr. Crary writes:

> Most of us have been socialized into thinking of intimacy and work as two separate compartments in our lives; intimacy takes place at home and work takes place at our place of employment. But for many people the realities of day-to-day experiences belie these rational arrangements of our worlds. Working closely together can create a sense of intimacy between people, or the creation of intimate relationships may be essential to performing the task itself.

Attractions at work may be quite natural—and even essential—to get the job done. Feelings of sexual attraction emerge spontaneously in an office setting, as they would in any other setting that brings people together. A marketing executive I surveyed said, "You don't turn off your feelings of sexual attraction just because you're walking through an office door. We are all human, and our hormones don't shut off between nine and five."

Gina, a forty-two-year-old real estate professional who participated in my survey, commented, "I think it is very normal to become attracted to someone with whom you spend more hours a day than with your spouse and with whom you have a great deal of common ground. Also, I think that many times men with whom you work respect and admire you as an equal in the industry . . . in a way that spouses cannot appreciate because they do not see you in action in the course of your work."

As this woman suggests, it is natural to expect that you would find yourself attracted to those with whom you work. *The workplace stimulates attraction.* Coworkers share common values and interests. Friendship leads to intimacy. Colleagues usually fall into the right age ranges, backgrounds, and qualifications for choosing future mates. Is it any wonder the statistics on office romance are on the rise?

The Facts That Foster Love at Work

Why is it, then, that we fall in love so easily in the workplace? I asked a number of women at an assertiveness training seminar this question.

- "The mere presence of good-looking men!" said one.
- "The pressures of making an important deadline arouse mutual excitement," said a newspaper reporter.
- "Power is sexy," said another.
- "Just being around people with whom you already have things in common," said a saleswoman.

All of their responses are right on target. Working closely together makes it easy for attractions to occur. Corporations informally spawn attraction as much as they officially discourage it. The long, hard hours put into working on an important contract, for example, can create an intellectually and emotionally stimulating climate. Shared commitments to a mutual cause can create a powerfully intimate bond. Corporate cocktail parties, business soirees, conventions, and travel assignments all add to the right ambience for romance.

According to a major report on interpersonal attraction written in 1969 by Ellen Berscheid and Elaine Walster, professors of psychology at the University of Minnesota and the University of Wisconsin respectively, *proximity* or propinquity is an important factor that explains why we become attracted to others.

When other factors are equal, the closer two individuals are geographically located the more likely it is that they will be attracted to one another.

"I know why Ellen and Spike got together," said one man I interviewed who told me about an office romance that emerged in his department. "It's because I constantly had them work together on the same types of projects. They both had the same expertise . . . but the long hours together working on the same projects really drew them together."

A February 15, 1988, *Newsweek* article reported that office romances are especially common in those professions in which employees are expected to spend long hours together on the job. Doctors in training, for example, who are on call twenty-four hours each day, often are confined to socializing mainly with other doctors and nurses. Associates in law firms, among journalists, and in some of the fast-paced financial professions on Wall Street all find that "shop talk often leads to pillow talk."

When you are so busy in your work life that you have little time for socializing, your primary friendship groups are formed at the office. When this happens, it is likely that romance will develop.

Two people whom I know became a couple after years of working together in the same entrepreneurial firm. "Joe and I did not start out on a romantic basis," said Veronica. "We were partners in the firm first. But after a while, we realized that our commitment to the business had developed into a commitment to each other. Dates with other men went nowhere. . . . They weren't interested in the same kinds of things that Joe and I were. After working together for two years, we realized that we were right for each other."

Robert Quinn, a professor of public administration at the State University of New York at Albany, agrees that proximity is an important factor in the formation of many office romances. For his article, "Coping with Cupid: The Formation, Impact, and Management of Romantic Relationships in Organizations," published in the March 1977 issue of *Administrative Science Quarterly,* he interviewed people in anonymous settings such as airport lobbies to define three types of office proximity that may lead to romance:

- *Geographic*, such a when partners shared the same office
- *On-going work requirement*, where partners were frequently thrown together due to task assignments, such as training, consulting, or supervising tasks, business trips, corporate socials
- *Occasional contact*, defined as meeting someone on a circumstantial short-term basis

Sixty-three percent of the romances he studied developed from geographic proximity. Seventy-seven percent of the cases developed from a shared task assignment. Very few romances were based upon short-term or occasional contact.[2]

My survey of executive women showed similar trends. Over two-thirds of the romances reported developed among boss-subordinate relationships or peer relationships in the same department. The close geographic proximity brought people together. Merely being together in an office working on the same kinds of assignments can lead to attraction. And through the bond that is created, love in the office sometimes can emerge.

PROXIMITY AND ATTRACTION: LAURA AND SANDY

I learned about the case of Laura and Sandy through a friend who watched this romance slowly build to its final crescendo. Laura and Sandy fell in love because of their proximity on an intense, highly politicized automation project in a large New York bank.

Laura said, "When I first met Sandy, I wasn't looking at him as a potential lover. It was strictly business. I knew enough about him to know he could do the job. I wanted the job done, that was all."

Because the automation project required an enormous amount of planning even prior to its implementation, Laura and Sandy soon found that most of their workdays were spent together. They worked many evenings on their mutual task, attending meetings, designing the appropriate composition for task forces, poring over the technical specifications. Rarely did they leave the office before seven-thirty or eight in the evening.

Often they ate lunches and dinners together. Both arrived at work before seven in the morning.

I wanted to know how the romance began. Laura described it in this way: "I'm still not sure how it happened. We just started talking, not just as coworkers on this new project, but as friends. I found that I could talk to him about anything."

Laura told me that one day she realized she was deeply jealous of Sandy's ex-wife, Jeanine. "During one meeting, my secretary came in with a message from Jeanine for Sandy. I became very upset, and told Sandy he should tell his ex-wife to call after hours. I was distant and argumentative for the remainder of the meeting. Afterward I thought about my extreme reaction to what ordinarily would have been a simple message. I knew then my feelings for Sandy had deepened more than I realized."

Meanwhile, the automation project captured the attention of upper management. Cocktail parties, business lunches, and trips to locations all over the country were held to preview the system. Laura and Sandy basked in the attention they were receiving.

"It was so exciting to be caught up in such a glamorous whirlwind of activity," said Laura. "We traveled together, met the CEO, gave presentations to the upper crust of the company, and were introduced to several board members. It was first class all the way."

One night, after a particularly late dinner together just before the system went on-line, Laura and Sandy lingered over their coffee. Laura said, "It got to the point where he knew everything about me—all about my work, my hopes, my dreams. And I wanted to know as much as I could about him. He knew more about what was happening with me than my own husband, who, as a lawyer, travels frequently across the country. I don't know when it happened, but one day I looked into Sandy's eyes and I knew I wanted him. After that, I could hardly concentrate when I was with him. I noticed everything about him—his hair, the color of his shirt, the hairs on his arms. I kept imagining what it would be like in bed."

The affair was passionate, loving, and intense. Laura said, "We would meet sometimes at a restaurant for lunch, and then go to his apartment. Everyone thought we were still at our meetings. Sometimes I would eagerly wait for my husband to leave on a business trip just so I could spend more time with him."

It lasted six months. But the tension produced by the affair caused Laura's driving ambition to falter. According to my friend, Laura lost a promotion she desperately wanted. "I think that was an important sign that things had to change," said my friend. "After that happened, she took charge of her life once more."

Laura broke off her affair with Sandy and simultaneously filed for a legal separation from her husband. Laura has since left the company, and now works for a real estate development firm in New York.

Intense Task Accomplishment Fosters Attraction

The mutual project that caused Laura and Sandy to meet put them in close proximity with one another, and this escalated the development of their romance. But proximity is only one part of the equation of falling in love at work. *Intensity* is another factor. Because feelings of success and accomplishment foster interpersonal attraction, the intensity with which we work to achieve success on projects also can lead to sexual attraction. Helen Gurley Brown, the editor of *Cosmopolitan* magazine, was quoted in Susan Jacoby's *New York Times Magazine* article on November 29, 1987, on this subject: "You can be sure that the more committed people are to their work, the more likely they are to fall for someone they meet on the job."

Have you ever been involved in a very intense, very important project which had to be completed by a tight deadline? Think back to how you felt about your colleagues at the time. Somehow, when we are involved in projects that require us to pursue our goals with single-minded dedication, the intensity with which we work fosters interpersonal attraction. We know we are working toward a common goal. A sense of bonding takes place. Especially when the project is successful, we feel physically and psychically tied to our coworkers. Sometimes, out of the bonding experience, a natural attraction ensues.

The film _Broadcast News_ shows how this can happen. The film's protagonist and news producer, Jane, was given a special assignment with Tom, a newly hired news anchor at her television network. Together, they worked at breakneck speed to make a deadline as news of the worldwide crisis arrived on the ticker-tape. Because Tom was a new hire, Jane did not believe he was ready to handle the special newscast, so she provided instructions via a wireless earphone to help him with his phrasing while on the air. Afterward, when the newscast was finally over, Tom met with Jane to tell her that the intense, highly pressurized experience they just went through was "like having great sex."

According to professors Bercheid and Walster, studies on interpersonal attraction show that intensity of the task and the act of cooperating with others toward the accomplishment of a common goal breed attraction. Doing things for others brings the norm of reciprocity into play. Ben Franklin used to say, "If you want a friend, let him do you a favor." When we work closely with others toward a goal that we share in common, the intensity of the experience causes us to like them more—and creates the foundation for sexual attraction.[3]

YOUNG DOCTORS IN LOVE: GERALD AND LINDA

Probably one of the most intense experiences of any profession is the work done in a hospital emergency room. This is the setting where Gerald and Linda's marriage was founded.

I met Gerald and Linda while searching for an investment home. They were selling, and my husband and I were buying. I noticed how complicated their child care situation was on one of my visits to preview the house. It was then that I asked Linda how she and Gerald met.

"In the hospital emergency room, working over a gunshot wound," said Linda. "Glamorous, huh?"

"Maybe not glamorous, but certainly unusual," I said. "Tell me what happened."

Their story was simple. Both Gerald and Linda had been assigned to complete their residencies at Yale-New Haven hospital. On a rotation basis, they were simultaneously assigned to emergency room duty. Although they knew each other through acquaintances, Linda had been seeing a medical school classmate whom she intended to marry.

"What impressed me about him at first was how he took charge of the situation," said Linda. "At the time, Dick was finishing his residency at Columbia-Presbyterian, so we hardly saw one another. Dick was not one to take charge, so the difference between them really came through to me."

"Sounds like it was a tough case," I said.

"It was one of those all-nighters," said Linda. "We split shifts watching over the patient. By working with Gerry on the case, I got to know him. We had a couple of lunches together that week, and for the next few months, when I saw him in the emergency room, we shared a special bond. Eventually we just started going out."

"How did others react?" I asked.

"No problem," said Linda. "This kind of thing happens in hospitals all the time. Doctors and nurses have affairs—you know all the stereotypes. The intensity of the work really brings people together. The only sticky situation was when I had to explain to Dick that I found someone else."

Similarity of Attitudes Also Breeds Attraction

Gerald and Linda's romance began because the intensity of their work together forged a common bond. But they also shared similar values, hopes, and ambitions in a way that Linda told me she and Dick did not.

Linda said that one of the reasons she chose Gerry over Dick was because "Gerry and I had a lot more in common. We worked for the same hospital, had the same specialties. Our philosophies about life and career were more similar than Dick's and mine."

Employees who work closely together often share comparable attitudes and values—and similarity breeds attraction. The more similar to us we believe that others are, the more attractive they are to us. The old adage "opposites attract" is only right for a small proportion of romantic friendships—and few of those last in the long run.

Adeline, twenty-four, who works for a video manufacturer, agrees that similarity is an important factor in attraction. "One of the things that first attracted me to Allan was merely the fact that we were very similar to one another. We had gone to the same schools, majored in the same major in college, and ended up in strategic planning through almost the same career routes. Our families even have equivalent backgrounds. . . . There was so much in common it would have been difficult *not* to become friends."

According to professors Berscheid and Walster, similarity of attitudes is a definite factor that promotes attraction. The saying "birds of a feather flock together" may have some merit when understanding the underlying mechanisms for attraction. When people share common attitudes and values, they are able to forge a solid basis for a friendship/romance.

The corporate world is notorious for selecting employees who are similar to one another to fit a corporate culture. If employees do not have much in common at the start of their employment, their attitudes become more parallel as they work together. This is referred to as the socialization process.

An employee at a well-known Silicon Valley computer firm, said, "There are a lot of benefits to dating employees in the same environment. The company serves as a good screening mechanism. Especially for companies with strong cultures, employees are chosen who are very similar to one another to begin with, the kind of people you'd like to date. They become even more homogeneous once inside."

COMMON AMBITIONS AND GOALS: LUCY AND LARRY

Two professors I know are a good example of the similarity and attraction. Lucy and Larry met while Lucy was an undergraduate and Larry was in graduate school working toward his Ph.D. I asked them to tell me the story of their romance.

"We met at a political meeting through friends," said Lucy. "Nothing unusual."

"What first attracted you to one another?" I asked.

"Well, Larry was doing something that I wanted to do— pursuing a Ph.D. Back in the Sixties, that took some courage.

We also were both rebels—you know, student demonstrations in the streets, that kind of thing. He was doing something I wanted to do, and that impressed me at the time."

I asked Larry what attracted him to Lucy. "Her politics," he said. "She made some strong statements that I agreed with. I admired her ability to stand up in front of a crowd and state her opinions."

They began their romance as students at the same university. But problems arose once Lucy applied for admission to Larry's doctoral program.

"Larry was a teaching assistant, and I was one of his students," said Lucy. "Everyone knew we had been seeing each other for over a year, because we had been living together much of that time. There were concerns about would he change my grade, that sort of thing."

They ironed out their difficulties by forcing Lucy to take classes in which she would minimize her contact with Larry. Larry also agreed to leave his grading at the office.

"Graduate programs, especially in politics, can be very competitive," said Larry. "It was an issue at the time."

Lucy accelerated her studies, and Larry took his time finishing his dissertation. They graduated the same year, and went on the job market together.

I asked if they had difficulties finding a job at the same university. "It really wasn't a problem," said Larry, "because once we got married, we marketed ourselves as a team. I would teach one semester while Lucy was writing, and vice versa. We shared the same position at the first two universities where we worked. It is only at the last university that we have held two separate positions."

The Sexiness of Travel

Lucy and Larry found each other because they shared similar values *and* were in the same location for a lengthy period of time. But sometimes attractions are acted upon as soon as employees *leave* the office. Travel assignments to exotic locations suspend office norms and bring people closer together through the shared experience. This is why travel is so sexy.

Undoubtedly you have heard many stories about "the convention caper." The general theme running through these anecdotes (and I'm sure many are exaggerated) is that conventions are a haven for sexual exploits and unprecedented lust.

Betty, fifty-five, a sales representative for a manufacturing firm, believes she has seen it all. "These sales conventions are a real ego trip for many of the men who attend. I've been in this business a long time. . . . For a number of years, I was the only woman around. I would routinely get propositioned as soon as the location of a sales meeting was announced. It was ridiculous."

Others disagree. Peter, forty-five, has attended many display conventions to showcase his product. "Maybe I'm really missing something, but I think a lot of this is hype. Most of the guys I know just go to their hotel rooms, order room service, and have a mundane evening watching television shows."

One thing is clear. If you are already attracted to someone in your office, and the feeling is mutual, travel provides an _opportunity_ for a sexual liaison separated from demands, pressures, and constraints of daily life. The cocktail parties that go along with out-of-the-office training sessions, the dinner meetings, and the "let's all go to the hotel bar after the session" mentality creates the appropriate ambience for romance. Because the opportunity is there, many people take advantage of it and embark on an affair.

In one case, told to me by a student, a couple had experienced a mild attraction for one another in the office, but had chosen not to act on their feelings. They went on a business trip together, and discovered that their hotel reservations had been mixed up due to a convention. They decided to share the one last room available to them. That night they decided to act upon their attraction. When the business trip was over, they returned to their offices and dissolved the romance.

As a corporate consultant, I often am called in to conduct a training session off-site for employees. Usually, during the daytime work session, I can predict the couples that might form—or at least who will get together with whom that night. Many times nothing happens, and everything is aboveboard. But occasionally something will.

THE SEMINAR CAPER: STEVE AND IRENE

Steve and Irene began their affair at a career development training workshop I conducted. I found out about the affair only because of my position as instructor.

The workshop was designed to run for two days. The firm had arranged for a series of small banquet rooms at a hotel in the Midwest that equalized the travel for all participants.

When I arrived at the hotel the night prior to the training session, I noticed a convivial group at the bar. Because they seemed to know each other, I guessed that they were my group.

I was right. I went over to a table near the bar and introduced myself. The woman with whom I spoke was Irene.

Irene and I had a lively conversation that night about leaving our husbands at home to do the dishes. After a half-hour of animated discussion, Steve joined in.

Steve was a plant personnel manager in the Southeast. He often networked with Irene, who was the headquarters compensation specialist, on personnel matters. Over the years, the two had developed a strong personal friendship.

I could tell they were attracted to one another from the way they teased each other about past exploits. Irene had a way of putting her arm on Steve's when she wanted to make a point.

When I asked what they meant by a term they used in conversation, they laughed. "Oh, that's just us, it's not a corporate colloquialism," said Steve. "Yeah, we play little word games all the time—like referring to the company headquarters as 'Mecca' when a new directive comes down."

They even had their own special language. Smiling, I excused myself for the evening. The next morning, Irene and Steve sat together for the training session. I noticed they had lunch together. When "homework" assignments were given out for the next day's session, they paired to complete the assignment.

That night, at a dinner given by the firm, Irene and Steve sat together with two other participants and me. All three of us noticed the attraction. Later, at the bar, more drinking and conviviality ensued. I excused myself to return to my hotel room to prepare for the next day's session.

It just so happened that Steve and Irene were scheduled to present their material first the next day. Realizing that I had forgotten to give them instructions about the first presentation, I decided to call Irene on her room extension an hour later to give her the special information. There was no answer.

Not wanting to disturb the festivities downstairs, I tiptoed down the hall to leave a note on Irene's door. I did not knock, thinking that she remained downstairs. As I reached to put the note on her door, it opened. Out came Steve in a bathrobe.

The three of us were a little embarrassed the next day. Irene and Steve were very quiet during the morning session. Only I knew why.

Lusting in Your Heart

Certainly, there are many workplace situations, like those experienced by Steve and Irene, that foster attraction. Travel frees inhibitions and opens opportunities. The sense of risk and the challenge of competition that takes place when you perform intense work tasks against a deadline can be very sexy. The sheer proximity of interesting, competent, and powerful people around you at work can serve as an aphrodisiac.

It is true that the workplace is conducive to intimacy. Relationships will continue to form on the job. People will fall in love, have affairs, and meet and marry their future spouses while employed at the same place of work. The new sexual revolution has made this inevitable.

But not everyone chooses to act on their sexual feelings. Some people choose to deepen their relationships with a sexual encounter, but others choose to "lust in their hearts," as former President Jimmy Carter once said. For example, Steve and Irene simply could have shared long conversations at the bar each night and parted as friends.

But suppose you decide to go ahead with a romantic relationship at work. What is it like to experience love—and attraction—in the office?

3

EXPERIENCING OFFICE LOVE

Imagine yourself falling in love with a colleague. Should you tell him or her about your feelings? Should you hide them? Should you continue to work along as usual, as if nothing has happened?

Doreen, thirty-two, currently is experiencing this dilemma. "As a medical technician, I am supposed to be professional and distant at all times. But I really like Danny, who works with me. I just don't know if I want to tell him because what if he doesn't reciprocate? I mean, I won't be able to face him again!"

For most of us, such questions bring forth our deepest school-day fears when we were first introduced to the opposite sex. The process of acting on your attraction at work can be equally intimidating, frightening, and confusing.

"I can't sleep, I can't breathe, and I can't think when I'm in the office because of him," said one woman. "I just wish I had the guts to do something about it!"

Many of the people with whom I spoke while researching this book were utterly bewildered about how to handle their feelings of attraction toward a colleague. Some became so distracted by their feelings that they could not continue their work. Others savored their feelings of attraction, but chose not to act on their feelings. Still others avoided intimacy in the workplace by refusing to discuss anything of a personal nature with colleagues.

Vicki, thirty-eight, said, "There are a number of men at my office whom I find attractive. But that doesn't mean I have to do anything about it. Being attracted to someone at work doesn't necessarily mean you will end up in a love affair with that person."

But Dolores, twenty-nine, disagrees. "Sometimes when you meet someone at work with whom you share a certain 'sympathique,' it's impossible not to let things become more intimate. It's hard to go against Mother Nature."

"The best solution, I've found," said a former accountant, "is simply to avoid anything personal altogether. The minute you start opening that door, you're bound for trouble."

Experiencing Attraction at Work

What is it like to experience an office attraction? How can you learn to cope with unrequited feelings for an office colleague?

Marcy Crary, an associate professor of management at Bentley College in Waltham, Massachusetts, has spent a great deal of time studying how people manage their feelings of attraction at work. She believes that coping with attraction is difficult because most people experience their feelings differently. Some are more aware of their feelings of attraction; others bury their feelings deep inside so that they can maintain a professional distance. In an article Dr. Crary wrote for *Organizational Dynamics* in spring of 1986, she describes one woman's recognition of the process of becoming attracted to a coworker. *

1. I'm first attracted to the person as a person—noticing his intelligence, the way he talks, etc. I'll find myself noticing something about his physical appearance (clothes, jewelry, hair) in the midst of a conversation.

2. Apart from his physical self, I may find myself remembering or ruminating over some personal data about him. I find myself thinking about something that is interesting about him, something that has piqued my curiosity.

3. The person may appear in my dreams. (This is an indication to me that I'm using him psychically, as a symbol of something in myself; he is becoming a source of my own growth).

4. At this point I start really to pay attention to him. I'm interested in him on a psychic level, interested in him as a person; I want to relate to him apart from the worker context. I've moved into a more active process at this point.

5. I begin to ask him questions about himself, watching how he is with other people, perhaps getting into conversations with friends at work about who's cute or not and thinking of him. This kind of talk with others helps to crystallize my feelings, making me aware of my own internal "ranking" of this person. The opinion of others also affects my interest in him, perhaps magnifying my attraction.

6. I am consciously paying attention to his clothing, watching how he moves, perhaps giggling at his jokes more, I notice what I like about his personality and his abilities.

7. I'll initiate more conversations with him. At meetings that he attends, I find myself stretching the "inclusion stage," the initial warm-up time in the meeting, by asking questions about his weekend, seeking more personal data.

8. At this point, if I'm really interested in him, I may covertly pass on information about my availability by not mentioning that I was with another person when I went to the movie over the weekend. I notice whom he mentions and whom he doesn't mention in his discussions of his weekend.

9. I move into a more personal state. I seek contact with him outside the workplace, or we might celebrate a

work event by going someplace outside the workplace.

10. Another signal of the intensifying of the relationship is his increasingly frequent appearances in my dreams. I may also be physically turned on by something h. tells me about himself.

11. At this point, I'm usually clear that I want to develop a friendship with this person. I can nurse such attractions and not act on them, but just enjoy them as they unfold.

The Sexual Dilemma

The description offered in this article, more so than any other that I have seen, richly demonstrates how fantasies and work experiences can intersect to foster sexual attraction. Sexual feelings, like the ones described by this woman, are basic to our existence. When you walk through your office door, such feelings are not immediately extinguished. But because the office environment requires a code of professionalism, distance, and objectivity in judgment, we learn to suppress our feelings of attraction.

Soon, we discover that this is not only impossible to do, but untenable to sustain. According to professors James Clawson, of Bentley College, and Kathy Kram, of Boston University, both experts on mentoring and intimate relationships at work who wrote a *Business Horizons* article on this subject in May 1985, we must balance between intimacy and professional distance along a continuum:

Intimacy   Distance

Neither too much distance nor too much intimacy may be a good thing, according to professors Clawson and Kram. But achieving the appropriate level of intimacy versus distance in any relationship is not an easy task. In cross-sex relationships, both people must define the boundary between appropriate levels of intimacy and romantic or sexual involvement. If the relationship crosses that boundary, the two people involved may agree not to act on mutual attraction in order to maintain a professional relationship. Or they may agree to go ahead with the romance.

The process of making such decisions—without knowing exactly how your partner feels toward you—causes people often to err on the side of conservatism and retain a sense of distance. But sometimes this can be bad for business. Some women complain that their bosses hold them at arm's length because of the sexual barrier, and this causes them to lose key developmental guidance. One woman reported, "If I were not a woman, and if this guy were not scared of his feelings for me, I'm sure I would have been sent to that convention. He took [Harry] instead."

Men complain about the opposite side of the spectrum— that women give off signals of attraction. Said one man, "I know this lady has the hots for me. I can read the signs—and this just isn't male ego talking, because others have noticed it, too. But when I approach her, she backs off. It's as if she's playing with me."

What Is—and What Is Not—an Office Romance

Playing sexual games of attraction in the office can be confusing, to men as well as women. The reason women sometimes back off is because they fear sexual harassment.

Sexual harassment takes place when one person engages in sexual behavior toward another but the other person is unwilling to reciprocate and work rewards are attached to the bargain. For example, if your boss says to you, "Sleep with me and you'll be promoted," this constitutes sexual harassment.

According to the Equal Employment Opportunity Commission (EEOC), three basic guidelines have been established to determine whether an act, including "unwelcome sexual advances, requests for sexual favors, and other verbal or physical contact of a sexual nature," constitutes unlawful sexual harassment.[1] These are:

• Submission to conduct is either an explicit or implicit term or condition of employment.

- Submission to or rejection of the conduct is used as the basis for employment decisions affecting the person who did the submitting or rejecting.
- The conduct has the purpose or effect of substantially interfering with an individual's work performance or creating an intimidating, hostile, or offensive work environment.

Romance in the workplace is very different. Romance takes place between *willing* parties who consciously make the decision to act upon their attraction for one another out of their own free choice.

Sexual harassment has no place in the office. It can be devastating for morale and productivity, and is entirely unethical. Most companies have developed strong policies to prevent harassment. But despite this important distinction between romance and harassment, people often confuse the two. Confusion exists because both romance and harassment concern sexual intimacy in the office.

"How can you tell the difference?" asked one man. "I mean, if I approach a woman, and she responds, that's romance. But if she decides she doesn't want to play the game, suddenly it's harassment and my career has gone down the tubes."

"I never was so surprised," said one source after his male office colleagues brought in a male stripper for a woman executive's birthday. "She was shocked we would do such a thing. She grew embarrassed, and then she turned mad. I never would have imagined having a little fun could be interpreted as sexual harassment."

The problem is that men and women view sexual innuendo differently. Women are fearful that the harmless flirting will turn to sexual harassment if encouraged, while men are surprised by what they consider to be exaggerated and overly negative responses on the part of women.

Gary Powell, a professor of management and organization at the University of Connecticut, conducted a survey reported in *Business Horizons* in July 1986 on beliefs concerning sexual intimacy in the workplace. He surveyed over one hundred MBA students to determine their feelings about sexual intimacy on the job.

Dr. Powell discovered that MBA students hold strong negative feelings about sexual harassment. Those surveyed agreed that some forms of sexual intimacy—romantic, willing intimacy—are acceptable in the workplace, as long as they are not extreme and have no adverse effect upon others. Women saw less positive value in sexual intimacy in the workplace, and desired more managerial action to discourage sexually oriented behavior.

As one woman who preferred anonymity in my survey reported, "I befriended a coworker and my intentions were misinterpreted. When I tried to sever the relationship, the man became a Mr. Jekyll. He persisted in harassing me at home and work with hang-up telephone calls for three years. Only when my company finally got the telephone company and the police involved did these calls cease. The experience left me with the attitude that it is not good to be associated with men at work other than on a professional level."

But others disagree. "The best experience of my life was when I was in love with a man in my office," said one woman. "The personal relationship combined with the work relationship created a wonderful rapport between us. I haven't had such an intense and fully vulnerable relationship since."

"I think it is difficult not to disclose personal feelings at work," said another. "If you hold back, then the same problems erupt as they do in any friendship or marriage. You have to spill the beans about how you're feeling or morale suffers."

Fears about sexual harassment aside, good working relationships are created when colleagues are able to share their hopes, fears, ambitions, and disappointments. It is natural that work environments foster attraction. In fact, in an American Society for Personnel Administration survey reported in _Personnel Administrator_ in October 1987, 70 percent of the employers surveyed said there really is nothing an organization can do to stop romantic attractions between men and women who work together.

Pete, a fifty-five-year-old human relations executive, put it this way: "I think love in the workplace is a good thing. I often feel attracted to the women with whom I work. It keeps me on my toes. I get excited just from knowing that I'll be in a meeting with an attractive woman. But I don't have to act on my feelings.

I am dedicated to my wife and family. I can just quietly enjoy them, treat them as fantasies, use them to energize me in my work."

But suppose you—and a *willing* colleague—decide you want to move beyond the stage of quiet fantasizing? What should you expect if you decide to experience office romance?

The Stages of Office Romance

My case research showed some interesting trends or stages that couples experienced as they moved from quiet fantasizing about a colleague toward an actual office romance.[2]

The first stage, *fantasy*, began with a sudden romantic interest in a colleague. Many people told me they became more conscious of their dress and work behavior at this time. They also made mental notes about their potential lover—the time he or she preferred to lunch, how he or she was dressed, and the way he or she moved.

Interestingly, the realization of sexual attraction and the allure of the intended causes a renewed interest in work. Productivity increases during this stage as a means of impressing the potential lover. You might be more willing to perform added work tasks because it may give you more time with your new-found love.

"When I was first interested in Gene, I became overly work-oriented," said Jeri, a woman I interviewed for this book. "I wanted to be around him, and he often worked late. I would join him and do extra work on my own."

"I wanted to show Rod how competent I was at my job," said Louise. "So I did extra homework just to impress him."

"I relished the overtime," said Simone, an interior designer. "Tomas couldn't meet me until after five P.M., and that was just fine with me."

The next stage marks the beginning of the relationship. Once the couple realizes their attraction is mutual, and there is movement toward an actual "date," the *honeymoon* period begins. During this stage, all good work intentions go out the window. Their concentration on their work often becomes muddled. The couple may find it difficult to concentrate on anything except each other.

"When I realized Mac was interested in me, and we first went on a date, I lost it," said Cindy, a recruiter. "Whenever he was near me, I couldn't stand it. I just wanted to play."

"The early stages with Jim were the best," said Maria, the friend I described in chapter 2. "But I don't know how I got through my classes . . . I winged it through several lectures, asking students to do special reports, that sort of thing. I spent most of my time thinking up gourmet dinners to cook for Jim."

Fortunately, inattention to work only occurs for a short period of time. Once the couple stabilizes their relationship, the third stage, *renewal*, commences. Concentration on work returns. The lovers experience a renewed interest in their work and in each other. Their now steady relationship moves along on an even keel.

"We had no problems working together once we became, in the true sense of the word, a couple," said Debbie, another woman I interviewed for this book. "We had a regular routine. In the morning we would meet for coffee, go to work, see each other at lunch, and then decide if we were going to get together for dinner. It was so businesslike it almost was as if we worked for two different companies."

Finally, the relationship reaches the *climax* stage. During this period, the couple realizes they must make a decision—to continue the relationship on a path toward an eventual long-term commitment, such as marriage, or to break it off. This stage is marked by many painful decisions. It is a time of self-evaluation—not only about the relationship itself, but about how this decision can affect your future career choices.[2]

"When our relationship broke up, it was one of the most difficult decisions I ever had to make," said Mike, thirty-one, who had just ended a relationship with his colleague and live-in lover. "When you fall in love at work, you really have to know what you are getting into. If you realize that you can no longer look that person in the eye and yet you have to see her at the office each day, you had better think about a new career."

Sometimes couples do indeed ride off into the sunset with a happy ending. In my research I met several couples who met at work and are now happily married and employed at the same firm. Some others have decided to go into business together.

"Because my husband and I run our firm together, we must ensure a sense of teamwork between us," said Linda, a fifty-year-old computer graphics entrepreneur. "We love working together. Everyone relies on us. We bring out the best in each other."

Ellen, forty-six, said, "John's work is the same as mine; we met in the office, then I left and returned two years later. The second time around our collaboration has been fantastic. We just know each other so well, we can anticipate each other. He catches my mistakes *before* I make them."

"We love working together," said Celia, a thirty-three-year-old financial analyst, " because we communicate well. I delight in our ability to be creative, to think well together. Now that we're married, our relationship is that much more enriched and full."

But enough of happy endings and fairytales. What about the day-to-day experience of romantic love at work? What is it *really* like to experience love in the office?

Living Love in the Office

Love in the office has its ups and downs. On the one hand, you can benefit from your close personal relationship with a colleague who really knows you well and can share in your work. On the other hand, there will be days where you may find work conflicts interfere dramatically with the quality of your personal relationship.

I interviewed Maggie on a day when she was experiencing great frustration over what I call the fishbowl effect. Maggie had completed an important presentation that morning, only to discover that she had ignored a key area that came up in a discussion after the presentation.

Maggie said, "I should have known they would have focused on the Clinton issue. That has been a problem for some time now. . . . I should have anticipated the reaction. But what I did not expect was Jim's response that the whole presentation would need to be revised."

Jim was Maggie's live-in lover. "Jim made that suggestion?" I asked.

"Yes," said Maggie. "It's times like this that I really hate the fact that we work in the same department. He knows how hard I worked on this presentation."

"So why didn't he support you?" I asked.

"It's just so complicated," said Maggie. "On the one hand, I understand his reaction. Because we don't want anyone saying that our personal life compromises our business judgments, he had to take that position in front of others. He had to show that he could be objective in the business sense. Otherwise people gossip. But he's my man, and I feel betrayed. It's natural to want my man to support me. Especially since he knows I've been through the wringer on this."

"So what happens now?" I asked.

"Well, I have to go have lunch with the gang, even though I'm angry as hell inside, just to keep up appearances. If I go to his office for a quiet chance to cry, everyone will think we are having a fight. So I can't go see him. I can only keep up appearances over lunch and work this thing out myself until we get home."

"That's putting a lot of pressure on yourself," I said.

"But I've got to keep up appearances. It'll be a hell of a day," said Maggie.

Office romancers live love in a fishbowl. Every move they make is constantly observed, discussed, and evaluated by coworkers' prying eyes.

This is what upset Maggie so much about the reality of her office relationship. "I really can't stand everyone watching us all the time," said Maggie. "It makes days like this that much more difficult to bear."

Love in the office is never boring. According to one woman who just ended a romance with a draftsman in her office, "We had the best of times and the worst of times. It was great because we knew one another so well that we really clicked when we had a chance to work together. It was the worst because we had the most amazing fights over petty issues that never would have come up if we didn't work together in the same office."

Romance at work is complicated because it requires a

balance between personal roles and professional responsibilities. For some the conflicting demands are too much, while for others the challenge can be stimulating, exciting, and rewarding.

Achieving Balance Between Personal and Professional Roles

Dr. Jeffrey Zimmerman, a psychologist at Connecticut Psychological Group in Hartford, believes this to be the central unresolvable dilemma that office romancers must confront. "In an office romance, personal and professional roles are interwoven in such a way that it is difficult for the couple to maintain a sense of separateness. How each member handles their roles—personal and professional roles—is crucial for the success of the relationship," Dr. Zimmerman told me.

The concept of *role* is defined in the social sciences as a set of expectations about behavior. For example, the role of "mother" suggests certain expectations about behavior. Mothers are supposed to care for their children, listen to their concerns, and watch over their growth and development. The role of the "boss" is another example. Good bosses are those who maintain high standards of performance while attending to their employees' concerns. They coach, guide, and counsel others while keeping their eyes on deadline demands. They support their employees and provide opportunities for growth and challenge.[3]

Romantic coworkers are caught in their own private Catch-22. They play dual roles in the office *and* at home. "What I found I really couldn't deal with was the dual personality effect when I was seeing David. I was supposed to be a caring lover in private and a distant, objective colleague in public. Sometimes I couldn't handle the change—it was as if we were four different people," said one woman who recently ended a two-year office relationship.

Many couples feel they are suffering from multiple personalities as a result of their dual roles. The problem is that expressing romantic interest toward one another at work violates the norms of professionalism. But ignoring each other to maintain professional distance compromises personal intimacy.

"He's my boss at work," said one woman. "So I have to respect his judgments. No one knows we are involved, but I do, and sometimes the decisions he makes make me mad. I want to tell him so but can't."

Problems occur when a crisis at work requires the personal and intimate support of the lover, or when personal life criss-crosses with business. This is what bothered Maggie the day of her presentation. She felt she could not turn to Jim for support. "Today we will be strangers," she said. "And I'll probably take it out on him tonight when we're in bed."

So Why Bother with Love in the Office?

"It's the best," said Laurinda. "Having my lover work with me has made us closer than peas in a pod. It's great."

"We haven't had any problems," said Kevin, half of a husband and wife research team. "The relationship has only enhanced our research work."

Said a real estate executive, now married to one of his former agents, "Marilyn and I are able to get more done than ever before. Because she understands my business so well, she truly has become my right arm in the partnership. I just caught myself . . . it's *our* business now."

The consensus reached by many long-term couples with whom I have spoken is that office romance, despite the compli-cations, is more than worthwhile. "I have been able to learn more about Marty from seeing him do his work," said one woman who recently became employed by her lover's firm. "Now I understand much more about the pressures he is under."

"As I work with Seth, I have grown to admire him more and more each day," said one wife who became a partner in her husband's accounting firm. "He has talents in areas that I never realized. When I watch him handle a high-pressure situation around tax time with a client, I can't wait to tell him how proud I am of him."

Having a lover, colleague, confidant, and friend all rolled into one can be "tremendous," in the words used by Noel, a thirty-two-year-old newspaper reporter. "Because Vinnie knows the same people I do, and because we face the same work pressures, we can sympathize—really sympathize—with each other's bad days. We have great dinnertime conversations [about] the people in our newsroom."

Many of the couples whom I interviewed for this book agreed that the dilemmas do not overshadow the advantages. "Sure, there are problems," said Vinnie, Noel's husband. "But we have learned to work them out an a day-to-day basis. A sense of humor helps."

Joella, a nurse who is engaged to a resident at her hospital, agrees. "When I'm with him I feel more in touch with the world, more caring, more alive. I am the better half of myself."

A MODEL OF SUCCESS: JOY AND ALAN

Some couples may experience a few rough spots before they are able to appreciate the advantages. Joy and Alan are probably the most successful example of a working partnership that I have seen.

Joy and Alan met while working on the same project together, started dating, and discovered that they shared common interests. They worked in a small company that makes VCR rental tapes from many of the major movie releases, and on their first date they went to a New York opening of a major feature film. They found they enjoyed the same bagels, the same restaurants, and the same types of vintage old movies. They knew they were off to a successful start.

"It was amazing," said Joy. "Here was this man, the picture of my ideal dreams, and he was telling me that his favorite movie of all time was *Notorious*! I just loved that movie. And I loved his bagels." Alan, upon hearing this, chimed in: "After all, what do you need in a successful marriage besides movies and bagels?"

Joy met Alan when he was hired into the company. Alan worked in the marketing department, Joy in procurements. They had some mutual friends who brought them together over lunch one day in the office, and they began dating.

Joy said, "When we first started seeing each other, I just never knew what to do. I wanted to run to Alan for comfort when I would have a fight with someone in the office. A few times I did."

Alan said, "A few times? Come on, it was almost every day for a month!"

Joy said, laughing, "Well, it wasn't quite that bad. But I did cause some problems for the office for a while. People started gossiping that I couldn't handle my work without Alan's help. That got me mad."

"So what did you do?" I inquired.

"Well, we had to separate ourselves from each other at the office," said Alan. "But because we worked for a small firm, this was difficult. We kept running into each other in the hallways. It made us feel like we were sneaking around."

Joy added, "The problem was that we realized if we did not talk to each other during the day, it would complicate things at home. For example, if I had a vendor who didn't deliver, and being an expressive type of person, if I had to vent my anger and couldn't, I would carry around all this pent-up anger with me all day, and by the time I saw Alan at home, I would project my anger onto him because he was unable to comfort me with my crisis. It wasn't his fault, of course, but he would get the brunt of it."

Joy and Alan made a pact about their relationship. They decided: "In the office, it's business, but at home, it's personal." They found this was the best way to manage their role confusion. In the office, they found time to socialize with colleagues, take them to lunch, and include them in their activities. At home they discussed the personal events of the day and their feelings toward each other.

Alan said, "We never display affection in the office. Sometimes, like once after she gave a big presentation, it took all I had not to go over and kiss her, but you do what you gotta do."

Joy continued by saying, "Working with someone you love can be great simply because he knows the personalities that you deal with on a daily basis. I can really trust his judgment. If I have a problem, once we get home we can discuss it calmly and rationally. He always helps me gain a better perspective."

Joy and Alan enjoy working together immensely. So much so, in fact, that once they got married, they decided to open up their own VCR rental store. "Being in business together has been even better than our days in the office together," said Joy. "Our personal relationship and business stake is now one."

Should You Romance Someone at Work?

Are you ready, willing, and able to handle an office romance?

Few people are. But for all of the reasons presented in this chapter, romancing in the office can be natural, enriching, somewhat complicated—and more than worthwhile.

Attractions at work are a natural part of the conviviality of daily office life. They should not be spurned nor dismissed as inconsequential. One of the consequences of the new sexual revolution is that men and women will meet, marry, and fall in love on the job. It is unrealistic to think otherwise.

But this quiet sexual revolution may be doing much more than simply contributing to a new landscape of personal relationships at work. It also may be contributing to improved office morale. Some attractions may enhance work relationships and improve office productivity. But others may bring a host of risks and disadvantages that are emotionally devastating to all concerned.

You need to know the benefits—and the risks—that office romance can bring. The next section will reveal what they are.

Part Two

WHY SOME OFFICE ROMANCES WORK AND OTHERS CAN BE DANGEROUS

4

THE POSITIVE SIDE OF OFFICE ROMANCE

Probably one of the scariest things about being a college professor is that sometimes your students may take you too literally. One day, after I had just given a brief lecture to graduate students on office romance, Nora, one of my best and most alert students, approached me. "I know that your research shows there are some benefits to office romance," she said. "But I just can't see it. I have seen too many women get pushed aside because they fooled around with the boss."

"Well, that's true," I said. "Boss-subordinate relationships can be problematic. But peer relationships often have many benefits."

"I just can't see it," she said.

A few weeks later, after class, Nora approached me again. "Does your research *really* show that there can be a positive side to office romance, as long as you go out with someone on your same level?"

"Yes," I said. "Provided that both participants conduct themselves in a professional manner."

She left without saying a word. I could tell something was up.

49

Nora was absent for the following week's class. I assumed that she, as a sales representative for a manufacturing firm, had been given a travel assignment and was unable to attend.

I waited two more weeks. Nora returned to class with a big smile on her face.

"Nora," I asked, "you have been absent for almost a month without a word. What's going on?"

"I've been doing research for you," she answered. "I've been having an office romance on the road."

"What?" I said, surprised at her response.

"Yes, it's true," she said. "There's this guy—another sales rep—I've had my eyes on. After your class lecture, I decided to see if he was interested. We have been dating ever since. And you're right—there are a lot of benefits!"

Most women and some men are reluctant to believe there is a positive side to office romance. Like Nora, even I had accepted much of the conventional wisdom about office romance before I began researching this topic. I expected to find that the risks outweighed the benefits by a landslide—that careers could be ruined, affections damaged, and productivity impaired. Instead, I discovered that my opinions were more jaded than I had realized.

There can be many benefits realized from a simple attraction—even if it remains suppressed—or an ongoing, overt office romance. My case research taught me that many of the people with whom I spoke had successfully negotiated an office romance. Some of their stories told of distinct improvements in company morale, satisfaction, and work relationships. In a few cases, romance had been openly encouraged—and supported—by colleagues.

The bottom line is that *attraction stimulates performance*. When love is in the air, people feel happier about themselves. Sometimes the feeling can be contagious.

One woman, a staff manager for a large fiber-optic company, said, "When people in the office are dating, morale improves. Everybody—not just the couple—is happier. I think socializing on the job is great as long as nothing gets out of hand."

A male manager who works for a sporting goods manufacturer agrees. "Romance on the job can be a great boost. People become much more motivated, not less so, to get to work on Monday morning."

According to the late Kaleel Jamison, a management consultant who wrote an article entitled "Managing Sexual Attraction in the Workplace" in the August 1983 edition of *Personnel Administrator*:

> Sexual attraction—a situation in which one person experiences the exhiliration or inclination toward another without the desire to diminish the other person—is different from either sex discrimination or sexual harassment. It may be disruptive, but the difference is that, if properly managed, it can be not disruptive but actually energizing and productive within the organization.

Based on my own research, I believe this is true. Attraction and romance at work bring out the best in all of us, as long as it is handled properly by the couple.

An executive woman commented, "I manage this couple in two of my departments, and at first, I was ready to transfer Sally or Joe—or both—out of my organization. But I decided to wait, and I'm glad I did. Although at first I thought this was going to be a disaster, they have really managed to keep their personal and professional lives separate. I think being in love even has improved their productivity. It [the romance] has been a welcome change."

The Benefits of Office Romance

What are some of the benefits that can result from love in the office? Who is most likely to benefit? How can these benefits be achieved?

Benefit #1

OFFICE ROMANCE CAN ENERGIZE WORKPLACE MORALE

It can be exciting to watch two people fall in love at work. In fact, it can be downright uplifting. When the spirit of love is in the air, everyone feels more energized, excited, and stimulated. Watching a romance unfold can do wonders for company morale.

Teri, twenty-eight, agrees. "My romance in the office had a very positive effect on everyone in the department. Most people, except my boss, were pleased that John and I were going out. We were happier, and everyone around us noticed the change."

There is something about a new, budding romance that is just plain fun. Few people can resist playing matchmaker when given the opportunity. We enjoy bringing together people who we believe deserve one another. When the match is successful, we can share in the excitement of their developing romance. We gain the pleasure of deflected love even when we are not direct participants.

In my survey, 34 percent of executive women recognized that romance can energize workplace morale. One woman commented, "What I have observed primarily is that people are calmer and more friendly if they are in a good love relationship. As long as this does not interfere with work, no one seems to mind. The best department I ever had as an administrator was very close in general; there was an affectionate camaraderie, and therefore good support. Whatever was going on in a person's life was fine."

The results from other surveys show that many people agree with this. The survey conducted by Carolyn Anderson and Philip Hunsaker, of the University of San Diego, reported in _Personnel_ magazine in February 1985, found that "the development of a romance may make work more enjoyable and can reduce stress and anxieties." Romance in the office can eliminate tension, create a happier work climate, and improve morale.

Leandra, a forty-year-old diplomat, believes this is true. "One of the things I have noticed is that love in the office reduces stress, just because you know you have a companion to whom you can turn when events become tense."

Mike, a fifty-two-year-old executive with a food processing conglomerate, said, "People are friendlier and happier when they're in love. [Their feelings] are bound to have a positive effect . . . on office relationships."

Cathy, twenty-three, a junior accountant with a small practice, said, "I don't understand . . . why people would think otherwise. Of course when you're in love, especially if it's someone who works with you, you feel happier. Your office colleagues also will be happy because [the relationship] will make you less of an office bitch. Morale is bound to improve!"

Let's look at one case from my research in which office morale improved because of the matchmaking efforts of co-workers.

AN IMPROVEMENT IN MORALE: MINDY AND AL

I met Mindy through a friend. She was a bright, talented, and serious young woman. I asked her to tell me her story.

Mindy said, "I met Al when I was assigned to a local grammar school to complete my practice teaching for my master's degree in special education. The principal liked my work, so he made a point to introduce me to Al, the superintendent of schools. Al told me that a special project he was developing for his school district would be ideal material for a Ph.D. thesis. He urged me to consider the opportunity."

Mindy applied for candidacy for her doctorate with Al's research project in mind. Together, they mapped out a research strategy for her dissertation. Al grew more and more interested in the project—and in Mindy. Mindy felt the same about Al. She said, "Here was a man who was willing to encourage me to pursue my dreams and at the same time, make me feel safe and secure. I thought he was great—a friend, work colleague, and mentor all rolled into one."

According to Mindy, the principals and teachers began to notice that Mindy and Al were attracted to one another. They also realized that Mindy and Al were reluctant to do anything about their budding attraction. So they decided to do something to bring them together.

"One day I casually mentioned to a friend, a teacher in one of the schools, that I was interested in Al. You know, girl talk. But immediately the grapevine went into action. One of Al's secretaries mentioned to him that there was a rumor going around that I was asking questions about Al. Al told the secretary that he thought any man lucky enough to be involved with Mindy should marry her right away, and this was reported back to me. I was never so embarrassed in my life. Suddenly I was the object of gossip. I had never been a gossiper myself, so it was really embarrassing for me."

But the efforts of the teachers and secretaries continued. Every time Mindy made a presentation at one of the schools about her research, Al was encouraged to attend. Mindy said, "Al and I couldn't do any work on the project without someone telling me about how wonderful he was or vice versa. When we worked behind closed doors, in one of the workrooms, everyone would wink at us. It got to the point where we could no longer do anything but go out on a date—just to satisfy those around us."

Finally, they did. Al took Mindy to a quiet restaurant. They talked until late. As Mindy told me of her date with Al, her eyes lit up with delight. "We had the most wonderful conversations on our first date. It was as if he poured his heart out to me, and I did the same with him. We talked and talked— about our mutual desires to have a family, about the school, about ourselves. It was just wonderful."

After their successful first date, Mindy and Al saw each other on a regular basis. The principals, teachers, and secretaries beamed at the result of their matchmaking efforts. Everyone was pleased.

I asked Mindy how the research project fared in the midst of all this romancing. "Oh!" she said, surprised. "The research was fantastic. I presented my results to my dissertation committee and received their immediate approval. In fact, one of my advisors commented that it was one of the best projects in special education they had reviewed that year. I was on Cloud Nine! They loved my work.

"And I know one of the reasons why it was so successful was because of Al. I didn't mind working hard because I knew it gave us something in common. He was a great help to me," said Mindy. "I worked a number of extra nights and weekends so I could not only get the research done, but so I could be really helpful to the entire school system where they needed it most."

But with her dissertation complete, Mindy needed a permanent job. Al had advertised a position vacancy for the job of an assistant superintendent, but Mindy hesitated to apply for the position. She feared that her personal relationship with Al would be a factor not well received by the school board. She and Al had grown closer, and were considering marriage.

Mindy described her dilemma: "There I was, with this wonderful opportunity staring me in the face. I knew I could be great in that job. But I wanted Al, too. I had found the two things that I had searched for my entire life—a good job and a wonderful man—and I feared I might lose both—or at least one, most likely the job—because of the circumstances."

The teachers and principals met to rouse support for Mindy. Mindy was nominated for the position over her objections. She told the school board that she would remove her name from consideration if the board had a negative reaction to her appointment because of her personal relationship with Al.

"I was so scared," Mindy told me. "Never before had I put everything on the line like that. I always was the wallflower type. This was the first time I had to fight for what I believed in."

At the next public meeting, the school board members appointed Mindy to the position on a temporary basis. The teachers, secretaries, and principals in the audience applauded. Mindy breathed a sigh of relief; so did Al. But the real surprise came next. Mindy said, "Would you believe that Al chose that moment to propose to me, right in front of everyone? Of course I said yes."

Their wedding became one of the most talk-about social events in the town's history. The entire town shared the credit for bringing two deserving people together. Mindy and Al went on to make significant contributions to their school district, which has gained a reputation as one of the most innovative in their state in the area of special education. She and Al are still happily married, and have two children of their own.

Benefit #2

OFFICE ROMANCE CAN MOTIVATE EMPLOYEES

Besides a newfound sense of departmental morale and *esprit de corps*, romance in the office may increase motivation as well. My survey results showed that in almost one-third of the cases studied, productivity *improved* rather than declined.[1]

This was an additional benefit that Mindy and Al experienced. "Looking back, it is amazing how much I accomplished in such a short time," said Mindy. "Usually I procrastinate when given a large project. I can't seem to separate the mountains from the molehills. But because I was in love, I finished the dissertation in only nine months!"

"One of the major benefits of my romance with Stanley was that I put more energy into my work than ever before," said Annette, a thirty-three-year-old retailer. "When things were good, they were _really_ good. I was happier and more motivated."

Bette, twenty-nine, agrees. "When I was dating my husband in the office, I was concerned . . . that others would view [the relationship] negatively . . . so I made sure that my work was outstanding. I worked extra hard because I wanted to be certain that no one was saying anything [about us]."

Most people with whom I spoke assumed that one of the disadvantages of an office romance would be that motivation would decline because the lovers would be so enraptured and distracted. But this was rarely the case. Many romancers told me that the romance caused them to become _more_ motivated in their work rather than less productive.

"I didn't want to be accused of putting pleasure before work," said Alfred, a health-care executive. "My boss kept giving me the eye. . . . There was some locker-room conversation about my relationship with Jeannie. So I made certain my work was in on time, and she did the same."

Other survey reports show that in some limited situations, productivity may increase. In the survey published in _Administrative Science Quarterly_ in March 1977 by Robert Quinn, a professor of public administration at the State University of New York at Albany, 17 percent of the men and 15 percent of the women studied became more productive. In the Anderson and Hunsaker survey published in _Personnel_ magazine in February 1985, similar results were reported. Twenty-one percent of the women and 9 percent of the men were seen as being more productive.

Productivity, however, may ebb and flow depending on the stage of the romance. As I reported in chapter 3, the stages of an office romance have an important impact on productivity levels. During the fantasy and renewal stages of office romance, productivity may increase.

A CASE OF IMPROVED PRODUCTIVITY: JUDY AND NEIL

I did not know Judy very well when I researched this case, and I had been acquainted with Neil only from a distance. Neil had gone to work for one of the major investment houses in New York, and was highly respected for his talents as a member of the merger and acquisitions department. Judy recently had been hired as a merger and acquisitions analyst.

From my first impressions, Neil was everything you would expect in an investment banker. He wore Brooks Brothers suits and the requisite red suspenders and club tie. Everything about him smacked of his Ivy League background. He blended in well with his investment banker colleagues.

Both Judy and Neil were highly dedicated professionals. You could tell, even from a distance, that these two were talented at their work. Neil already had established his reputation; Judy was just beginning hers. In fact, she felt lucky to be working with Neil.

Judy told me that she and Neil began dating after working together for a full year. "We were concerned at first, because the firm tends to look down on personal relationships. At this place they think they own you. We also were concerned about how we would handle a breakup, should that happen, so we just had a few dates from time to time. It was a real slow start."

"How did things get going?" I asked.

"Well, we realized that this relationship could be something more if we would only give it a chance. We had been meeting at a number of far-out places where no one would see us. One day we decided we were tired of it all—all the tentativeness, the sneakiness, the guilt—and that we wanted to give the relationship a chance. So we moved in together, into Neil's apartment. I kept my old place, though, which I shared with three roommates, as my actual address."

Ironically, once they made the decision to live together, they were both simultaneously assigned to a highly publicized merger deal for two major corporations. Because the deal had to be worked on in a short time span, and since a lot of money was at stake, the merger was considered a hot property in the office. It was the kind of deal that could make or break a young investment banker's career.

Judy said, "Work on the merger was intensive. The project required not only the standard eight A.M. to eight P.M. workday considered reasonable in most merger and acquisitions offices, but also many hours of grueling work on weekends to make the deadline. The office became totally chaotic."

Not only did the project involve one of the firm's biggest clients, but the amount of work that had to be done in the available time was staggering. Tensions ran high.

Neil and Judy were as aware as anyone else about what was at stake. But they were unconcerned about the pressures in the office. Why? Because Neil and Judy already were involved in a personal relationship, they did not resent having to spend their weekends, as well as long workdays, together. In fact, because they spent so much time together as romantic partners as well as colleagues, they were delighted to put in extra time to make the deal optimally successful.

"We worked weekends, we worked weeknights, and we virtually slept at the office. We did what we had to do. We flew to the headquarters of the major corporations involved, and flew home on the red-eye flights. But the funny part was that we didn't care as much about the pressures as the others because we knew we were together no matter what. It wasn't the kind of thing where you feel guilty because your wife or husband is home waiting for you."

Their relationship allowed them to perform the work required—without costs to their personal relationship. And their efforts paid off. They were able to find a loophole in the deal that allowed the offer to be presented so it was completely attractive to both companies.

"There's always a key in the deals that you can find—it's like a big puzzle," said Neil. "But because we were working creatively together, and didn't mind the hours, we were the ones who found the key. We both received a lot of support from my boss for our final solution."

Judy and Neil's romance caused them to put more effort into their work than was reasonably expected. While others in the office were complaining about the long, hard hours and time spent away from their families, Judy and Neil were able to optimize their personal relationship to benefit office productivity. They both have since been promoted, and are still living together in New York.

**OFFICE ROMANCE CAN ENCOURAGE
CREATIVITY AND INNOVATION**

Judy and Neil's experience shows how motivation and productivity can be enhanced from an office romance. An added benefit they found was being able to work creatively together.

"One of the things I really loved about the whole experience," said Judy, "was how our minds worked together. I really admire Neil's mind. Our thought process was wonderfully creative."

Most people in love maintain that being in love makes them more creative. Love can make you quite ingenious.

"Some of the best times we had were when Ben and I were on the XYZ company audit," said Barbara, a twenty-six-year-old accountant with a Big Eight firm. "We spent all our time thinking up new ways to get the work done faster, so we could have more play time together after five. We found a creative way around the messiness of the audit without compromise."

"I loved our ad campaign meetings when Steve and I first were attracted to one another," said Melanie. "We came up with some really wild ideas. I think we were testing each other to see how far the other would go."

Many psychologists believe that a creative synergy emerges between two people who are attracted to each other. That synergy can lead to innovation, brainstorming, and the courage to apply new, risky approaches to old problems. Sometimes work performance can improve as a result.

In one case I studied, one member of a couple who worked for a different but related department from his partner had been given a challenging assignment: to restructure a small subset of a larger division for his boss. Usually this type of assignment is reserved for executives, but it had been delegated down the chain of command. According to David, "The question was how could lower level input be achieved without upsetting office politics? This [project] could potentially backfire easily. It was a difficult problem."

Working at home for several nights in a row, the couple put their heads together to identify strategies to approach the assignment. Even though they worked for different departments, they knew the important players in each. Together, they had a brainstorm: Why not take some of the engineering functions from Department A and put them in Department B, and vice versa? This type of reorganization had never been done before, but it made sense, given the work flow of the two different but intersecting departments.

"What we did was to talk to the members of our own respective departments," said Lee. "This way we were able to marshall the support needed. Then David went to his boss, who mulled it over, and later made a presentation to the division level."

The division managers were pleased. They commented that this reorganization represented a significant innovation that only could have been achieved from a bottom-up decision-making process. David was congratulated for his efforts.

Many of the women I surveyed commented upon this benefit. Thirty-four percent of those who mentioned benefits believed that an office romance improved creativity and innovation.

A publishing assistant said, "Somehow, when you're in love, you're willing to take more risks. The best ideas are the crazy ones that you never would have dreamed of alone. Talking over ideas with a lover at work can really stimulate the creative process."

HOW CREATIVE SYNERGIES ENHANCE PERFORMANCE: JESSICA AND ED

Jessica and Ed arrived at the doorstep of their advertising firm's Los Angeles division just in time to make the firm's early morning staff meeting.

Jessica said, "I knew right then and there that we had something in common. Who else besides a procrastinator would take a red-eye from New York?"

They had been called to the Los Angeles office to develop a new public service ad campaign for AIDS research. The campaign would use a number of media celebrities in nationally viewed television spots.

"We had to be in L.A.," said Ed, "because many of the people we were signing were in that location. The spots were designed to be individually tailored to the personalities signed."

They had a monumental task. To complete the campaign, they had to develop twelve different spots for the celebrities chosen. Each one had to enhance the celebrity's reputation and image with the public, yet communicate the central theme.

I asked them how their affair got off the ground. "We were assigned to the task of chasing around after press agents and publicity managers of the stars," said Jessica. "We couldn't get the spots going until we knew who we had signed. Ed and I drove all over L.A. going to breakfast meetings at different restaurants. Neither of us knew anyone else in L.A., so we often had dinner together. One day, we had worked up the storyboards for two celebrities in an all-day meeting, ate dinner together, worked some more, and had to meet with another agent the following morning. Somehow it was easier to stay together for the night in Ed's hotel room before the breakfast meeting."

"What attracted you to each other?" I wanted to know.

Said Ed: "Her sense of humor."

Said Jessica: "His procrastination! We were so alike, and so different from my husband and me."

At the time of the affair, Jessica and Ed both were married. Ed was separated from his wife of thirteen years.

"How did you feel working together on the campaign?" I asked.

"Fantastic!" said Jessica. "Our creative juices were running high. I could tell what he was going to say even before he said it."

"And I often finished her sentences," added Ed.

"We ran through the spots like magic. Some days we did two or three workups—which is unheard of. The creative process is very sexy."

They remained at work on the campaign for three months. After returning to New York, they resumed their affair. Jessica left her husband, and both are now living together—and working together—in the same New York office.

Benefit #4

OFFICE ROMANCE CAN SOFTEN WORK-RELATED PERSONALITY CONFLICTS

Because a little romance can go a long way, it is not uncommon for an office romance to have a major effect on the personalities, interaction patterns, and personal styles of the couple.

"People in L.A. could tell we were involved," said Ed. "Even though they didn't know us well. We were happy and crazy—just crazy—together. Our work relationship was very fluid."

Being in love causes us to wake up and smell the roses. We feel good about ourselves. The mere knowledge that someone cares helps us to gain a different, broader perspective. Romance teaches us to be flexible. We are no longer bothered by daily crises; after all, what can be more important than being in love?

Some of the cases I have researched have shown me that romance can be beneficial in the workplace for this reason alone. In my survey, many women (41 percent) who observed actual cases agreed with the statement that a romance made participants "easier to get along with." The Quinn survey published in 1977 by *Administrative Science Quarterly* reported that 25 percent of the men and 28 percent of the women were reported to have improved work relationships as a result of a romance.

In the Anderson and Hunsaker survey published in 1985 by *Personnel* magazine, one woman was reported to have become more open, readily expressing criticism to the man with whom she was involved about the way he was running the organization. The romance in this case improved the quality of work life for the work group, according to these authors.[2]

Susannah, twenty-nine, responded to my survey by saying, "I'm all for romance! I used to have to work with this real bitchy coworker. But now that she's dating, her whole demeanor has improved. Our office is much better off. . . . We dread a breakup!"

Another woman, Marcie, a twenty-three-year-old secretary, said, "My boss is much easier to work for now that he is in love again. After his divorce I thought I would have to leave the firm because things were so bad. He couldn't remember his appointments . . . but now he's back on track."

A little romance can go a long way in this regard. One case with which I am familiar concerned a rigid, inflexible professor of mathematics. To her, students were always irresponsible, undermotivated, and unwilling to be challenged. Nothing they could do would suit her expectations, so they rarely attended her classes. But once she became involved in an office romance, everything changed. She became more flexible and understanding of the concerns of her students, and her classroom attendance improved markedly.

AN IMPROVEMENT IN ATTITUDE: MARTHA AND HENRY

Martha and Henry aptly illustrate how a romance can soften personal conflicts in the office when love is in the air. Martha worked for a private foundation that provided grants to the disadvantaged. According to the source who told me the story, Martha felt almost like one of them.

"Martha was a complainer," said Larry, my source. "She complained about the cost of living in the area, her problems finishing her MBA, the low pay in her new job, about relatives and friends who never called her. She found people unfriendly. She disliked her apartment. She had too much work to do in too little time. We couldn't stand all the complaining because she was so difficult to work with."

But one day, Henry came on the scene. He was hired as the head of one of the foundation's grant-giving departments, in an area that intersected with Martha's job, but not directly as a part of her department.

"Henry was an accomplished, attractive man, in the process of getting a divorce from his wife of fifteen years. A man of action, you know the type? Within a few months, he had created more innovations in his department than the foundation had seen in years," said Larry.

In many respects, Henry was the direct opposite of Martha, both in personality and in outlook. Henry viewed himself as a leader who preferred to act rather than react. Martha, on the other hand, let her life control *her*. Henry was very suave politically, Martha was not.

Larry told me, "We couldn't believe it once they began dating. Those two? What a combination. We predicted it wouldn't last more than two weeks. Who could put up with her? But soon, we were all hoping—earnestly—that their relationship would become more permanent. The romance made Martha change into a whole new person."

She became happier, more open and caring with others. She bounced around the office and completed her work efficiently and productively. Martha's productivity increased, and she no longer complained about all the details, pressures, and issues related to her work. She was a much happier person to be around.

"My boss—and everyone in the office—was floored by the change," said Larry. "We couldn't believe it. I even started asking her to lunch again."

In fact, at the time I met Martha, she seemed wonderful. Happy, helpful, funny, and joyous would be the words I would use to describe her. Henry also had a glow about him.

As a result, the romance had a spillover effect upon the morale and working relationships in the office. Martha finished her master's thesis, became more productive in her job, and generally wowed everyone around her with her accomplishments. So did Henry. Together these two made an unbeatable team.

Benefit #5

OFFICE ROMANCE CAN IMPROVE TEAMWORK, COMMUNICATION, AND COOPERATION

Yet another surprising benefit I have found is that sometimes office romance can have a beneficial effect by increasing the teamwork, communication, and cooperation between departments. If the members of the couple hold jobs in different departments, their personal relationship can serve as a channel for communication.

In my survey, 27 percent said that improved communication, teamwork, and cooperation existed among departments as a result of an office romance. One woman commented, "Now [because of the romance] I can get action out of the marketing department when I need something from them."

It is not uncommon for departments to engage in in-house wars over competing goals and priorities on project assignments. Much of the political game-playing in corporations results from interdepartmental strife. When the work flow between the departments is hampered, turf battles ensue, and goals and priorities are questioned.

The problem is, when departments are set against one another, they stop communicating. In fact, poor communication between departments is often how they get into trouble in the first place.

When this happens, an office romance can be helpful. I have seen several cases in which the involved couple worked in different departments for the same company, and a conflict over work flow processing occurred. Because of the personal relationship, the couple was able to communicate the concerns of their respective departments and keep the spirit of teamwork and cooperation going. As a result, many conflicts were eliminated before they grew out of proportion.

One case with which I am familiar concerned a woman staff trainer who developed skill training programs and a man in research and development at a telecommunications firm. When new equipment was given to the field personnel, it was the mandate of the staff training department to develop appropriate programs to train field personnel on the new equipment. But for years the quality of training had been poor. The reason for this was a history of conflicts between the staff trainers, who complained they never received accurate and timely information from the corporate research and development staff, their arch-enemies. When this couple became an item, the conflicts between the two departments de-escalated and the quality of training improved overall.

Other surveys show positive benefits of this type as well. The 1985 survey conducted by Carolyn Anderson and Philip Hunsaker published in *Personnel* magazine showed that 21 percent of those surveyed said the relationship had a positive impact in the organization. Positive impacts were defined as increased coordination in the work group, lowered interdepartmental tensions, and improved work flow.

Catherine, a thirty-seven-year-old telemarketing specialist, agrees. "Now that my boss is involved with a man in one of our customer service departments, we no longer have to wait for quick response. She tells him directly about a customer problem that has surfaced and it gets his immediate attention."

A CHANGE IN COOPERATION: TOM AND DEBBIE

Sometimes, a romance can benefit the flow of information in the workplace and improve teamwork and cooperation among departments. Tom and Debbie did exactly that.

Tom and Debbie had become involved in an office romance while working for the same company. Their firm was a small manufacturing company in the toy business. Tom was an engineer who designed new computer games for children to play, while Debbie worked in the marketing department, dreaming up ways to sell the games to children.

Tom and Debbie met at a local bar one night after work. Debbie said, "We didn't even know we worked for the same company at first—we just talked. I asked Tom to accompany me to a corporate dinner with out-of-town vendors the next night, and was surprised to learn that Tom worked in the engineering department of the company! I was so embarrassed that I hadn't thought to ask first! I was sure he thought I was some kind of airhead."

That dinner marked the start of their romance. They met for lunch; they spent as many nights after work together as they could. "Our romance just blossomed," said Debbie. "Tom may not agree, but we were so comfortable together I think even then we knew we would be married someday."

Tom laughed. "Maybe *you* knew," he said. "But I sure didn't!"

I asked them how it felt to be dating someone at work. They told me everything was fine until one day when they were spontaneously assigned to the same task force.

Usually, the marketing and engineering departments had little to do with one another, but it just so happened that a new task force was being created that required the input of both departments. A new, very special game with unique software had been created, and the marketing people had no idea how to approach the test market. Marketing needed the exact specifications from engineering before they could talk to advertisers intelligently about the uniqueness of the product.

Debbie said, "The initial meeting of the task force was a disaster. Engineers like Tom, especially computer design engineers, have their own language that permits them to talk to one another in shorthand. We marketing professionals also have created our own lingo. The result when the two groups get together can be a mess. The engineers had difficulty explaining the specifications to us as the marketing people. And we really needed to understand the demands of the new software to sell the product."

Tom continued: "It *was* a mess. The marketing people were very image-oriented, wanting to know about the positioning of the new product, and talking about market tests and geographical tests and that sort of thing. On the engineering side, we had little patience. First of all, we all hated meetings of this type. Second of all, we couldn't understand what they wanted from us. Their job is to go out and market the product. Ours is to create it. But sometimes, especially when you're the creator yourself, it is really hard to separate yourself from what you've done. It's like having a cook explain the details of an unwritten recipe that has been in the family for years and that she can make in her sleep, but has no real quantitative way to assemble."

Tom and Debbie found themselves caught in the middle of this conflict. After a particularly frustrating task force meeting one day, they discussed the issues over dinner.

"It became really frustrating," said Debbie. "We couldn't get a decent word out of them that we could use. One night, after a particularly bad meeting, Tom and I couldn't help discussing the problems. We talked all night until we each understood what was going on. Then the next day we went to our respective task force colleagues and explained, in our own language, what the other side needed."

The next task force meeting was highly successful. Success was largely attributed to the efforts of Tom and Debbie, who were able to use their personal relationship to improve communication on the task force. Cooperative relations among the task force members were re-established.

Benefit #6

OFFICE ROMANCE CAN ENRICH PERSONAL RELATIONSHIPS

Many of the couples with whom I have spoken have said that their personal relationships have been enriched and strengthened by working together in the office. Most couples believe working together with a spouse or lover adds dimension and sparkle to their personal relationship.

One man, a personal friend of mine who is married to a woman in his organization, said, "Before Leslie came to work here, we had separate careers. When she left her job, and applied here, we discussed all the pros and cons of us working in the same firm. I was nervous—so was she. But now we wouldn't have it any other way. I can go home and talk about the people we both know, and she can give me her perspectives in a way she couldn't before. . . . We help each other out because we understand each other's pressures and demands. Working together has strengthened our marriage, not broken it apart."

Having a lover, friend, romantic partner, and coworker all rolled into one can have a number of surprising benefits. Many couples say that their mutual work relationship helps them to understand one another better. An added advantage is that you may be able to empathize more with each other's work commitments.

"There's a real sense of mutual understanding now that Liz and I work for the same organization," said Paul, forty-four, a political analyst. "And it's fun because sometimes she surprises me with her views. We challenge each other at the office and at home. I feel I know her better as a person and as a professional. She also understands now why I must work late some nights."

Married couples who work closely together, such as Bonnie Bartlett and William Daniels of "St. Elsewhere," and Jill Eikenberry and Michael Tucker of "L.A. Law," the NBC television shows, have publicly stated their personal relationship has only enhanced their work relationship.[3] Because they understand one another so well on a personal level, couples working together can predict and interpret each other's reactions in a way that others cannot.

Of course, there are couples who maintain that the opposite is true. They have found that their work styles are so different that working together in the office is a mistake for their personal relationship. But this is not always the case. Couples who work together may bring a dimension of understanding to the work relationship that is unequaled. And there often is a positive "spillover" effect on the personal relationship as well.

Joy, a woman I interviewed for this book, talked frankly about this benefit. "It is my nature to blow off steam and jump to conclusions. Alan is entirely opposite—he waits, patiently analyzes a situation, and objectively states his concerns. Alan can give me a better sense of perspective on my crises because he knows the people with whom I work. He understands them, knows their personalities. Therefore, I can trust his judgment. On more than one occasion, he has prevented me from acting rashly."

In one case with which I am familiar, a woman was having great difficulty dealing with her boss. One day, after a particularly upsetting conflict over scheduling, her lover interceded. Bob, her lover, said, "Mark is a good guy. I knew that what Joan was telling me couldn't be the whole truth. So I called him up on the phone, told him I thought there was more to the story, and let him vent. I then let him in on a few of the pressures Joan was experiencing . . . he was very understanding." Because of his intervention, his lover and her boss were able to repair their damaged work relationship.

A spouse or lover's intervention can be most welcome at times like this. Especially for those couples who work in fast-paced, highly politicized office environments, having an ally in the office may be a priceless treasure.

A partner in a law firm who works with her husband said, "A year ago, the politics in this office were so thick you could cut it with a knife. That's not a bad analogy either, since a lot of backstabbing was happening. There was this situation that involved my husband and his evaluation of one of the junior partners on a case. He needed an ally. As it happened, I agreed with him, and was able to work with some of the others to help them come around to his judgments. My interventions really strengthened our relationship at a time when he felt he had nowhere to turn."

TOGETHER IS BETTER: CAROLINE AND WILLIAM

Caroline and William are college professors at the same university. But it didn't start out that way.

They met when Caroline decided to take a night course toward her MBA at the local university. William was her instructor.

"At first I didn't even notice him," said Caroline. "I was older than many of the students in the class, and quite nervous about the workload. I simply was concerned with passing the course."

William noticed the attractive, accomplished woman sitting at the back of the room. Her dedication to her coursework impressed him.

Caroline grew fascinated with one particular aspect of the course that she knew could help her in her job as a staff manager for an insurance firm. She met with William to gain additional information.

"As I got into it, I began to realize that what I really wanted was an academic career," said Caroline. "With William's encouragement, I applied for the doctoral program."

Their relationship remained platonic. But Caroline had made an impression.

William said, "I always looked forward to having her in class. She has a great mind . . . and her research instincts were stellar."

Caroline's chosen area of research dovetailed with William's. One of her seminar papers was outstanding. William encouraged her to publish it after he polished it. It was accepted in a major financial journal.

"We loved working together," said Caroline. "We still do. Our personal relationship has added a depth to our research that others only can envy."

Caroline and William continued to work together. He chaired her dissertation committee. After several years of a platonic relationship, at the end of her studies, they started dating. They were married two months later.

Caroline said, "There was no reason to wait. We already knew everything there was to know about each other. We were best friends, colleagues, and lovers."

Caroline applied for a position in William's department. But their colleagues demurred on her appointment. They were reluctant to appoint her because, they said, they were uncertain how much William had contributed to her research and what Caroline could accomplish on her own.

"I was fighting mad," said Caroline. "After all, they knew me. I already had begun establishing my own reputation in the field. I think petty jealousies were the underlying reasons for their reluctance. Some still are jealous. It took William everything he had to make me not go into their offices and tell them to take the job and shove it."

William encouraged Caroline to play the game. She went through a new round of appointments. She had letters of recommendation sent from faculty members outside the department attesting to her contributions.

Meanwhile, William intervened with his colleagues. He recommended if they had any concerns, he would share his faculty appointment with his wife, and during off semesters they would individually pursue their own research. "I was tenured, so I didn't have much to lose," said William. "Besides, the mutual offer was one they could really benefit from."

They accepted the offer on a one-year trial basis. It worked, and now Caroline has her own appointment—and tenure—at the university. "Working together has been wonderful," said Caroline. "We really understand the demands of each other's schedules. Now I know what it is like to teach and do research at the same time. I understand how all-consuming it is. I can appreciate that in William, and he can in me. We wouldn't have it any other way."

Benefit #7

OFFICE ROMANCE MAY STABILIZE THE WORKFORCE

A final benefit arises in many of the conversations I have had with corporate executives on this topic. Romance in corporations may be used as a recruitment and retention device to stabilize the workforce of certain firms.

Recent demographic trends show that geographic restrictions are complicating the career path choices of many employees. Dual career marriages often mean that when one spouse needs to find a new job, employers lose a valuable employee in the form of the other.

"It killed me when Joe left," said one research and development laboratory administrator. "And I knew he didn't want to go. He was our most valuable—or at least one of our most valuable—scientists in this division. But of course he had to go to the Midwest with his wife."

Some corporate executives have told me that they are changing their policies about married couples working together as a means to retain valuable personnel like Joe. "If only we could have found a job here for his wife," sighed the administrator despairingly.

Cable News Network (CNN) has long been known in the news business as a haven for married couples. Several couples have been employed as co-anchors. According to Steve Haworth, Director of Public Relations at CNN in Atlanta, "There are no formal policies to employ or not to employ a spouse, but, occasionally, we have offered employment to a spouse as part of attracting an employee to come or stay here. We do our best to find positions for those who are qualified."

Office romance may not only improve a firm's ability to retain valuable employees, but may also help the firm recruit them. "We knew her husband was a superstar," said one academic administrator about a newly hired faculty member. "It was our hope that if his wife came to work here we later could entice him as well."

This may be because, as one source at AT&T said, "We believe the workforce will dramatically change in the 1990s. There will be more women, more minorities, more international employees, and we may be faced with a workforce shortage. Developing anti-nepotism policies may cause us to lose valuable employees in the future."

Some corporations realize the benefits that office romance can bring for productivity, morale, and motivation—and unofficially encourage developing romances in their midst. "In this firm, management has the attitude, 'That's great' when you arrive at a corporate function with another employee," said a manager who works at a well-known Silicon Valley firm. "Secretly they hope if the romance works out, you probably will produce more together than apart. Besides, they know you will be less likely to leave the company for a competitor."

Believing in the Positives

All managers want to find ways to stimulate creativity, improve morale, increase productivity, enhance teamwork, and recruit the best of talent. What could be better than an office romance for encouraging all of this?

I think women—and men—need to become more aware of the benefits that office romances can bring to the workplace. It is my belief that they have been judged too harshly.

Even Mary Cunningham agrees that love in the office is worth the trouble. In her book, *Powerplay: What Really Happened at Bendix* (New York: Linden Press/Simon and Schuster, 1984), she states:

> The problems that can ensue within a corporation because of these romantic liaisons must be admitted. But those can be solved with a little creativity and ingenuity. And it is possible to balance both dimensions as long as a couple adopt certain considerate ways—such as no longer functioning as husband and wife the minute they walk through the corporate door. Bill and I have adopted this approach on our current projects, and, with few exceptions, it works well. And it actually allows us to devote more time to our jobs.

Not only may the personal relationship be enriched from the experience of an office romance, but the firm may discover a number of unrealized benefits. Women in particular need to realize that some very real advantages exist.

But there also can be an equal number of disadvantages. Risks to career and the potential for conflict with colleagues are serious concerns that should not be overlooked or discounted. In some firms, gossip and innuendo will follow you at every turn should you become involved with a colleague. And if the corporate risks are not sufficiently threatening, what about the personal risks? What is it like to sustain a long-term relationship—both in the office and at home—with a colleague who also is your lover? Can feelings of competition ruin a marriage?

The new sexual revolution does not come without its price. The next chapter reveals the hazards and perils of which you should beware.

5

THE REALITIES AND
THE RISKS

I can still see Cassandra as vividly as when she was sitting across from me at the lunchroom table in her stark, whitewashed company cafeteria. Having just led a difficult and draining morning workshop session on career development, both of us were exhausted. The afternoon session still was ahead of us. All we could do was stare at our food as the joggers passed by our brightly lit cafeteria window in the midday sunshine.

As one man in particular jogged by, I noticed she became more attentive. I followed her gaze. Cassandra watched the man as he rounded the corner. She noticed his build, his bearing, his posture. She sighed deeply once he had cleared out of sight, and went back to playing with her food.

Looking for any topic of conversation other than career development, I decided to ask her about her reaction. Tentatively, I said, "A friend?"

"No," she responded. "But I wish he were. His name is George, and we did a lot of project work together on the X-19 marketing initiative last year. He is solid, dependable, has a great body—couldn't you tell?—and he even has a promising future with the company. He's everything I am looking for in a man."

"Sounds good," I said. "So why aren't you doing anything about him?"

"Are you kidding?" Cassandra responded, with disbelief in her eyes. "Ruin my career with this company after ten years of hard labor getting to where I am today? No way!"

Let's face it. Popular opinion doesn't materialize from thin air; there is usually some basis to such fears. Despite the benefits, there are serious risks that should be carefully considered.

One woman in my survey wrote, "I don't care what anyone says. Love in the office just isn't worth the risk. Women are still left behind, and it's awful to break up with a coworker. Dating your boss can be a real mistake."

Another woman said, "I was involved in an office romance and I am now sorry I was. My professional reputation was diminished [at that firm] because of my actions—and my lover's as well. We both had to leave the firm because relationships [with others] were strained, even though we never did anything unethical or wrong."

A television producer commented, "My affair . . . with another producer caused tongues to wag and problems in the office. We worked really well together but no longer can because there was so much gossip about the affair. My relationships with the people I work with are now strained. They keep wondering what I know about them—you know, what he told me during the affair—whether I will use the information politically . . . and so on."

According to the 1988 Bureau of National Affairs report, office romances cause nervousness among employees who worry about:

- Whether the liaison means unequal treatment for others in the office
- Whether the executives' thinking and decision-making abilities are clouded because they are in love
- Whether the balance of power in the corporation will be upset because of the personal alliance between the lovers
- Whether the channels of communication will be scrambled as a result of the romance

These are significant concerns. Imagine working for a boss who is befuddled by love. If the cause of your boss's confusion is your best friend and coworker, watch out! You might find yourself reporting to her—indirectly—before long.

The risks that people fear may result from an office romance are real and should not be minimized. Most of the women who responded to my survey indicated a far stronger response on the risks than the benefits. At least two-thirds of the women identified risks. Only one-quarter to one-third noticed any benefits.

A poorly conducted office romance can spell trouble for not only the couple but for colleagues as well. Reputations can be jeopardized, productivity may decline, and management may intervene in the affair for the sake of office morale. Coworkers, the couple, managers, and the organization may suffer needlessly. This is what many of the women in my survey feared.

The Seven Risks to Avoid

Specifically, what are some of the risks that people fear? Here are some of the more difficult ones.

Risk #1

OFFICE ROMANCE CAN THREATEN CAREER ADVANCEMENT

Probably the number one concern that many people share about office romance is that career advancement will be threatened. In this age of cut-throat competition in career ambitions, few people are willing to accept this risk.

"My romance spoiled any chances I had," said one woman who desperately wanted to become part of her firm's high potential list. "Because of my affair with Charlie, upper management started wondering about my judgment. It was a major mistake for me that cost me my career in this firm. I'm looking for another job now."

In my survey of executive women, 63 percent of those surveyed felt that careers could be compromised by an office romance. More than half felt this risk was too much to bear.

Most people wonder how the short-term gains of an office affair could possibly outweigh some of the longer-term risks. Especially for those employees who are only interested in a fling, a question arises: Is a fling with a colleague worth sabotaging your career?

One woman, a plant manager at a chemical processing firm, reported, "My office affair [with a subordinate] cost me my career. The affair really didn't mean all that much to me—just an attractive guy from whom I wanted some companionship—not marriage or anything long-term; I'd been through all that. But the rumors that were generated really messed me up. I am now going for a transfer to start fresh in another location."

Gwen, a thirty-year-old health care director for a medical conglomerate, agrees. "The problem with office romance is that it is so damn messy. People accuse you of everything—especially when you're sleeping with the boss. And if he's married or if you are, you might as well kiss your career goodbye in this company."

The kind of risks you experience depends on the politics of your firm, the culture of your company, and in particular, the circumstances of your liaison. Extramarital affairs cause discomfort among coworkers and bring into question issues of morality, judgment, and ethics. Boss-subordinate relationships often create jealousy on the part of coworkers, who fear favoritism. Office morale may be disrupted if the personal relationship is manipulated for professional gains.

"We hated it when Nellie was dating Larry," said one colleague who observed a boss-subordinate romance in a small manufacturing firm. "We watched them closely—too closely, I think, because nothing ever really happened. But the mere fact that they were seeing one another made us suspicious."

Kathy, a twenty-eight-year-old mail order service representative, believes this is a necessary caveat. "The old adage 'Don't mess around in your own backyard' is definitely true for boss-employee relationships. There is too much at stake. Even if nothing bad is going on, people assume it is, so the whole situation is a mess. You can be used in that type of situation."

HOW NOT TO RUIN YOUR CAREER: STEPHANIE AND MARK

I met Stephanie only after much cajoling from her friend, Betty, who was a student in one of my classes. Betty told me she had a friend who had slept with a subordinate. In the process, her career had been ruined.

Curious, I gave Stephanie a call. At first she didn't want to talk to me, but after promises of anonymity, she gave in.

I asked Stephanie how the romance began. "I met Mark when he was assigned to my department. Mark was a new hire from another company, and he was different from the standard college graduates I usually hired. Mark had corporate experience, and was considerably older than his peers."

When Stephanie met Mark, she said, "One of the first things that attracted me to Mark was his experience. I was working with all these college kids at the time, and being with Mark was a refreshing change. He had this calm, cool look about him that I found terribly appealing."

Stephanie recognized that Mark had specialized expertise that could be utilized on a project she was considering. She asked Mark for his input. He suggested that they get together for a series of meetings to discuss solutions. Their meetings were scheduled for late in the day, and often ran through dinner.

Stephanie said, "I really looked forward to our work sessions. I was able to learn from Mark as much as he was able to learn from me. We had this mutual understanding. . . . We were able to be really creative together, to discuss all the issues, to come up with a number of innovative ideas. Working with Mark was play, not work—I would go home and get depressed afterward because it had been so much fun. I hated to leave."

Both were single, available, and interested in each other. One day, Mark suggested that they go to a local bar after their meeting. That night, they ended up in bed.

Stephanie said, "For the first time, there I was, timidly inviting a colleague—and a subordinate—to my apartment. It was so strange. . . . We knew so much about each other from our work relationship, but he didn't even know where I lived! And as I was driving home, I wasn't sure I really wanted to tell him . . . but we knew that we were destined to be together that night."

They drove to work together the next day. Stephanie was concerned about letting news of the romance leak out; Mark proudly made it known that they had slept together.

"I was embarrassed," said Stephanie. "We had gone to bed as private lovers. For me it was a personal thing. But Mark wanted to shout the news of our relationship from the rooftops. He told some of the people in the office even before we had a chance to talk about it and plan a strategy."

They continued to work on the special project. Stephanie spent a great deal of her time with Mark. They had lunch together, held meetings behind closed doors, and worked exclusively with one another. Coworkers grew resentful of all the attention Mark was receiving. They felt abandoned by their boss.

My student, Betty, told me, "The problem was that Stephanie was a good developer of people but she was spending all her time concentrating on Mark. I think some of her subordinates simply became jealous."

The special project culminated in a presentation to the marketing director of their firm. Mark made the presentation, with Stephanie's coaching behind the scenes. The marketing director was impressed, and gave Mark the go-ahead on the project.

Mark received considerable visibility and recognition for his project efforts. Rumors started flying that Mark was up for a promotion. At the time, he had only been employed for three months. Coworkers were indignant at the news and made their anger about it known. Morale declined and departmental productivity hit a standstill. The standard joke was, "It's not what you do that gets you promoted around here, it's who you sleep with."

Betty said, "Things went from bad to worse. All kinds of ugly rumors started. Stephanie was accused of being a Svengali."

After two more months of colleague resistance, Stephanie decided that she had had enough. She made the choice to end the romance for the sake of her career. She retained deep feelings for Mark, however, and was deeply hurt when he started dating another woman in a different department.

Stephanie said, "I couldn't believe it when it was over. He

was dating this other woman—and I was extremely jealous. I would get depressed just thinking of the two of them together. It felt like my whole life had crumbled to pieces.

But Stephanie's personal pain was augmented by management's reaction to the news of the romance. Stephanie's boss called her in for a discussion about her personal conduct. He asked her if the personal relationship had anything to do with Mark's assignment to and performance on the special project. She said no. Taking this as a falsehood, he transferred Stephanie to another division. Mark was promoted to her job.

According to Betty, "The decision . . . was especially ironic because their romance was over at the time. And her boss was known to be sleeping with his secretary on the side, even though they were both married!"

Risk #2

OFFICE ROMANCE CAN RUIN PROFESSIONAL RELATIONSHIPS

Stephanie's relationship with Mark was not only traumatic because she jeopardized her career, but also because she had to go through a painful breakup. Stephanie said, "Between ruining my career and losing a man for whom I cared deeply, I wasn't certain I could go on. It almost was too painful to bear."

Endings are normally messy, but they are especially so when they involve the dissolution of an office romance. You must continue to see your ex-lover on a daily basis. He will be a constant reminder of the failure of the relationship.

As one woman manager in my survey stated, "When my personal life was not going well in the past, I always could escape into my work life, and vice versa. One of the things I found most difficult was the end of the romance. I still have to work with Walter and maintain a collegial relationship, even though we are no longer involved."

Next to career risks, most people have told me they fear an office breakup. Sixty-five percent of the women I surveyed said they believed the romance could ruin professional relationships in the office. As one woman told me, "Breaking up with a coworker is an impossible thing to do. Your professional relationship can be ruined forever."

Dealing with the aftermath of an unsuccessful romance in the office can be messy. And blending your personal and professional lives can make your romance more complicated. But neither is impossible.

Said one woman, "I always believed office affairs were too messy to handle. But then I met and fell in love with a manager in one of our stores. . . . I was very concerned—almost panicked—about what would happen if the romance did not work out. As things happened, it didn't, for a variety of reasons. But we still manage to work together well. In fact, my former boyfriend remains my best confidant in the office."

Because so many people fear a breakup, those who are involved sometimes feel they must protect themselves against this eventuality. A friend of mine, who recently became involved with a man in her office, came to see me three days after their first date. She laid out an elaborate plan of transfers to other departments, the possibility of leaving the company, the when and the where. She said, "I must plan ahead. This man is important to me. He can do some damage to my life if things don't work out."

Responsible couples develop contingency plans should their romance sour. They make decisions—_in advance_—as to whether one member of the couple will request a transfer, and who will accept that burden. Or they determine how they can isolate their professional relationship from personal feelings should the romance fail. Couples must recognize that professional relationships must be maintained for the good of the team—regardless of how they work out.[1]

BREAKING UP IS HARD TO DO: SHEILA AND SAM

One romance that illustrates this problem is the story of Sheila and Sam.

Sheila and Sam originally met on a business trip to the annual meeting of their professional association. Both Sheila and Sam held Ph.D.s from respected universities and had taken positions in different chemical research and development laboratories. Their research interests were similar—both were study-ing applications of polymer chemicals in industry.

At the association meeting, Sheila and Sam were on the same panel to discuss their separate research findings. Both had presented a paper on the subject, and had attended the same conference sessions.

According to Sam, they noticed one another right away. He said, "I saw this great-looking gal go up to the podium. I swear she looked right at me. Then she started talking about things that were directly related to my specialty. Kind of floored me, you know?"

The conference session led to a heated debate. Sam and Sheila defended the differences in their findings. The session lasted longer than anyone expected, and was emotionally charged. You could feel the challenges, the tension in the room. But Sam and Sheila fought on. A truce was declared, and the conference session was adjourned.

To make sure no feelings were injured, Sam asked Sheila to dinner. He was impressed with this woman who dared to ques-tion his research. Sheila flirted with Sam, toyed with him, and made him disclose some areas of his research that he never thought he would tell anyone. One thing led to another, and that night, Sheila and Sam shared the same hotel room.

Sheila said, "It was just one of those things, you know? We had a lot of fun together, and sleeping together that night was a way of continuing the fun. We were just playing around."

Both thought that when the conference ended, so would their romance. But Fate stepped in and rearranged the circum-stances. Sheila discovered upon returning to her lab that the company's strategic direction had changed and they would no longer be emphasizing research on chemical polymers. Upset by the change, Sheila applied for research jobs at several chemical companies.

Sheila said, "It wasn't planned, but it just so happened that my best offer came from Sam's company. I felt I would be a fool not to take the offer. I said yes."

She was concerned, however, about Sam's reaction to her presence. Sam was unaware that Sheila had been hired for a new position; he was so involved in his research that he only had a vague recollection that someone new was being hired, and that was all. Imagine his surprise when Sheila showed up in his laboratory one day!

"I couldn't believe it," said Sam. "At first I thought she was in the neighborhood and had stopped in to say hello. I was away when she was interviewed, so I knew nothing about her appointment. I almost fell off the bench when my group leader told me we would be working together."

Fortunately, after a brief period of awkwardness, they were able to rekindle their passionate romance. Sheila said, "It was a little odd at first. I mean, here was this man I had slept with, and now suddenly I had to get to know him as a colleague. Once you've known someone in the biblical sense, it can be a little weird. But we talked it through, and didn't rush into anything. I had been employed full-time for two months before we did anything about it."

For a short while, everything was rosy. Sheila and Sam both thought that they had met the partner of their dreams. But little things began to grate on each partner.

Sam was a neatnik who hated clutter and confusion; Sheila thrived on it. Sam liked to read books and professional journal material on his own time at night; Sheila preferred to watch TV. Sam enjoyed fishing; Sheila hated it. Sam would sometimes get so wrapped up in his research that he would refuse to come home at night; the only way Sheila found she could be productive was by taking a break and clearing her mind before moving on to the next problem. Sam hated parties; Sheila thrived on them.

They began to realize that although they had a great deal in common in terms of work interests, their personal styles did not match. But they still had to work together.

"We didn't realize how opposite we were," said Sam, "until much later. We fought a lot about stupid, silly things. The relationship just wasn't working. But the professional collaboration was."

The project to which Sheila had been assigned was housed in Sam's department, and there was no way that Sheila could move to another area. They were stuck together. So they had to grin and bear it.

They broke off the romance after six months. Sam said of

the breakup, "Yeah, it was tough. I mean, there we were, thinking everything was going along well, but we both knew that the romance couldn't last. We should have ended it in that hotel room. I think because of the work we forced ourselves to stick it out longer than we should. But we didn't want to deal with the ending."

Sheila and Sam still work together in the same lab. They managed to put their feelings aside for the good of their collaboration. Their coworkers have been surprised with how well they handled the situation. Sometimes a breakup works out for the best.

Risk #3

OFFICE ROMANCE CAN CAUSE COWORKER CONFUSION —AND SCORN

Because office romancers live love in a fishbowl, the prying eyes of colleagues are ever present. They are as much a part of the office romance as the couple.

Sheila said, "The tough part was letting everyone in the lab know we were breaking up. I think some of them took the news much harder than we did when it finally came out!"

Colleagues usually are as confused as the couple about how to react to the news of a personal liaison. A coworker who observed the Joy and Alan romance reported in chapter 3 expressed her concerns in this way: "Both Joy and Alan were well liked by all of us in the office. We were pleased to see them get together. But even though we were all friends, as well as peers, we just didn't know how to respond. I mean, when you see them walking in together in the morning, do you joke about it? Do you pretend not to notice?"

Because colleagues are confused over whether to treat the couple as individuals or as a team, they often mistreat or misjudge the couple. One woman I know complained that the one thing she really disliked about her office romance was that her lover's subordinates always came to her to see if she could get him to change his mind about unfavorable decisions. For example, on one occasion, his subordinates wanted to get her to change the location of their Christmas party. Her reaction was,

"If they want a different kind of office party this year, they should tell him themselves!"

Another woman told me that she resented her boss going to see her husband to find out how she was doing on the job. Her reaction was, "He [her boss] should have come directly to me to ask that kind of question. Why did he feel he had to go to see my husband? And I further was angry at my husband for giving my boss *his* opinion on how *I* was doing. I can speak for myself!"

Even worse is a guilt-by-association problem that colleagues—and bosses—sometimes levy against office romancers. One woman told me, "My live-in lover . . . is known for being a real rebel—taking radical stands on the issues, raising hell. He is not well liked by the administration for this reason. I found myself in a compromising position when I wanted to be hired for a position [in his area]; they assumed that I too would be a hell-raiser [and were] reluctant to hire me for that reason."

Marisa, thirty-nine, had a similar story: "Geoff was brought in as a division manager in charge of public relations with a resume as long as your arm. But when the chemical spill fiasco broke, his neck was on the line with the press. In the company's view, he didn't handle the situation as well as he could have, so he was suddenly *persona non grata*. But I had nothing to do with the whole mess, and yet people were on my case to tell Geoff what to do and say."

Sometimes coworkers scorn the relationship altogether. It is not uncommon for an entire department of employees to ostracize a romantic couple—especially if they behave unprofessionally.

A friend of mine told me about one couple who created havoc in the office because they constantly had knock-down, drag-out fights with one another if something went wrong in their personal relationship. My friend surmised, "Either this couple enjoyed the opportunity to stage a romance in front of the others, or wanted us to serve as referees. Of course, we backed off. But it made life really uncomfortable."

One woman told me that because her office partner had broken up an affair with a colleague in another department, she constantly had to be the one who would courier paperwork from his department to hers and vice versa because her friend refused for fear of seeing her old lover. "I was angry," said Catherine, "because I was placed in the middle. I found her behavior to be very unprofessional."

Still others told me of smooching in the office hallways, pats on the back, or fondling under the table in meetings that turned colleagues sour on public displays of affection. Watching people act in unprofessional ways causes you to lose respect. You begin to wonder if you misjudged them or their abilities.

"C'mon, let's get real," said one male manager. "Christ, if you have a romance in the office, at least tell people to keep it to themselves. All this kissy-kissy around the office makes me sick."

FIGHTING IN THE OFFICE: MAX AND CHERYL

Max and Cheryl were a passionate but troubled couple. Their romance was distinguished by horrendous fighting and intimate loving. This was a problem for coworkers because much of their fighting—and loving—occurred within the confines of their small office. I heard this story from one of their peers, who endured their behavior for several months.

According to my source, Belinda, Max and Cheryl were a couple who believed in fighting first and making up later. Their screaming, knock-down, drag-out fights in front of coworkers were legendary. "If Max and Cheryl were having a good day, everyone had a good day. If Max and Cheryl had a problem, everyone suffered," said Belinda.

One day, Cheryl was so upset with Max's behavior the previous night that she screamed when she saw him enter the office in the morning, and proceeded to punch him out. They continued yelling and screaming in the halls, all the way out to the parking lot.

Another day, Cheryl wanted Max to pay more attention to her. To get his attention, she started flirting with a colleague. Max became so angry and upset that he tore up a report she'd spent months preparing. On yet another occasion, when Cheryl spotted Max talking to an attractive sales representative, she decided to get even. She sprayed shaving cream all over his car.

"Their antics were entertaining to watch—at first, anyway," said Belinda. "We watched from our window seats in the office and anxiously awaited the outcome of each fight." The romance went on like this: fighting, making up, screaming, yelling, making up again. After a while, the romance caused so much stress for colleagues that they could not stand it any longer.

Belinda said, "We had to go to the boss. He was fully aware of what had been going on. I think he was just waiting for an excuse [to do something]."

A transfer to different departments was arranged for both Cheryl and Max. They were given no choice in the matter.

I believe this kind of a lack of separation between personal and professional lives—and generally unprofessional behavior—is what causes the most trouble. If a couple cannot develop a blend of professional distance and personal intimacy at home, there can be many problems—for the couple, colleagues, management, and the total organization.

Risk #4

OFFICE ROMANCE MAY CAUSE WORK PERFORMANCE TO DECLINE

As in the case of Max and Cheryl, sometimes the pure passion of the romance can distract the couple from their job tasks, causing them to lose their concentration on their work. This can be deadly.

Because colleagues are like family, they notice mood changes and attitude shifts. When you fall behind your usual work performance, coworkers notice even before you do because your work typically affects theirs.

Any change in performance may cause suspicion and distrust. It's almost as if there is an unspoken code that says, "What you do on your own is your own business, but if it affects my work, watch out!" The very next minute they may be in your boss's office telling her the same thing.

Geraldine, a forty-three-year-old personnel manager, agrees. "I can tell when two people are involved. Usually they are slower getting their work back to me. There's a lot of paperwork in this job, and it's the kind of paperwork most managers want to delay. But when I have to call eighteen times to get the paperwork, that's a different story."

I said in the previous chapter that performance sometimes may increase depending on the stage of the romance. But the reverse is true as well. The honeymoon stage of the romance can lead to inattention and productivity declines. Performance problems also may surface during the climax stage if things are not going smoothly.[2]

"When I first fell in love with Joe, I couldn't concentrate," said Patricia, a graphics artist. "Just being around him made me crazy. I stared into space a lot. My boss teased me about it."

Helen, forty-two, echoed this sentiment. "After my divorce, everything fell apart—my work, my relationships with my kids, everything. But then I got back my concentration . . . until Tony came along. Then it started all over again, but I had to get control of myself because my performance had slipped so badly in the past year. I couldn't afford any more mistakes."

In the Quinn survey reported in *Administrative Science Quarterly* in 1977, 14 percent of the men and 17 percent of the women were reported to have produced lower quality work as a result of the romance. In Anderson and Hunsaker's 1985 *Personnel* magazine survey, a lower quality of work was attributed to 24 percent of women and 14 percent of men. In my own survey, however, less than a quarter of those involved showed a productivity decline, yet more than half the women I polled expected work performance to decrease as a result of romance.[3]

A CASE OF POOR CONCENTRATION: ANNE AND GEOFFREY

Anne and Geoffrey found that once they became involved romantically, they simply couldn't concentrate upon their work. I did not personally meet Anne and Geoffrey as part of the research for this book. But I did get an earful about this romance from one of the employees of their design firm who directly observed the effects of the romance upon the couple's productivity. His story was so vivid that I decided it deserved a place in this book.

According to my source, Anne recently was divorced and

in her mid-thirties; Geoffrey was a younger man in his twenties, a design whiz from a well-known trade institution. They met while working for the same upscale design firm that primarily served high profile corporate clients in the San Francisco Bay area. The company was doing very well, as you could tell the moment you walked in the door. Chrome, glass, steel, peach and gray velour, and expensive modern paintings decorated the lobby.

Anne and Geoffrey were both part of the design staff. Their work required creativity as well as strict attention to detail. They needed to know everything about their clients: their tastes in music, art, literature, color—anything and everything helped to determine the appropriate design atmosphere for a particular firm. They had to judge a client's personality from a brief meeting about color and decor. And they had to get it right.

One day, after a particularly taxing session with a corporate client, Anne and Geoffrey decided to go to a local bar to discuss concepts. One thing led to another, and they decided to spend the night together. The next day, according to my source, "all hell broke loose in the office."

My source said, "They couldn't get enough of one another. At work, they would pat each other on the rump, and take a pencil and draw on the other's body. They would physically massage one another at their desks. Anne took to wearing the sexiest, most open, flowing blouses she could find. One day I walked in and found Geoffrey's hand on her breast."

They frequently made excuses to leave the office for exceptionally long lunches together. Or they would come in to the office unusually late in the morning. Just as often, they would leave in the middle of the day supposedly to visit a corporate client. On occasion they never made it, and had to reschedule the appointment with a fuming corporate executive.

Their performance began to slip. They started missing appointments with important clients. They could not concentrate in their meetings with clients when they did attend, because they were so passionate for one another. They had to reschedule meetings and call back clients to determine which color the sofa was to be.

My source said, "In the office, their work piled up. Nothing was getting done. It was a real mess that the rest of us had to clean up after the fact. We were all so angry, and felt abused. Their behavior was unprofessional to say the least."

Because they were courting each other in the office, they both found themselves missing critical details that were essential for the quality of their work. My source continued, "They were forgetful. They were inattentive. They lost their ability to concentrate. In a short period of time their jobs were in jeopardy."

In desperation, they asked coworkers, like my source, to cover for them. On one occasion, they asked him to substitute for them in a meeting with one of the firm's best clients.

He said, "You couldn't, wouldn't believe the antics of these two. It is beyond description. It was as if they were caught in some sort of a mystical passion, like some of the scenes in a porno movie. In fact, I think they got their kicks out of displaying their sexuality in the office. They wanted everyone to know they had the hots for each other."

Their mistakes grew more noticeable, and corporate clients were calling to find out when their design masters would be ready. Colleagues found that it was impossible to cover for them; there were so many mistakes as a result of their inattention. Finally, when the situation grew entirely out of hand, their boss stepped in and asked them to leave.

Risk #5

OFFICE ROMANCE CAN LEAD TO SELF-DOUBT AND LOST OBJECTIVITY

Not only may performance decline, as in the case of Anne and Geoffrey, but another risk that couples must confront is that of self-doubt and lost objectivity. Sometimes, because of the politics and gossip that surround a romance, their competence and professionalism is undermined.

In the majority of cases, these questions are spurred as a result of petty jealousies. But in some situations, there may be an actual basis to the rumors. Overtly, most couples will staunchly defend their professional decisions as having nothing to do with their personal relationship. But some couples have confided to me that secretly they wonder if there is an unconscious basis to the rumors.

One woman who worked for a recruiting firm commented in my survey, "My theory has always been that it's a bad idea to date anyone at work. However, three years ago I fell in love with my boss. My boss (who is my fiance) is stricter with me than with other employees because he wants to be sure no one thinks he's playing favorites—hence he's unfair to me! So, I think I'll stick with my original theory!"

Because "love is blind," many couples wonder if their personal feelings are clouding their professional judgments. This can destroy self-esteem and self-worth. When I interviewed Peggy, a woman who became involved in a romantic liaison with her mentor, Bill, she felt this way. At the time, she wondered, "Did I really receive the promotion as a result of my performance? Or did Bill influence the decision?" Peggy maintains that she remained grateful to Bill for his help, but in part, her gratitude destroyed their romance. Peggy never could shake her feelings of self-doubt until she took another job away from Bill to prove to herself—and others—that she could do the work on her own.

One woman commented anonymously in my survey, "I have a very talented female friend who will never work to her potential because she always goes to bed with her boss. . . . She has lost her self-esteem. . . . No amount of reinforcement has stopped the repeated actions on my friend's part. I would like to see her regain her sense of self-worth, and handle her workplace as work and her personal life outside it."

A CASE OF LOST OBJECTIVITY: JOHN AND SUZANNE

John and Suzanne illustrate how lost objectivity can compromise careers.

John, Suzanne's boss, was considered an up-and-coming manager, effective at his work and known for bringing innovative marketing approaches to his company. John was a go-getter. In his thirties, he had the air of a distinguished gentleman. He had inner strength. When you were with John, you felt secure.

Suzanne was a twenty-five-year-old college graduate who

wanted to get ahead without really doing a lot of work. Suzanne wanted all the trappings of success—with minimal effort. Her charge accounts were astronomical. She relied on funds from "Daddy" to pay her bills.

Suzanne was the sort who did her job competently but was not motivated to take the initiative to go beyond the boundaries of her job description. In fact, she confided to a friend that she really would just like to be somebody's mistress so she could have what she wanted—a nice apartment, dinners at the best restaurants, a mink coat—with as little effort as possible.

John, for whatever mysterious reason, became attracted to her. He felt sorry for her. She complained to him that no one recognized how wonderful her work was. She said that the company was anti-women. She used every excuse in the book to be perceived as the poor little girl in John's eyes.

John was captivated. Wanting to make things right, he said he would find a way to make a change. He attempted to persuade others at his level that Suzanne's work had improved to the point where she was truly deserving of a promotion. In reality, nothing of the kind had occurred.

John said, "I wanted to help her out a bit. I gave her a highly visible marketing project to work on which I felt would show others what she could do. But boy, was I wrong. Blinded by love, I guess."

Suzanne was out of her league on the project. She had to consult with everyone she could to get even some of the initial information she would have needed to evaluate the project objectives. She grew frustrated and asked John for his help. Many nights John stayed up and did her work for her.

But even with John's added help, there was little that could be done. It was clear that she was not executive level. John himself began to see that this was true.

"I couldn't deny it any longer," said John. "I tried coaching her, counseling her, doing some of her work for her—because her performance reflected on my judgment. I got mad—at her, and especially at myself—for not seeing things the way they were."

But by the time he realized what was happening, others around him already had written him off.

John decided he could stand it no longer. When he broke

off the relationship, Suzanne started arriving late and leaving early. When she was in the office, she sulked and hardly did any work.

John was not about to let his career go down the drain because of a misjudgment. He encouraged Suzanne to take a job in what was generally known as a dead-end area of the company. She did.

John said, now in retrospect, "This girl . . . if I had only seen it coming. I guess sometimes love is blind. She was a spoiled little kid. She had it coming to her."

Risk #6

OFFICE ROMANCE MAY GENERATE COMPETITION AND CONFLICT

On some days, dealing with your lover in the office environment can be quite trying. You may find yourself disliking his behavior in a meeting. Your department may be fighting against his. He may resent your attitude about how he handled a particular project. Colleagues may come to you complaining about him—or they may complain to him about you.

"There are some things about Bob's style in the office that I really object to," said one woman about her fiancé. "He can be very overbearing with employees—he pushes them like the workaholic he is. I'm more flexible. People come to me and complain about him all the time. It has caused a number of fights between us at home."

Probably the greatest type of conflict couples experience is peer competition over career paths. There is always a danger that one will advance at a faster rate than the other. In fact, the specter of career competition is enough to turn many people off the idea of an office romance.

A man I know well who works in the energy industry said, "When you are involved in a relationship that has the potential for competition—especially if you work in the same department—there is always the possibility that one will be promoted over the other. This can have a spillover effect onto the personal relationship, and in some cases your personal intimacy can be compromised."

One woman who responded to my survey said, "I have been involved in several office romances (unfortunately) since my divorce. . . . My relationships basically don't work after a somewhat short period of time because of the fears that surround my status as well as my position—I'm the number one representative in the entire company, out of five thousand employees. This is incredibly threatening to a man. Of course there is no reason whatsoever for them to fear me—how outdated a notion."

Having your lover turn into your enemy can be almost too difficult to bear for married couples who believe that spouses are supposed to be best friends and allies. I know of three relationships in which one member was promoted to the exclusion of the other, creating havoc in their personal relationships.

One woman told me: "Our relationship . . . has not been the same since my last promotion. Even though my lover will not admit it, I know that he feels emasculated [by my promotion]. I don't know what to do."

Competition occurs in various guises. Overt competition for promotions is only one form. Competition over the size of the paycheck is another. More subtle forms—such as who is better liked by coworkers, who has better relationships with clients, and who is likely to be mentored by the boss—can also occur.

One woman entrepreneur I know who works with her lover finds that they are always jockeying for the affection and loyalty of subordinates. "We get along, but there is this unspoken tension if our management people prefer his ideas to mine, or mine to his. It must be difficult for those who work with us."

Another woman said, "Last year, when my bonus was greater than my husband's, I was almost afraid to suggest that we go out to dinner to celebrate. . . . I didn't know whether to be happy for me or sad for him."

One woman who lives with her partner said, "The only thing we have found that works is to back each other up all the way, even if one of us disagrees with the other. We run a small entrepreneurial business, and we can't allow ourselves to get jealous or competitive or concerned about who has the most control. When a decision needs to be made, even if we disagree, we decide on the best choice for the business and support one another completely. It is good for business to do so, and that's that. Case closed."

As one man I know dealing with the difficulties of relocation said to me, "It's a no-win situation. Either she moves with me so that I can get a better position, and she may lose time in her career, or I stay here and support her. One of us is going to lose at some point."

A CASE OF COMPETITION: HELEN AND ERIC

Helen and Eric almost lost their marriage because of career competition that threatened to destroy their relationship. Helen, one of my students, came to class one night obviously upset. During the break, I asked her what was wrong. She related to me that she and her husband had met in the office and recently married. Now that their lives had just begun to get settled, the company had decided to shut down its local office and move the company headquarters to the Midwest. She was afraid that only one of them would be promoted, that the company was about to leave the other behind. I asked her to tell me the story.

Helen and her husband, Eric, had met when they both were hired at the company just after completing college. They worked for a computer software firm that had gained a great reputation over the past ten years, and were excited by the fast-growing technology and abundant opportunities presented in such a firm. They dedicated themselves to their careers in this firm to gain the opportunities for advancement they felt they both deserved.

Helen said that the first time she was promoted it was no big deal, because there were rumors that Eric would also be promoted around the same time. "At our company, it was pretty standard that unless you really screwed up, you would have a chance at the next level. We both knew that in time, we would each get our chance. So our first promotions occurred within a six-month period. We were just dating then, and we were each happy for the other's success."

In time, their personal relationship deepened. They chose to get married. Helen believed that their decision caused the dynamics of competition to set in. "For some reason, as soon as it was known that we were going to be married, Eric started thinking that he had to be the primary breadwinner. Anyway, an opportunity came up and he got the job. It gave him a lot of visibility with the executive level, and we were no longer reporting to the same boss."

However, Eric continually made references to his career potential at home. Helen was excited for him, happy for his success, but continued to plod along in her own work. She received several favorable performance ratings. Her bonus was greater than Eric's. Her concern that night in class, she confided in me, was that she would soon lose her husband.

Because her evaluations were so favorable, she was considered the more valuable member of their "team." The company was moving its headquarters to a location in the Midwest, and it was possible that Eric—or Helen—would be fired or promoted as a consequence.

"I am afraid the company only will give me an offer to move," confided Helen. "What will this do to our marriage?"

The following semester, I ran into Helen at lunch. I asked her what had happened.

Helen told me that Eric wasn't promoted, nor was she. Instead they were transferred to the Midwest corporate headquarters as a team.

She said, "It was really tough there for a while. Eric and I were so competitive with one another, we couldn't even have a dinner conversation without discussing our career potentials in the company. I was jealous of him, he was jealous of me. But we talked it out. Now that everything's settled, we're back to normal. We have made a vow never to let our careers get in the way of our marriage ever again."

In their new job situation, Helen and Eric have become the best of colleagues—and friends. "Now we really pull together as a team. We help each other with our work. Eric is a fountain of good ideas for me, and I have helped him resolve a few political situations. . . . Now we view our careers as *our* career, not his and mine. What's good for one is good for the other. The funny thing is, once we resolved the competition thing, we both were promoted. We are very happy now."

Risk #7

_____

OFFICE ROMANCE CAN CAUSE PROFESSIONAL CONFLICTS OF INTEREST

One of the things that makes coworkers (and management) uncomfortable about married couples like Helen and Eric—or any other couple, for that matter—is the possibility of "pillow talk." Certain work information may cause a conflict of interest.

One academic couple whom I know well is constantly confronted with this dilemma. As professors in separate schools of the same university, they are often at odds with one another over funding for each university division and the goals and priorities of each of their schools. Voting on common faculty issues sometimes yields differences of opinion. I asked them how they resolve these issues.

Said Liza, "People assume that we discuss everything at home. But they would be surprised to find how rarely we do. We talk things out and then make up our minds as individuals. If we vote differently on a matter, then we both learn to respect each other's viewpoints and leave it at that."

Adds Ed, Liza's husband, "But we try to stay away from those areas where there is a direct conflict of interest. For example, if Liza wants to run for a position on the faculty senate, I will absent myself from consideration. We prefer not to engage in a direct conflict of interest if that is preventable. But if an issue arises on which we differ, we discuss the problem, and make up our own minds."

Managers are most concerned about the damage that conflicts of interests can do to business—and to the couple. Said one executive in the banking industry, "It is the policy of this company to separate and isolate couples from working together, because we don't want them to do damage to their marriage if there's a problem. And we especially do not want security leaks or private information to be discussed by the couple."

In fact, Eliza Collins, a former editor of *Harvard Business Review* and a writer on this subject, believes that office romances should be treated as a conflict of interest. In her September 1983 article, "Managers and Lovers," she says, "The top manager needs to be clear in his own mind before he can help the two people involved that their love affair represents a conflict of interest in the organization. In talking to couples, managers must stress that they are going to deal with the romance as they would any business problem—as equitably as possible."

Many of the managers with whom I spoke said that should a conflict of interest appear, such as in auditing relationships or in departments such as personnel which hold confidential information, it may be necessary to transfer one member of a couple. But they also recognized that some interdepartmental relationships may be naturally synergistic. For a couple holding jobs in a mergers and acquisitions department and publicity, for example, there may be no need for management to take immediate action. Their work performance may improve as a result of their personal communication.

I think—and many others agree—that the best way to deal with conflict of interest issues is to prevent them from happening if they are at all avoidable. Recently, I was offered an opportunity to serve as a management consultant to my husband's company. My husband and I discussed the problem, and the manager and I discussed the circumstances. Together we made a mutual decision that the conflict of interest issues presented would create many more problems than was worth the trouble. I recommended someone else for the job.

Do the Risks Outweigh the Benefits?

Is office love worth these risks? Most office romancers to whom I posed this question responded with an emphatic but qualified "Yes."

Mary, a thirty-nine-year-old accountant said, "I was against office romance until I had one. I have since realized that it is possible to have a productive office relationship and at the same time be lovers. Of course you are putting yourself and your lover at risk if you smooch kisses at each other in front of your boss. But if your conduct in the office is professional, few people raise an eyebrow."

Many of the people with whom I spoke said that as long as conduct in the office was professional, the value of a romantic relationship at work exceeded any disadvantages. One woman in my survey put it this way: "I'm not sure if the risks outweigh the benefits, but I know that if you conduct yourself in a businesslike manner in the office, there is less of a problem."

Melissa, twenty-six, said, "I'm all for office romance despite the disadvantages. The quality of the sharing in the personal relationship is well worth it. Where else can you find someone who knows you so well?"

Lisa, twenty-nine, said, "What I have learned from Dave has been wonderful. He has taught me how to manage. I never would have accepted such criticisms from anyone else but a lover."

James, a division manager for a Fortune 500 firm who recently met and married another division manager at his firm, summed it up this way: "Life is made of challenges, and I view office romance as one of those challenges. If you are a reasonable person, and if you can handle the personal aspect while acting as business colleagues, then your professional relationship will be on solid ground. The challenge of an office romance is making sure it doesn't interfere with business. In reality, the risks you take with an office romance—or any romance—are within yourself."

A number of couples also told me that maintaining an outstanding work record is your best offense against potential threats to your career advancement. "Because my work performance has remained strong, there have been few reprisals," said Nina, a thirty-three-year-old corporate manager for a Fortune 500 corporation. "All anyone cares about in business is that you do a good job. The minute a relationship gets in the way of that, then you put yourself at risk. My work performance has been my best defense against reprisals."

Objectivity in business decisions also guards against co-worker animosity and management reprisals. One woman I know actually found she had to dismiss her lover during a reorganization. Both handled this decision with integrity and dignity. "It was tough," said this woman, "but it was necessary and we both knew it. To do otherwise would have compromised the business, our professional reputations, and our colleagues' respect."

Additionally, plans anticipating breakup strategies, conflicts of interest, or problems with competition help to maintain the personal relationship on an even keel. Gina, a forty-three-year-old real estate developer, has kept this in mind in her relationship with Brian at her office. "We know exactly what we will do should we break up or should we get into competition with each other for the same projects. And we work hard to make sure that everyone around us knows the personal relationship has not caused any loss of objectivity in our business decisions. My performance has improved since my relationship with Brian. As a result, there have been few risks, only benefits to this office relationship."

Your Best Defense Is a Good Offense

There is no doubt about it. Your best defense is a good offense. If you want to minimize the risks associated with an office romance, anticipating potential problems is one of the keys to success. Maintaining excellence in your work performance is another.

How can employees weigh the benefits and risks to determine whether an office romance is feasible? Although there are many advantages, there also are a number of drawbacks. The attitudes of colleagues and management may further complicate matters. In the next section, the issues that accentuate the risks—the conservatism of the corporate culture and the special concerns of women—will be explored.

PART THREE

THE HIGH RISK FACTORS: WOMEN AND CONSERVATIVE CULTURES

6

CORPORATE CULTURES

O n a recent consulting assignment, I queried a district manager about attitudes toward office romance in his company. "There are none," he answered. "At least, if hanky panky is happening around here, we don't know about it. There's no way anyone's going to let the cat out of the bag. Not in *this* company!"

A few months later, I asked another manager in a different firm the same question. "Sure, it goes on here all the time," he responded. "No one blinks an eye. In fact, we encourage it."

I was surprised by the differences in their responses. Why would one firm encourage office romance while the other denies its existence?

The answer concerns differences in each firm's corporate culture. Some companies have open norms regarding office romance; others hold strict policies against fraternization.

Once upon a time, a single word of warning covered the dos and don'ts of office romance. Simply put, that warning read, "Don't date your secretary." But with increasing numbers of women working side-by-side with men as a consequence of the new sexual revolution, the situation has become much more complex.

Companies differ in the strength of their internal cultures, their management's attitudes about office romance, and the politics associated with non-traditional behavior. *The values, norms, and philosophies of a firm's culture directly affect the degree of risk—and potential benefits—that will be experienced by couples involved in an office romance.* But before I can explain how I arrived at this conclusion, I first need to describe what a corporate culture is.

Corporate Culture: What Is It?

Corporate cultures are the sum total of the attitudes, beliefs, values, philosophies, norms, and standards of behavior that evolve for those who work in a corporation. Just like people, companies develop equivalent "personalities" all their own. Some cultures are action-oriented, creative, and innovative. Others are more traditional, reactive, and conservative.

According to professors Terrence Deal and Allan Kennedy, authors of the book *Corporate Cultures: The Rites and Rituals of Corporate Life* (Addison-Wesley, 1984), corporate cultures are determined by a number of factors:

- *The company's business environment:* fast-paced and competitive or slow-paced and monopolistic
- *Values personified by key employees:* traditional and conservative or creative and innovative
- *Heroes, anti-heroes, and legends:* successes and failures in the corporate political network
- *Rites and rituals of behavior:* such as a standard address from the chief executive officer at a certain time of year
- *The informal network:* how employees use informal communication channels to discern changes and exchange information about key players

Professors Deal and Kennedy believe organizational cultures are strongly influenced by the business environment of their industries. Some industries, such as the computer graphics industry, are fast-paced, continually dynamic, and ever changing.

Other industries, such as some utilities, experience slower growth and more conservative rates of change. Companies in these industries tend to adopt more traditional values and norms. Values are reflected by the legendary rites and rituals of the culture. Often there are company "heroes" who personify key company values through their actions.

As an example, a strong and unique corporate culture exists at Tandem Computers, a Silicon Valley firm and a highly successful producer of mainframe computers. Tandem prides itself on an absence of rules and formality. Employees are treated on an egalitarian basis. Everyone is expected to contribute to the corporate goals. When they do, employees are rewarded with generous stock options and performance benefits.

To communicate the company's norms, values, and philosophies, a number of corporate rituals have evolved. One is Tandem's traditional "Friday night beer bust." As described in a June 28, 1982, *Fortune* magazine article, nearly two-thirds of the firm's employees drop in at an informal beer party to mark the end of the week. "Incredible Hunk" contests—a headquarters-wide beauty contest for male employees—heighten the merriment. Flexible work hours, six-week sabbaticals in Nepal or other exotic places, and a company-sponsored recreation center all are advocated by the founder and hero of Tandem, Jim Trybig, the current president of the firm, to improve employee morale and productivity.

And it works. Though some of these rituals have changed slightly since that time as company size has increased, Tandem has remained extremely successful. Recent stock quotes are testimony to this company's continued success.

International Business Machines (IBM) is another example of a unique corporate culture. In some circles, IBM jokingly stands for "I've Been Moved." Employees are often sent on tours of duty around the country to learn the business. Loyalty is rewarded. Company personnel must represent company values on and off the job. Strict adherence to deadlines, corporate codes of dress, and meeting etiquette is observed.

For many years, a strict no-drinking rule was applied to employee behavior—on and off the job. Employees who were caught drinking were, in some cases, summarily dismissed. One such story was told to me by a former male employee at IBM's Seattle office. "One day," he said, "the head of our office saw myself and a woman employee walking down the street nearby our office. Across the way was a bar and hotel. He approached us and said, 'You're *not* going into that bar for drinks, are you?' As a joke, I said, 'No, but we're going into that hotel to make love.' He said, 'Fine.' "

The no-drinking rule was so steeped in the IBM culture that for a moment, prohibitions against sex on the job were momentarily repressed from this manager's awareness. He didn't even realize a joke had been made.

How Corporate Cultures Affect Romance

In my survey of executive women, I asked questions about the relationship between company cultures and attitudes, actions, policies, and norms concerning office romance. More than three-quarters of the women I surveyed said that their company did not have formal policies regarding office romance. Only a small number—12 percent—said their firms had developed a formal policy on office romance, as distinguished from sexual harassment.

But when I compared their results to descriptions of the degree of conservatism or liberalism in their corporate cultures, I found several surprising results:

- *Eight-six* percent of those surveyed who said they worked in company cultures characterized as "traditional, reactive, and conservative" said that their company informally discouraged office romance and/or had adopted policies *against* romantic liaisons on the job.
- *Fifty* percent of those surveyed who said they worked in company cultures characterized as "action-oriented, creative, and innovative" felt that their company *neither encouraged nor discouraged* office romance.

What these results suggest is that conservative cultures discourage office romance. More innovative, action-oriented cultures are more accepting of romantic liaisons among employees.

The reason for this is simple. Innovative, action-oriented cultures tend to adopt values that are in congruence with the new sexual revolution. Conservative cultures remain steadfast in traditionalist beliefs regarding women's roles and are less flexible concerning norms of appropriate employee behavior.

Perhaps this is most clearly illustrated when cultural attitudes across different industries are compared. One male source, a friend of mine who has worked in both the investment banking and entertainment industries, said, "There are distinct differences across industries. . . . In the investment banking and Big Eight firms, where everything is so conservative, office affairs go on all the time but they are widely discouraged. In fact, I know of one case where management broke up a couple by transferring the man to the Midwest office. In the entertainment industry, it was more open, and at times it was almost as if sex was for sale. I would hear stories of parties where young girls—actresses and models—were hired to jazz up the interest of corporate clients."

Another source, a man who has worked in both the computer industry and a large automotive manufacturing plant in the Midwest, said, "In the computer industry, there tends to be a large proportion of younger employees fresh out of college. There is a greater tendency for people to become involved because they are of the right age and mentality to do so. But in manufacturing, there is a greater spread of ages and interests. Especially in the automotive industry, where corporate layoffs are frequent, there seemed to be less of a tendency for people to get involved. It might be too much of a risk."

Departmental cultures within companies also may vary in their propensity and openness toward office romance. According to one source who had worked in both the marketing and finance areas of four different corporations, "Office affairs are much more acceptable and commonplace in marketing areas than in the financial ones. In some of the marketing departments where I worked, some of the salesmen picked up women routinely while traveling—almost as a badge of status. . . . In the financial areas, office affairs still take place, but they are more secretive, more covert, about them."

Diagnosing the Climate for Romance

Why do companies—and departments—vary to such an extent regarding their attitudes about office romance? From discussions with managers, my survey research, and the cases I studied, I identified eight factors.

COMPANY VALUES

In more conservative firms, certain corporate values may be in conflict with the liberalized sexual mores associated with office romance. Companies whose corporate cultures reinforce such values may ban office romance altogether. Religious organizations, for example, may find their traditional core values of integrity and morality in conflict with the extramarital office romancers. Educational organizations, which value the trust and development of young students, may frown upon teacher-student romances. For example, a public school has strong expectations about appropriate teacher behavior. Should a teacher become involved with a student, all hell could break loose.

One source told me, "In my school district, there was a romance between one of the English teachers (a woman) and a young impressionable male student. The woman was married at the time. We called an immediate school board meeting and fired her. There was no way we could let a romance like that continue."

WORK STYLES AND ETHICS

In some professions, such as the advertising business, creativity is a necessary part of getting the job done. In other professions, conservative work styles provide the best approach. Romancing in the office may be widely discouraged in a mainline financial environment, for example, because it may not contribute to productivity in the office. But in advertising, where job tasks require creativity, love in the office may be encouraged.

"Affairs happen around here all the time," said one advertising executive. "It's part of the business. The only thing that is discouraged is a relationship with a client. But within the office there are a number of people who have fooled around and no one cares."

STATE OF GROWTH

The state of business evolution in a firm, or the firm's point in its growth cycle, also may have an impact on attitudes in the corporate culture toward office romance. Newer companies are more likely to have liberal policies and may use them as a recruiting tool. Smaller companies are characterized by more open, flexible, organic cultures that are less likely to hold negative attitudes toward office romance.

One company, Quadgraphics, a large printing concern based in Wisconsin, originally developed an anti-nepotism policy. However, management soon realized that this policy was hampering its attempts to attract and retain competent personnel. Hiring relatives and spouses may be the only way for such companies in the early stage of growth to remain competitive.[1]

DEMOGRAPHICS

Companies in industries that have higher percentages of women relative to men are more likely to have more flexible attitudes toward office romance. This is because there is a greater likelihood that office romancing will occur.

Companies that have a younger group of employees who are at the stage where they are looking for future partners will tend to have more open attitudes toward romance for the same reason. Said one male employee at a software development house where the median age is under forty, "Employees routinely fall in love and break up around here. We're all around the same age, so dating [in the office] is considered commonplace. In fact, just this week two different women asked me out on dates."

COMPETITION

Many companies remain genuinely concerned that office romances in highly competitive companies may lead to conflicts of interest should one person leave and become employed by a rival concern. This will undoubtedly be a factor against office romance in their corporate cultures.

The now-famous lawsuit brought by Gina Rulon-Miller against IBM illustrates this problem. Ms. Rulon-Miller was dismissed by IBM once it was discovered she was dating an employee of one of IBM's competitors. IBM was forced to pay a $200,000 award to Ms. Rulon-Miller, though she was fired from the firm for conflict of interest reasons.[2]

PRECEDENCE

Companies that have had a successful history of office romance are less likely to develop policies prohibiting love in the office. But in companies that have been burned by love, the opposite is likely to be true. Heroes and heroines need to be visible in the corporate culture to demonstrate that office romance can be managed successfully.

One woman told me, "My relationship with the man who later became my husband was a pioneering attempt at office romance in our firm. Because our romance was successful, I now informally counsel other couples in the company who come to me seeking advice."

RITES AND RITUALS

Some companies actively encourage socializing between employees on and off the job. When management believes that people are a corporation's greatest asset, certain rites and rituals may develop to support this value. When employees are socializing together, romance is likely to follow. Some companies even develop regular rituals that _promote_ the socializing between employees. Firms that follow regular sales meetings with lengthy cocktail hours reserved for socializing are more likely to encourage office romance.

These factors suggest that there may be a number of predictable reasons why certain firms develop more conservative attitudes, while others actively promote socializing between employees. For those firms in which office romancing is good for business, there is likely to be more openness and less reluctance.

But ironically, the attempts of more conservative managers to stem the tide of romance in their firms may be futile. Falling in love on the job, no matter what the culture, is inevitable. Office romance does not decline in more conservative firms; it only becomes less visible. A ritual of secrecy is enforced to protect lovers against undue risks.

Conservative Company Cultures Force Romancers to Go Underground

"In my company, no one would dare let it be known they were seeing another employee," said one woman who works for a conservative law firm. "The upper management of this firm is likely to fire you if you let your romance become public. Kissing in closets is the only way around here."

Conservative cultures only force romancers to go underground. In my survey, of those who characterized their firms as conservative and reactive, nearly half of the romances described to me were a secret. Only a little over a quarter of those who worked in more creative, innovative, or liberal environments felt compelled to hide their liaisons.[3]

"We don't have a thing to worry about in this firm," said one woman who recently met and married her husband at work. "Everyone here is involved—or has been involved—with someone in this office. No one blinks an eye."

For those who work in conservative firms, the decision to go public creates confusion and trepidation. "We were so afraid that someone would find out about us," said Trisha, an investment banker, "that we kept our romance secret for two and a half years. Even though we lived together, no one knew about it. It wasn't until I left the firm that news got around about our engagement."

Sometimes, those who boldly go public with their romances become company legends in their own time. One couple I know were uncertain of management reaction toward their romance in a conservative firm. But because their job performance was solid, they felt they could take a risk and let their romance become public knowledge. They did. Management called them in for a discussion about their romance, but no warnings, transfers, or terminations were levied against the couple. Shortly thereafter, other couples went public. The company has since grown more tolerant toward romantic liaisons.

Women Have More to Lose in Conservative Cultures

The values of the corporate culture may affect more than the secrecy of a romance. I also found that the degree of conservatism affects the risks of an office romance—especially by women.

For those who characterized their firm as conservative or reactive, 68 percent said that the risks were greater for women than for men. Less than a quarter of those in such cultures believed men and women were treated equally by management when their romance was discovered.[4]

"I wouldn't attempt a romance in this firm," said one woman who works for a well-known family-run financial corporation. "It would be used against me in career discussions."

"I know one woman whose career was ruined because news of her romance leaked out," said an accountant. "Mixing pleasure with business was her fatal mistake."

But for women who characterized their companies as action-oriented and innovative, 48 percent said the risks applied equally to men and women. "There's no problem here," said a manager for an aircraft engine firm in California. "Women and men meet, fall in love, and marry on the job all the time. In fact, I think it gives you some additional visibility when you do."

One woman in a more liberal firm was encouraged by her subordinates to date a male manager at her level. "They said to me, 'Go out and get him!' " said this woman. " 'Come on—you can make action-oriented, risky business decisions, so why not do the same for your personal life?' "

The new sexual revolution has made headway when women are no more penalized than men for engaging in an office romance. This is a hopeful sign for the future.

Corporations Are Becoming More Lenient

Office romances are becoming more and more commonplace. As the new sexual revolution takes hold, even those firms that have retained "stuffy" attitudes are likely to change their tune.

One woman in the banking industry who responded to my survey said, "When my husband and I began our 'clandestine' office romance thirteen years ago, there was one married couple in our large corporation—at opposite ends of the state. Discretion was necessary. Four years later, when we were married, we were one of only three married couples in the company of three thousand employees. We were encouraged, but not ordered, to work in different departments and in fact, as much as we love working together, we chose personally to work apart in different divisions. That was nine years ago. . . . We're still happily in love. And there are at least seventy-five to a hundred married couples in the company now, but it's still not encouraged in the same department, which in banking makes a lot of sense from a security standpoint. We've come a long way, baby!"

Yes, we have. But many women continue to believe that office romance is more trouble than it is worth. Some believe that regardless of the flexibility of corporate culture attitudes toward office romance, the risks of office romancing are greater for women than for men. The new sexual revolution has not yet generated equality for women in the same sense as men in this regard. Although women are rising to the top of many corporations, many men—and women—believe that an office romance may be the fastest way to put a woman's career in a downward spiral.

Despite the prevalence of office love throughout the corporate world, many women remain fearful that an office romance will ruin their lives—and their careers. The central question many competent, professional women are asking themselves is: Am I willing to risk it all—my career, my future, my ego—for the sake of an office romance? Can today's woman really have it all—love in the office and at home?

7

THE SPECIAL CONCERNS
OF WOMEN

My friend Liz is one of those people who steadfastly agree with popular opinion. Regardless of the corporate culture, Liz believes the risks of an office romance outweigh the benefits for most women like herself.

When I met Liz, she was a newly hired staff manager at a large corporation in the telecommunications business. She met two men to whom she was attracted in her department. But despite her feelings of attraction, she decided against a romantic pursuit with either one.

She announced to her female friends, including myself, "There was no way that I would ever allow myself to become involved in an office romance! My career is important to me, but a romance on the job? No way. More trouble than it's worth, if you ask me."

Although I have since tried to convince Liz otherwise, I do have to admit that because of her opinion, I personally benefited. Liz introduced me to one of the men, and he later became my wonderful husband.

But Liz's complaint is a common cry among women. She is not alone in her steadfast belief that women have more to lose from an office relationship. Many women believe the risks of partaking in an office romance are greater for women than for men.

One woman, a technical staff professional in the chemical industry, commented, "I've never been involved in an office affair but I have observed several. . . . In one case the woman was made to leave after they married because company policy ruled against husband-and-wife teams working in the same company. In the other case the woman left two years after her marriage because she felt stuck in her career track. In neither case did the husband suffer."

Glenda, fifty, said, "My own romance ended badly, and I was the one made to suffer. . . . There was a lot of legal and political maneuvering to make me leave. It was very cruel and damaged careers and morale. The irony of it all—my boss, who cornered me into resigning, was having an affair with his assistant."

Jane, a corporate planner, said, "I have observed several romances in three different companies—and in almost every case, it was the woman who suffered the brunt of the gossip. Some men got burned, too. But I know of two situations in which the women will never be promoted because they were fooling around."

Eliza Collins, a former editor of *Harvard Business Review*, believes this is indisputable. In a controversial September 1983 article entitled "Managers and Lovers," she reported that among the executives she studied, women had the most to lose when it came to an office affair. Said Collins in her article, "Until more women are at high executive levels, the woman will usually be the prime victim when two executives fall in love, even if she is a senior member in the organization. Although it is realistic that the least valuable person leave, because that person is so often a woman, it is a sexist solution."

Betty Lehan Harragan, the author of *Games Mother Never Taught You* (Rawson Associates/Warner Books, 1977), put it much more graphically:

> The female physical presence is tolerated as a primal adjunct to glorification of the phallic symbolism which represents power, virility, strength, and domination.

In the deep recesses of the male-conditioned unconscious, male-female relationships are dictated like
moves in a checker game. The conquest of a woman's
anatomy, by whatever seductive or commanding means
. . . gives the male player possession of the captured
playing piece. Any temporary gains the female may be
allowed are inevitably used to crown her partner's
"kings" and make him undisputed lord of the playing
board.

Ms. Harragan obviously believes that women should avoid
sexual relationships in the office because men will use such
relationships against women.[1] But what do you believe? Is it
really true that women have much more to lose than men? Or is
this an antiquated notion in the face of the new sexual revolution?

The Strong Anti–Office Romance Beliefs of Women

Many women remain absolutely convinced, even today,
that the risks are greater for them than for men. My survey of
100 executive women showed that even as recently as 1988,
women believed that the risks associated with office romances
are much greater than those for men.

For example, some of the women I surveyed commented:

- "Engaging in an office love affair is like stepping into an
  uncharted mine. . . . The rules of the game are set up to
  favor men."—_Bank vice-president_
- "It can be a real problem, especially if you are working in
  the same office and break up the relationship later—how
  do you work with that person? Your only choice is to get
  out."—_Cosmetics executive_
- "I've seen some romances that have worked, and others
  that haven't. . . . It depends on the couple involved. But
  usually there is more to be lost than gained, both in
  personal pain and professional advancement."—_Sales rep-
  resentative_

- "Not many benefits that I can see, except that at least you're guaranteed a free lunch!"—*Insurance company executive*

But I noticed a telling discrepancy when I compared the results reported on my survey (when I asked respondents to tell me about their *perceptions*) to the actual cases they reported. When asked about their perceptions about office romance, two-thirds of those who responded showed concern about the risks. For example, 63 percent believed an office romance would be a risk to their careers, 55 percent worried that work performance might decline, and 65 percent claimed professional relationships could be ruined.

But when I asked them to think of a case they actually had observed and to describe what had happened, their results changed. Of the ninety-four cases gathered in the survey, negative effects occurred only from 20 percent to one-third of the time.

For example, only 10 percent of the cases made participants "more difficult to get along with." Less than one-quarter actually experienced productivity declines.[2]

This means that in most of the cases, problems did not occur as much as women thought. In only a few cases were people really more difficult to get along with because of the romance. Few problems and risks actually were realized. The rest of my survey showed the same discrepancy. For example, approximately one-third to one-half of the cases showed that participants were happier, more motivated, and more confident in their work.

What this means is that *women may exaggerate the risks because they fear the consequences.* They are out of step with the new sexual revolution in the office. The discrepancies I found in my survey show that women still adhere to the popular misconceptions on this subject. The conventional wisdom still lives on: Men are to be admired as macho if they play around, while women are compromised.

Why Women Resist the Benefits

Although women have gained access to corporate middle management positions, recent Bureau of Labor statistics suggest that they still face an uphill climb. Even in 1988, less than 15 percent of board memberships in major corporations are held by women. In a survey of Fortune 500 companies conducted in 1986 by Mary Ann Von Glinow, a professor of business at the University of Southern California, only 1.7 percent of corporate officers were women. This figure dropped to 1.3 percent when the companies studied were narrowed to the Fortune 50.[3]

As the popular Virginia Slims cigarette slogan says, "You've come a long way, baby"—and this is true—but women as a group still have a long way to go. Until women are fully accepted as upper level executives in their own right, they will lack the same degree of power and influence granted men.

According to a recent study on executive women by Ann Morrison, Randall White, and Ellen Van Velsor at the Center for Creative Leadership in Greensboro, North Carolina, women managers must negotiate a narrow band between their femininity and professionalism. As these authors reported in their book, _Breaking the Glass Ceiling_ (Addison-Wesley, 1987):

> This narrow band of acceptable characteristics and actions reflects the multiple expectations of corporate women and the challenge they face of blending very disparate qualities. It is clear that much behavioral territory is off-limits to executive women. Only certain characteristics traditionally accepted as "masculine" and some traditionally thought of as "feminine" are permitted through the narrow band.
>
> The unacceptable area comprises the extremes that would make an executive woman too much like traditional nonprofessional women or too much like women trying too hard to be like men. . . . Certain "male" kinds of behavior are not only allowed but required. Some savvy insiders wanted to see toughness demonstrated by a woman on an executive track be-cause they believe, as a rule, that women aren't tough

enough to handle the job. Sometimes people require executive women to be more "masculine" than men in certain ways to be accepted. One executive said that the chief executive officer told her, "You're tougher than most of the men around here. Can you go find some more of you?"

Because of these attitudes, many women believe that falling in love with a colleague destroys a woman's already tenuous credibility. An office romance, in other words, causes a woman to fall off the tightrope of the narrow band. By showing her emotional, romantic side, a woman may violate the norms of professionalism in the workplace.

Grace, a forty-three-year-old financial analyst for an investment banking firm, commented, "Office affairs place women in a very vulnerable position. . . . Sometimes it seems men want the women to make the first move, which, I feel, increases the female's vulnerability. A secretary may be taken by other males in the office as 'easy' if one or more of the male bosses [find] out she had an affair with one of the other bosses, or even with a peer."

Sound like traditional stereotypes at work? It is. Professors D. Anthony Butterfield and Gary N. Powell, of the University of Massachusetts and the University of Connecticut, respectively, conducted a study on stereotypical characteristics of female versus male managers. In their research (published in the *Academy of Management Journal* in June 1979), they asked students to describe the characteristics of a "good" manager, and then to describe stereotypically female and male manager profiles. They discovered that the "good manager" description was not androgynous, as they had hoped; instead, the good manager profile was more closely associated with stereotypically male characteristics.

Because men have defined the norms of acceptable behavior in the corporate culture by their historical presence, women have been forced to fit in with this traditional male model. Women managers are expected to act aggressively, to be harsh in their judgments, and to function decisively—just like men. There is little room for consensus-seeking or cooperative efforts—the traditional attributes of women. The narrow band of acceptable behavior precludes any expression of sexuality.

For most women, sexuality is intimately intertwined with femininity. Women who believe they have more at risk than men in an office romance believe that any expression of sexuality in an office setting would be considered "unprofessional." Such women also believe that any slip-up on the part of one woman reflects upon all women, so rather than accept the benefits, they steadfastly maintain a narrow course of behavior to avoid any risk. They *allow* the challenges of the new sexual revolution to steadily pass them by.

Are Women Really at Greater Risk Than Men?

I have spoken with a few women, and several men, who believe things have changed. Thirty-five percent of the women I surveyed said that they believed that "risks and benefits are equal regardless of gender." Only 10 percent said that they thought the benefits were greater for men.

One woman who has worked at several Silicon Valley firms said, "I have participated in two different office romances, and at no time was I concerned about benefits or reputation. There is no pressure out here, no feeling that anything negative could occur for a woman or a man if you date someone in your same company."

Another woman, a manager in a northeastern cosmetics firm, said, "Office romances can work equally well for men and for women if the people involved are mature and discreet. People in love who are not involved in a romance don't show their feelings at work; why should those involved do it? There is a difference between discretion and denial. . . . If the romance is conducted properly, the risks are minimal."

A third woman stated, "I used to fear the 'she slept her way to the top' scenario, and was very cautious when I was involved with a man at my law firm. But in my second firm, where I had another affair, I realized there was little to fear. We really have come a long way from traditional stereotypes."

What explains these differences in attitudes? Certainly,

there is something to be said for the degree of professionalism with which a couple conducts their romance. But there is a second, more deeply seated issue that directly explains the degree of risk experienced by women—the issue of organizational *power*.

Power Minimizes Risk—for Women and for Men

Sandra Monroe, a former manager in finance and marketing for such companies as Honeywell, Pfizer, and RCA, summed up the dilemma like this: "Women know instinctively they will be the ones who are hurt. But I don't know if this is because they are women *per se*, or if it is really a power issue. It just happens to be that women have less power than men. They still tend to be the subordinates, so they have less protection."

I believe that women are *not* at greater risk than men. Those who lack power are. Today's executive women who have power cannot be manipulated in this way. The truth is that sex in the office *is* a power game. Women who are powerless can be used as the pawn of men. But those who have power cannot. Their power protects and insulates them from risks.

I remember one example very well which illustrates this. A source told me about a woman "who was the best thing this company ever had as a manager. She cut deals like you wouldn't believe. Everyone respected her, everyone wanted to be on her team. But she had this habit of dating the new young male recruits to the firm. Ironically, though, no one cared about her sexual exploits because she was so good."

I asked why no one cared. He continued, "When you're good, you're good. No one is disputing her professionalism. She has become so valuable to the firm I'd bet they'd set her up with an escort business if that was what she wanted. She has widespread influence in the firm—the kind of influence that can make or break careers. No one dares say anything [harmful] about her."

According to Rosabeth Moss Kanter, Class of 1960 professor of business administration at Harvard Business School and the author of *Men and Women of the Corporation* (Basic Books, 1977), "Power wipes out sex. A woman who does acquire power stops arousing the same level of concern about whether or not she will be wanted as a leader. People who want to attach themselves to power may not even notice [her] sex."

Power not only wipes out sex, as Kanter notes; it also obviates risk. This dictum applies to women as well as men. Men and women who have power have little to lose. Those who are powerless, however, are vulnerable.

Let me tell you a converse story to make my point. A man, not well liked by others in the firm, had an affair with a subordinate. Because he had antagonized his boss a few years before by not delivering a project that was of great importance to his boss's career, he had no political allies to support him. When the romance soured, the woman subordinate maligned him on charges of sexual harassment. Nothing of the kind had occurred. But his boss and others in the firm saw the incident as an opportunity for his dismissal. Because he had no power, no political allies, and no clout, he was terminated shortly thereafter.

Another man, a research scientist, had a passionate affair with a woman in his laboratory. Because his research was not considered central to the firm's corporate objectives, he was sent to another corporate location to break up the romance. The woman was promoted to group leader because of her excellent research efforts.

So it can work both ways. This is one of the benefits of the modern sexual revolution. *Only those who are powerless have a lot to lose—regardless of gender.*

MARY CUNNINGHAM SUFFERED BECAUSE SHE LACKED POWER

From my perspective as a professor who teaches about power, I believe the primary reason Mary Cunningham had to leave Bendix was that she never established a power base of her own in her position as William Agee's assistant. Without power—true power—she was vanquished by Agee's enemies.

In her book, *Powerplay* (Linden Press, 1984), she writes,

> Powerplay—that was the name of the game. You go
> after what you want and you use any piece of weap-
> onry, any piece of ammunition you can, to get it. That

I happened to be the most convenient pawn around was merely coincidental. . . . My fortunes were inextricably tied to Bill's. If he fell, I went too. Conversely, his survival didn't necessarily insure mine. And part of the problem was that I didn't work at cultivating power. . . . Probably my biggest error was ignoring all the warning signals in the name of duty or loyalty. . . . With four of the five men I interviewed obviously hostile to me from the start, what made me think I could survive in such an unfriendly environment? What made me think I could change it?

Cunningham made a number of fatal mistakes in her naivete. Because she had built no power base early on, she was unable to hush rumors about her sleeping her way to the top. She allowed herself to be vulnerable.

Ironically, Cunningham, like many others at the upper levels, made a fatal assumption—that her title and level in the hierarchy meant she had power. But this is rarely the case. Although you may be named a CEO of a major corporation, the title may be misleading. Only those who have achieved power through contacts, information, and alliances are able to establish a power base. Those who do not can be rendered ineffective and powerless as easily as anyone else.[4]

In a July 1979 *Harvard Business Review* article entitled "Power Failures in Management Circuits," Rosabeth Moss Kanter writes:

Despite the great resources and responsibilities concentrated at the top of an organization, leaders can be powerless for reasons that are not very different from those that affect staff and supervisors: lack of supplies, information, and support. . . . Leaders who are cut out of an organization's information networks understand neither what is really going on at lower levels nor that their own isolation may be having negative effects.

Your power and credibility, therefore, depend on the goodwill of others. Even those at the top can fall into a trap of powerlessness if they do not carefully cultivate their allies.

In Cunningham's case, her credibility was diminished well before the rumors began. She was unable to protect herself because she neglected to consider one very important fact: Despite her high-level title and position, she was vulnerable.

Women Have Misinterpreted the Problem

For women who do have power and influence and the allies that come along with it, such risks are minimized. A source who works on Wall Street told me a story about a woman and man who were "both being groomed to go places. She was a Wharton MBA superstar and he had a Northwestern MBA. Their romance was hot and heavy—so much so it was obvious. But *he* was the one who was shipped out to Cincinnati to break up the romance. She was the real star of the firm, so they protected her, not him."

Another story I heard concerned a powerful female general manager who "made a practice of sleeping with every one of her executive assistants. But her position and her credentials never were questioned. She is in line for one of the executive vice-president slots and is rumored to be the first choice to take over one of the corporate subsidiaries as president."

These examples, and a few others I have heard like them, suggest that women have misinterpreted the problem. *Women do not have more at risk than men. Those who are powerless are more at risk.*

We will know that women have "come a long way, baby" when they are able to openly engage in sexual activities with no more adverse effects to their professional reputations than is experienced by men. Women need power to achieve equality both in the bedroom and in the boardroom. Once women gain the power they lack, sexual equality will reign supreme.

Part Four

WHEN OFFICE ROMANCE
INVOLVES A POWER GAME

8

LOVE BETWEEN UNEQUALS

Jennifer, the woman I discussed in chapter 1 who first made me aware of the dilemmas of office romance, had made an unresolvable mistake. She risked it all—and suffered the consequences—not because she was a woman, but because she was a subordinate who fell in love with a manager above her in the corporate hierarchy.

Jennifer did not leave her firm after all. She was persuaded to stay where she was. But this decision complicated her personal relationships at work.

"What has made all of this so difficult is because our love is unequal," Jennifer told me one day. "If only Greg wasn't my boss's boss," she said, sighing. "Then everything would be perfect."

"What do you mean?" I asked.

"Well, everyone around me thinks that I'm some kind of a charlatan. You know, that I've only made it so far in my career because of Greg's help. I know that's what my boss thinks. He probably thinks I'm sleeping my way to the top, and that's what makes him so nervous."

"C'mon, Jennifer," I said. "Your boss and colleagues know you better than that. You have a proven record of accomplishments. You have gained widespread support for your professionalism."

"You'd be surprised what people really think," she said. "Everyone assumes Greg is favoring me too much—even though my performance record has remained strong. My boss is jealous of our relationship. I've been branded a homewrecker [Greg has since divorced his wife] and a sexpot. I really care for Greg, and want to make a life with him, but given what I've been through, I wonder if it will be worth the risks I've taken."

The perils of office romance are many. Not only does the corporate culture and the relatively low power of women in the hierarchy cause added risk, but in some forms office love can be emotionally devastating and destructive to careers. This is particularly true for boss-subordinate or hierarchical romances like Jennifer's. "I never would do this again," said Jennifer. "The price I have paid is too great to bear."

Many women have told me they agree that boss-subordinate relationships spell trouble. "Messing around with the boss is career suicide," said Nicole, a forty-two-year-old staff manager for a communications firm. "A friend of mine did, and she got into so much trouble her boss eventually had to transfer her elsewhere."

"When I was dating this guy two levels above me, all hell broke loose," said a female sales representative who participated in my survey. "I couldn't walk into the cafeteria without everyone whispering. Even people I thought were friends."

No matter whether you are a secretary, middle manager, or busy corporate executive, one principle about office romance should be inviolate: *Romantic relationships between hierarchical levels should be avoided.* All of the risks I outlined in chapter 5—career threats, performance declines, lost objectivity, conflicts of interest, ruined professional relationships—apply most directly to boss-subordinate romances. Because of the competitive, pyramidal nature of modern corporations—and the quest for power that drives so many people within them—such liaisons are suspect.

"The problem with a boss-subordinate romance," said Marcie, a twenty-eight-year-old retail sales representative, "is that it causes jealousy because people suspect you really are favored by the boss—even if this isn't true. This breeds resentment in a way that peer relationships do not."

According to the 1988 Bureau of National Affairs report:

> The type of romance considered to be most disruptive of office routine and most negative in its consequences is an affair between a supervisor and a subordinate. . . . These romances cause jealousy and suspicion among coworkers and can result in lowered productivity. Such involvements can lead to charges of favoritism when the two parties to the romance are not of equal rank. Coworkers of the romantically linked pair can have feelings of jealousy, anger, and abandonment.

I agree strongly with this statement. Boss-subordinate romances are very disruptive—for coworkers, for other subordinates, for the couple, and for the total welfare of the firm. Your whole reputation is on the line. You really can lose it all.

Why Dating Your Boss Exaggerates the Risks

Whether you are a man or a woman, dating your boss spells trouble. My survey results show clearly—and unequivocally—that boss-subordinate relationships should be avoided at all costs. Of the ninety-four cases reported in my survey, 78 percent of those who reported "coworkers resented the romance" were talking about a boss-subordinate relationship in their office environment. Only 21 percent of peer relationships were similarly resented.

One of the women who reported she resented a boss-subordinate romance in her office described it like this: "In my office, a woman was hired into the company while dating our boss. Management was aware of the romance before the woman was hired, [but] I feel it was an extremely out-of-line decision and makes working with this woman awkward for other employees. The woman has preferred treatment as to time off and salary arrangements. I totally disapprove and management has hit the bottom of my respect scale."

I analyzed the survey results further. Coworkers who complained of work performance declines, disruptions in morale, and general dissatisfaction with the relationship, were referring to boss-subordinate relationships 79 percent of the time. Less than one-quarter of peer relationships were evaluated in a similarly negative manner.[1]

What these results are saying is that boss-subordinate relationships bring out the worst of the risks associated with office romance. *Risks to career are exaggerated when a boss-subordinate romance takes place.* Whether the relationship involves a man or a woman in the subordinate position does not seem to matter. Morale actually can decline in an office when a relationship between a boss and subordinate evolves. Coworkers may not only become resentful, but may grow angry and dissatisfied.

AN INNOCENT BOSS-SUBORDINATE ROMANCE: ADRIENNE AND JERRY

Let's analyze one case from my research to show you why boss-subordinate relationships are so problematic—the story of Adrienne and Jerry.

I met Adrienne when she attended a career planning seminar I was giving for technically trained personnel. She is a beautiful woman—blonde, intelligent, and gregarious. She had worked as a scientist in a well-known R&D laboratory for a number of years, and felt that she had proved herself through her innovations on a number of high-level projects. In fact, she had been responsible for a scientific breakthrough that would, in time, earn the company a significant profit.

I asked Adrienne how she met Jerry. "Jerry had been brought in from one of the outside manufacturing plants for a tour of duty in the lab before moving along the career path to the corporate headquarters. I felt pleased at first when I learned that he was to be my new boss. I was even more pleased when I learned from a friend that he was interested in me."

"What attracted you to him?" I asked.

"Jerry was strong, comforting, attractive, and intelligent. I really respected his ideas, his intuition. In the lab, things move slowly, but at the same time they are really intense, so you get to know your colleagues well. Jerry was the best kind of boss for that situation. I admired him—I still do."

After a few weeks of working together, they went out on a date. "It was a Friday night dinner-and-movie type date," said Adrienne. "But we never got to the movie. We had such fun just talking over dinner that we closed the restaurant!"

Their date turned into a full weekend of romance. "We did not spend that Friday night together," said Adrienne. "But Saturday we had a really fun day together, shopping and going to the zoo. Being together that night seemed natural. I think that was when I fell in love."

Quietly Adrienne and Jerry let it be known to friends that they were seeing one another. I asked Adrienne if secrecy was an issue. She said, "Not usually, but much of the lab work we do is confidential, and somewhat political. We were just a little nervous whether the relationship would work out or not, so we kept a low profile."

Soon enough, everyone at the lab knew. Colleague reaction was somewhat "standoffish," said Adrienne. "I was surprised. In this day and age I figured no one really cared about these things. But boy, was I wrong. I was naive!"

In Jerry's lab, there were projects that were considered highly desirable to work on—and others that no one wanted to be a part of. From my consulting experience in research and development laboratories, I was well aware that project assignments are highly political. Backstabbing and infighting are not uncommon to gain necessary resources and laboratory time. I asked Adrienne how she and Jerry handled this.

"Badly, I think, as it turned out," said Adrienne. "Prior to Jerry's arrival, I had finished one of the 'hot' inducer projects that gave me a lot of visibility at headquarters. But Jerry assigned me to another hot project soon after. That really got tongues wagging."

Rumors started to fly that Jerry was favoring Adrienne unfairly. Others in the lab wanted their shot at the new project. Adrienne said, "I really believe, even now, that our personal relationship had little to do with the decision Jerry made to assign me to the surfactants project. It was just the right decision, objectively. But the fact that we had made our romance known caused others to scrutinize Jerry's and my behavior a little more closely. We should have known that we would get some flack."

"Were there any other allegations of favoritism?" I asked.

"There was this major issue over a conference presentation I made," answered Adrienne, "that caused me and Jerry a lot of problems. I put in [to attend] the conference because this paper I had written was directly related to the scientific material. Jerry said I could go. But then Rusty [another scientist] said he should be the one to present the paper because it relied heavily on his findings. Jerry relented and let him go in my place."

Colleagues at the lab began sniping about the romance. "We became an issue," said Adrienne. "We couldn't even sit together at lunch without people whispering about us. They said that Jerry was favoring me, that I was using sex to get ahead with the boss, that Jerry was doing more of the work on the project than I. Except I didn't know this at the time. I thought they were just jealous because I was dating an attractive, powerful man."

Meanwhile, she continued to work on the project. But a new development occurred. An announcement was made that the lab would undergo downsizing to reduce costs and remain competitive.

Morale in the department sagged at this announcement. Everyone was running scared.

Adrienne said, "One of the early warning signals that I should have paid attention to was when we had all those cutbacks and a coworker said to me, 'Well, you won't have to worry. Jerry will take care of you."

Before the announcement, Adrienne previously had expressed an interest in moving away from the bench and into the marketing end of the business. "I had put in for a transfer months before Jerry arrived because I wanted a broader exposure to marketing the product. You really can't understand this business until you've dealt with the customer. I wanted to expand my horizons. And with all the sniping that was going on about the relationship, it seemed a good idea."

But nothing came through for several months. Meanwhile, Adrienne and Jerry deepened their relationship. "We started living together more openly. We figured by that point the whole lab knew, and what they were saying about us could not be controlled anyway. We thought we could rise above the gossip. But I kept a separate address just in case the relationship didn't work out."

After more than a year of waiting, Adrienne was called into Jerry's office one late afternoon. "He had this big grin on his face. I thought it was because we had planned a weekend away in the country. But instead he showed me this piece of paper that said I would be moving to corporate headquarters."

But the surprise to her and to others was that her move was not just a lateral transfer. It was a promotion. True, she had been working at the bench, doing a fantastic job for a number of years. Yes, she had just completed her MBA degree, and was one of the most qualified women in the company at her level. But the promotion came as a total surprise.

"You could have blown me off the chair with a feather," said Adrienne. "I mean, I expected the transfer, and I had kept my transfer application alive during the time of my romance with Jerry just in case our romance blew up and I had to leave the lab to save face. When the downsizing occurred, I figured I would make a logical move to headquarters. But a promotion? No way."

Coincidentally, Jerry also returned to corporate headquarters at precisely the same time as Adrienne's move. Due to downsizing at the labs, they no longer needed him there; his tour of duty was over. But because of their personal relationship, and the timing of both moves, nasty rumors started that Jerry had arranged for the promotion for Adrienne due to their personal relationship.

"Rusty, who really had it out for me, started saying in public that the promotion was Jerry's doing. At one point he and Jerry almost came to blows physically. It was a horrendous scene," said Adrienne.

But nothing could have been farther from the truth. As it turned out, Jerry had little, if anything, to do with Adrienne's promotion; the promotion had been in the works well before Jerry took the job as Adrienne's boss. But many people ascribed Adrienne's good fortune to her romance with Jerry rather than to years of hard work.

I asked Adrienne how she handled all the sniping and backbiting once the promotion was announced. Adrienne said, "I handled it fine up to then—you know, rise above it and all that. But when the promotion came through, everything changed. Everyone wonders if I really deserved this promotion, and I did. I'll have to live with that."

"What was Jerry's reaction to all this?" I wondered out loud.

"That's what really bothered me," said Adrienne. "Jerry also suffered. Even though he had nothing to do with the promotion apart from signing his signature on the actual papers, his judgment was questioned. People wonder if I somehow made him do it, or if he has lost objectivity in his judgments about personnel issues where I am concerned. It makes me really mad, because it is so undeserved. Neither he nor I deserved that kind of grief—especially Jerry."

Because rumors were so strong, Jerry and Adrienne decided to break off their romance the moment they both moved to headquarters. They wanted to make sure that in the new location they would be recognized and respected for their individual efforts.

Adrienne said, "The breakup was hard. But by then the relationship was spoiled by all the sniping around us. We had to make a decision. So we did."

While talking with Adrienne, I had the distinct feeling that she regretted ever getting involved with Jerry. She said she did. "The whole situation really taught me a lot about people in corporations. I'll never get involved with another man in my office again. I'll certainly never get involved with my boss again! There was just too much grief to take. Okay, the romance was great. But was it worth the corporate politics and innuendo? I'll never know," she told me.

Love Between Unequals Disrupts the Power Structure

Why did Adrienne, and Jennifer before her, experience such difficulties with an office romance? Romantic relationships between bosses and subordinates are problematic because *it is only across hierarchical levels that sex can be traded for power.* Love between unequals disrupts the power structure of the firm. Coworkers fear collusion between the couple. Suspected favoritism causes gossip.

Another woman who was placed in this delicate position said, "Three years ago I fell in love with my boss and have been living with him for one and one-half years. Our relationship caused great turmoil in the company—which is small—and all peers (three of them) have since quit. Even though we weren't playing favorites, coworkers saw us as some kind of a power base. They worried that he would favor me, even though he never really did."

According to Eliza Collins, a former editor of the *Harvard Business Review* who published a September 1983 article entitled "Managers and Lovers," "Love between managers is dangerous because . . . [it] challenges—and can break down—the power structure." When sex can be traded for promotion, the normal channels for advancement in a firm are no longer viable.

But what exactly *is* power? Many sociologists and psychologists have spent their entire careers researching this question. Interestingly, lack of power is directly related to one's relative dependency on others. Conversely, having others dependent on you creates the perception of power and influence.

Richard Emerson, a sociologist at the University of Colorado who studied power and exchange relationships extensively, was the first to recognize this relationship. In an article that appeared in the *American Sociological Review* in 1962, he defined power as the inverse of dependency; that is, the more dependent others are on you for resources that you control, the more power you hold over them. Conversely, the more dependent you are on others for resources that you require, the less power you have in that particular social relation.

In other words, if you are interested in a promotion, you know that your boss has power over you to evaluate you favorably and help you achieve the goal you desire.

What most people fail to realize is that many different types of power-dependency relationships abound in daily organizational life. Because of the way organizations are structured, coworkers are dependent upon one another on a daily basis to perform their tasks to produce the company product. In my own research, I have referred to this as *task* dependency. For example, workers are dependent upon one another to share crucial project information. Managers are dependent upon their subordinates to outperform departmental quotas; departments are dependent upon one another for their inputs and outputs.[2]

Corporate relationships also are structured in terms of *career* dependencies. Managers who want to gain additional visibility to enhance their careers are dependent upon the evaluations of their superiors to grant them that visibility and recognition within the corporation. Political game-playing normally occurs between managers and subordinates who wish to achieve their desired goals.

But once a sexual dimension is added to a normal collegial relationship, the standard balance of power in the task and/or career domains is threatened. It is for this reason that boss-subordinate relationships are so upsetting to coworkers. Colleagues fear that one member will trade sex for promotions, raises, or favorable project assignments.

Morale declines when a boss-subordinate romance occurs for this reason. As one woman, Margo, an executive in the pharmaceutical industry, said, "The worse situation [I experienced] was when my boss fell for this sexpot in my office. He stopped paying attention to the rest of us and spent all his time with Heather. They spent a lot of time together—it made me sick. And then she was promoted! I saw the handwriting on the wall and got out."

To coworkers this is an unfair exchange, one that crosses the boundaries of propriety, equity, and justice.

Margo continued, "What upset me and the others most was how blatant the situation was. I mean, let's get real. Suddenly Heather was doing barely no work—and she was promoted into a senior position. It was blatantly unfair. We had no way to compete."

Coworkers even fear the *potential* misuse of power. Whether it is real or imagined does not seem to matter. For example, even though Jerry had little to do with Adrienne's promotion, coworker reactions were negative because they suspected favoritism.

Adrienne said, "Maybe Rusty was justified—to some extent—about the conference paper. At least I should have named him as a co-author, and I'm deeply sorry about that now. But all the *angst* about my promotion was unjustified. Jerry had nothing—really nothing—to do with it."

Love Between Unequals May Create Potential for Sexual Harassment

Occasionally the higher level member of a boss-subordinate relationship will use his or her power in a dangerous way—to force the lower level member to behave in ways that are unethical or immoral.

Sexual harassment in an office setting is unconscionable. It occurs when one person misuses the power of a position to cause another to comply with his or her wishes. If those wishes are of a sexual nature, blackmail, deceit, and illegal acts can take place.

One woman who worked in a small family business reported, "I used to be involved with the boss's son, who also was my boss. I decided to break up the relationship . . . and then the son started coming after me. He couldn't stand being rejected in front of his family. And he knew he was protected. . . . I had to suffer through lewd comments, hushed conversations, and his stopping by my desk at all times of the day just to check up on me. Sometimes he would follow me out to my car, and once I saw his car parked across my street, watching me. His family did nothing. I finally had to get out."

The American Association of Personnel Administrators survey published in *Personnel Administrator* in October 1987 showed that personnel managers found affairs between superiors and subordinates to be more of a problem for their companies than affairs between coworkers. Over 30 percent of those surveyed believed it probable that a romance between a superior and subordinate would turn into sexual harassment.

I received a number of complaints in my survey about romances that had turned into sexual harassment. Most of these concerned relationships between unequals. One woman told me that she had been denied a promotion because of an affair with her mentor. "My mentor really screwed me over—no pun intended," she wrote. "I had no idea he would use the affair to blackmail my credibility."

Another described a situation in which her lover, the president of the company, took several legal steps to make life uncomfortable for her in the office after they broke up. "He did some political and legal maneuvering. It was very cruel and damaged my career and morale."

A third told me a tale of lost bonus points, unfair evaluations, and increased quotas in her sales goals once she broke up her affair with her boss. "My lover couldn't handle the breakup. He refused to give up on me, and used the power of performance appraisal to increase my sales quotas to make me look bad. Somehow he thought it would make me go back to him."

Love between unequals should be avoided for this reason alone. The case of Bruce and Sandra shows why.

LOVE TURNED UGLY BY HARASSMENT: SANDRA AND BRUCE

Sandra was a bank teller supervisor, and Bruce was a branch manager at the same branch. Sandra was a single woman in her late thirties who had never found a mate; Bruce was a forty-four-year-old man who had established a family at an early age.

According to Sandra, their close interaction at the bank as branch manager and teller supervisor led to their attraction to one another. "I fell madly in love with Bruce," said Sandra. "I looked forward to every working day as an opportunity to be together. But he didn't feel the same for me. I found that out later."

Their romance continued for many months, even years. "I had resigned myself to never being married, and decided I was better off as Bruce's mistress than alone by myself," said Sandra. "Now I would never think that way. It shows how weak I was at the time."

As their relationship progressed, Bruce encountered a number of financial problems. He began to receive signals from the bank management that he would not be considered for promotion. Two younger MBAs were promoted to the position he desired in the same year. He began to despair that he was destined to remain a branch manager forever.

"Bruce was upset all the time," said Sandra. "I hurt just looking at him."

Bruce grew increasingly angry with his lack of career progress and his financial woes. Little by little, he came upon an idea. Why not take a little extra money from the bank branch accounts each day? After all, he was the branch manager. He could do it—with a little help from Sandra. He rationalized that he truly deserved the promotion, so taking some money from the branch coffers was the least he could do. The bank brass should look the other way—after all, he reasoned, he was the boss.

"Bruce manipulated me into helping him embezzle the money," confessed Sandra. "Now it's all been publicly disclosed, so I don't mind talking about it any more."

Sandra provided Bruce with fixed numbers from the bank computer accounts; Bruce collected his purse at the end of each week. They only embezzled small amounts from their corporate accounts at the end of each interest period; they realized that customer accounts would be too suspicious.

Because of her love and deep-seated need for Bruce in her life, Sandra decided to look the other way. "I knew what we were doing was wrong," said Sandra. "But I wanted to make him feel better. Besides, he was using the money for me—he was spoiling me."

Bruce, feeling guilty, used some of the money to purchase expensive presents for Sandra. Sandra enjoyed the attention. They went along in this secret transaction for a number of months—until the relationship went sour. I asked Sandra what was the turning point for her.

"Well, it started when he upped his demands," said Sandra. "He wanted me to take more money than I felt was prudent from the corporate interest accounts."

Sandra began to protest. In fact, she downright refused to go along any further. She had a big fight with Bruce one night after hours and ended the relationship.

"I had been thinking about everything, and realized I couldn't do it any longer," said Sandra. "It was wrong. I also realized, more importantly, that Bruce was no longer interested in me as a person. He only wanted me as a tool to get money for him."

But they still had to work together. Sandra said, "I could barely get myself to go into the office each morning. I couldn't look at him. I could barely concentrate."

Bruce began to turn his attentions toward another recently hired young teller in the branch. Sandra wanted to fire her. Bruce wanted her to stay.

"I knew what he was doing," said Sandra. "He was going to get her to take my place. I wasn't about to let that happen again."

Bruce threatened Sandra that if she told anyone about his embezzlement, he would expose their romance. Sandra realized that if news of the romance became public, she would have no hope for advancement. Furthermore, Sandra was a co-conspirator.

"I was backed against a wall," said Sandra. "He was harassing me at that point, and I didn't feel I could tell anyone because I had participated in the wrongdoing. I knew my career would be ruined. So I maintained my silence."

So she continued embezzlling for Bruce. But she no longer was involved in the affair. "Just thinking about him turned my stomach," said Sandra. "I couldn't believe I had been so naive."

The situation came to a head when a sharp accountant from one of the branch's corporate customers realized that his branch accounts did not cash out. Most corporations would look the other way if small amounts were missing, but this accountant did not. When he and the bank brass investigated the records, they realized something was awry. They discovered the problem after interviewing the branch tellers.

Sandra said, "I was so relieved that I came forward at that time. I told them everything that had been going on. I was glad to accept my punishment."

Both Bruce and Sandra were fired from the firm. Bruce also was brought up on charges of sexual harassment and embezzlement. Sandra has since found another job.

Love Between Unequals Also Can Levy a Blow to Your Ego

But love between unequals not only disrupts the power structure of the firm and causes potential for sexual harassment. Love between unequals also can cause you to become a victim of self-doubt. According to Dr. Phyllis Hopkins, a Connecticut psychiatrist in private practice who has counseled women in this area, "One of the significant psychological dilemmas that women must confront is that she may always wonder if her promotion was due to her relationship or her abilities."

Dating your boss also may cause coworkers to lose respect for your credibility. This is what Jennifer feared about her situation. "It's as if all my good work has gone down the drain," she said. "Now everyone thinks anything I do is the result of Greg's help."

In my survey, 49 percent of those who said they lost respect for coworkers because of a romance referred to a boss-subordinate relationship. Only 13 percent of peer relationships caused coworkers to lose respect for the couple.

When others lose respect for your credibility, you may become a victim of self-doubt. Jennifer said to me one day after a long discussion, "I know this is silly, and I should be stronger, but all the whispering sometimes has caused me to wonder if it's true. Am I using my relationship with Greg to get ahead? Has my performance slipped?"

I assured her it had not. But I know many lower level subordinates who become involved with upper level managers wonder the same.

Adrienne wondered the same. "I kept reviewing the situation, over and over, in my mind," said Adrienne. "After a while, I started doubting myself and my abilities. But then I realized it was just petty jealousies that were causing the problem."

A well-known line of research in the social sciences, called attribution theory, suggests why self-doubt happens. Attribution theory is a model for describing how it is that we *explain* the causes of behavior. It can be applied directly to the reasoning we offer for successful task accomplishment or failure.

Psychologists Kay Deaux and T. Enswiller were among the

first to research attribution theory, in a 1974 article in the *Journal of Personality and Social Psychology* called "Explanation of Successful Performance on Sex-Linked Tasks: What Is Skill for the Male Is Luck for the Female." Their research showed that a woman's success was more likely to be attributed to factors that vary, such as effort, task difficulty, or luck. A man's success was more likely to be attributed to fixed factors, such as ability and competence. This research since has been mired in controversy, but the central principle remains.[3]

If it is true to say that we attribute causes of performance in this way, then we are more likely to explain a successful woman's promotion by saying, "She had a good mentor helping her" or "She slept her way to the top" than by recognizing that she had the abilities to do the job. Women who sleep with their bosses are allowing themselves to be victimized by such statements.

I believe this may be another factor that may have affected the Mary Cunningham–Bill Agee fiasco at Bendix. Cunningham was considered a superstar of the Harvard Business School, and she had all the talent required to make it to the top. But as she indicates in her book *Powerplay*, others around her felt the cause of her success was not her own efforts—but those of her mentor, Agee. Her competence was attributed to finding a good mentor rather than to her own abilities or effort at her job(s). Petty jealousies emerged, and the story broke in the midst of internal political strife. She had little choice but to leave the company.

"Execusex" Can Be Dangerous for Upper Level Managers

As Cunningham discovered, romancing an upper level manager comes with an additional price: overnight celebrity status. But it often turns into something more like notoriety than mere celebrity.

Elena, a forty-six-year-old television producer, said, "My romance . . . with a network executive caused me more problems . . . than I ever imagined. Suddenly I was the scarlet woman whose programs were getting first consideration from the network."

This was the dilemma Jennifer experienced. "What I learned is that you never should get involved with an upper level executive in your firm. It's just too visible. People who don't even know me suspect something untoward is going on because they know Greg in his position in the firm and they know he is getting a divorce."

One woman in my survey said, "Several years ago, I was involved with my boss's boss's boss—a man several levels up in the hierarchy. We met at a bar one night and became close. . . . But the work situation grew intense. My boss and I got along, but he felt really uncomfortable knowing that I was seeing this guy. It put a lot of pressure on him, and on me, just because he was so visible and well known politically."

There is sometimes a temptation to use the power an upper executive can wield if you are involved in a romance with one. Diana, thirty-eight, said, "My romance with a vice-president in my former firm got tongues wagging because everyone thought I was using the relationship somehow. I wasn't, but sometimes there was a temptation. There was this one time that the bureaucracy bogged down and nothing was getting done. I knew all I had to do was tell my lover about the situation and he would straighten it out with a quick phone call, but I just couldn't use his power that way. Even though I didn't, others still assumed I did, and were always afraid that I was tattling on them because of our personal relationship."

Even if your relationship with a member of a higher executive echelon of your company is aboveboard, dating him or her can be a risk to one's reputation. In my survey, I asked, "Are the risks greater for higher level managers in your company?" Sixty-three percent of those who responded said that this was true. Only 6 percent reported that they believed "dating down" involved the same risks.

Eliza Collins, author of the September 1983 *Harvard Business Review* article on the subject, agrees. She writes, "In a company where the two [involved] are high level managers who are supposed to work together as equals, love's old sexist hierarchy is disruptive. Also, because the lovers are managers, their romance affects the organization's power alliances."

Other survey reports concur. Surveys by both Robert Quinn

(published in _Administrative Science Quarterly_ in March 1977) and Carolyn Anderson and Phillip Hunsaker (published in February 1985 in _Personnel_ magazine) showed that the greatest dissatisfaction among coworkers occurred when romances crossed organizational levels. If an upper level manager was involved, or, even worse, a direct reporting relationship between an upper level boss and subordinate, coworkers were highly suspicious of and uncomfortable with the romance.

In my research, I discovered something that surprised me. Not only are the risks exaggerated as you assume higher positions in the organizational hierarchy, but the risks actually may be greater for executives than for subordinates. Executives who romance lower level subordinates subject themselves to gossip and innuendo about their judgment because of their visibility.

One male source in the oil industry said, "The major sin an executive can make is poor judgment. This can affect your reputation, everything—and at the upper levels, you depend on your reputation. Sometimes a romance is used as an excuse _not_ to promote someone who deserves it, so you can push your own candidate for the promotion. I've seen this happen in succession-planning discussions."

He continued, "When this happens, the intentions are reasonable at the time. Some managers may overcompensate to help the firm avoid trouble later by avoiding such situations. It's for the good of the company, because the company has so much to lose if reputations are ruined at the upper levels."

Another woman, who works for a well-known insurance company, said, "At the lower levels, romance is more acceptable because it is less disruptive should something go wrong. I mean, if you have two people working on CRT screens inputting insurance claims, there is a whole lot less to lose than two executives arguing in the boardroom because they argued in the bedroom."

"Execusex," as some people have called it, is problematic because of its potential for disruption. Any personal relationship forged between unequals casts doubt on their ultimate allegiance: to the firm or to each other?

Secretarial Relationships Do Not Disrupt Power

Ironically, one of the sexisms I heard, over and over in my research, was "Dating your secretary doesn't seem to present much of a problem."

This bothered me. A boss-secretary relationship is a boss-subordinate relationship and should be subject to the same conditions and problems as other such relationships. So why were secretaries so special? After I heard several stories about bosses fooling around with their secretaries, I began to realize what the real cause was.

Secretaries have no power. Secretaries assist their bosses. They are not considered big-time players in the power games of their corporations. Without power to wield, they cannot do damage to anyone's career. They do not call into question concerns of equity and justice with other members of the work group on the same career track. The sentiment seemed to be that they present a minor inconvenience when they are involved with your boss, but otherwise, don't worry.

According to Betty Lehan Harragan:

Everybody knows that long-time affairs between secretaries and their bosses can go on without repercussions, always providing the woman remains in her subservient, noncomplaining role of the dutiful doormat. Those sexual relationships are possible because secretarial jobs have no place in the hierarchy; as presently constituted, they are extraneous servant positions. A secretary has no upward mobility and the job is not a team position.

Everything changes, however, if a secretary uses her relationship as a means for advancement. One man told me a story about a secretary who started out as an assistant, was promoted to claims manager, then became head of the personnel department—all due to her relationship with a division head of the company. Coworkers were upset once they realized promotions were at stake. But they were not upset earlier.

Because romancing a secretary is not viewed as a power

issue, such romances raise few eyebrows. But if the power dynamics should be disrupted as a result of a boss-secretary romance, watch out.

Love Between Unequals May Compromise Women More Than Men

For all these reasons, whether you are a secretary, a highly placed executive, or a staff supervisor, dating your boss should be taboo—especially for women. I believe that love between unequals compromises women more than men.

The reason for this is that a woman is more likely to be accused of sleeping her way to the top. At the present time, because women remain relegated to the lower and middle levels of the corporate hierarchy, few romances take place between women bosses and male subordinates. Most hierarchical romances involve a more traditional scenario—a man as boss and a woman as subordinate.

The Anderson and Hunsaker survey published in February 1985 by _Personnel_ magazine bears this out. More than half of the romances studied involved a man in a higher position, 30 percent involved peers, and only 8 percent concerned a woman in the boss role.

I said earlier that power equalizes risk, for men and for women. This is true, and it will become more evident as more women gain power. But for the moment, because more women remain in lower level positions, more women will be accused of sleeping their way to the top. This is what Jennifer discovered.

"I'm not having this trouble because I'm a woman," said Jennifer. "My credibility remains intact. The real problem is that because I have been involved with a higher level manager, people are suspicious. I'm sure if the roles were reversed the same would be true for Greg in my place."

One woman, a retail sales representative, agrees. "When women date their bosses, they run into the old saying 'She slept her way to the top.' The woman finds that her credibility is destroyed—so much so that she has to leave the firm. I speak from experience, because this was exactly what happened to me in my last job. But the same can happen to men if a woman is in the more powerful position."

In *Games Mother Never Taught You,* Betty Lehan Harragan voices strong opinions on this delicate subject:

> Once you've slept with your boss, you've ended your upward mobility in that company—and the reason has nothing to do with sex. That particular career path is closed because you violated the chain-of-command relationship. . . . A prior or current sexual affair between a male boss and female subordinate also carries horrendous complications into the functioning of the rest of the team. Male subordinates who are equal colleagues of the offending woman will hate her for taking "unfair advantage" of her sexual attraction. Other women will also hate her for much the same reasons. Her boss's superiors will automatically classify her as a sex-servicing instrument, not a candidate for recognition on her own merits.

Hierarchical romances compromise women more for this reason. Because women hold less power than men in the corporate hierarchy, they can be victimized more easily. If a mentor relationship is involved, a woman is likely to be dealt a double-edged blow—she will not only lose her reputation but her professional identity *and* her mentor's protection. A female financial analyst in an investment banking firm put it this way: "Why would women want to humble themselves in this way? When one woman fails it hurts us all."

Why Love Between Unequals Should Be Taboo

Office romances between bosses and subordinates, or mentors and proteges, or for that matter any unequal hierarchical combination, strike a responsive chord of fear in the hearts and minds of colleagues. Jealousy, favoritism, petty strife, and lost objectivity follow such romances around like a black cloud. Should you enter into a relationship with someone above you in the corporate hierarchy, you will become a target for gossip, especially if you are a woman.

When you date your boss, the normal rules of political game-playing are suspended. Sex can be traded for promotion, and everyone knows it. Gossip mills come alive like never before. Friendships are threatened. *Love should be taboo between unequals becauses it can break down—and break apart—the power structure of the corporate hierarchy.* When this happens, the entire organization can grind to a halt, and effective business decisions may reach a standstill.

9

MENTOR AND PEER RELATIONSHIPS

Romances between mentors and proteges are especially vulnerable. Mentor relationships represent an unequal power relationship that has all the disadvantages of boss-subordinate relationships—and more.

Amanda, a twenty-eight-year-old retail store owner, agrees. "When I first got into this business, I apprenticed to an older, more seasoned store owner. We became friends and then lovers. He showed me how the business operates, and for that I am grateful. He was my first mentor. But I knew I had to end the relationship and start something fresh on my own. He was suffocating me."

Jill, thirty-three, an investment banker, said, "I was so dependent on my mentor it scared me. I was afraid I couldn't make deals on my own. It became a self-fulfilling prophecy—because I was so attached to him, I made myself incapable of doing my own work. Eventually I had to get out."

Katherine, a fifty-four-year-old management consultant, said, "My mentor and I came to blows over the ending of our relationship. But I was tired of everyone saying that I was nothing more than his protege and couldn't develop my own clients. It was a very painful ending."

151

Ironically, although mentor relationships should be avoided for all of the same reasons as boss-subordinate relationships, *the conditions that spawn attraction are most likely to be present in mentor relationships.* Having a powerful man or woman pay special attention to your work can be seductive. Your gratefulness for your mentor's special attention may spur you on toward a romantic relationship.

Let's examine mentor relationships to discover why and how so many of these developmental experiences turn romantic, and why they should be avoided.

What Mentoring Is

Mentor relationships are a very personal experience. Researchers who have studied mentor relationships understand that the dynamics of these relationships are very complicated. Dr. Kathy Kram, a professor at Boston University who has studied this subject, believes that mentor-protege relationships provide specialized development. In an article she published in the *Academy of Management Journal* in December 1983, she reported the two primary functions of mentor relationships as career guidance and psycho-social functions (or self-development).[1]

Mentors also provide important introductions to key movers and shakers in the firm. This alone makes the relationship a special and valuable experience.

"The good thing about my mentor," said one woman, "is that I can never thank him enough for improving my visibility in this firm. If I wasn't being mentored I never would have gone this far."

What few people realize, however, is that mentors gain as much from the relationship as their proteges. Mentors measure their own power in the firm by what they are able to accomplish for their disciples. If they place their proteges in important positions, then their own power is assured. Each is dependent on the other.

"I always felt guilty because I thought I was the one who had the most to gain," said one man who recently has become a mentor for some of the younger members of his accounting firm.

"But now I realize that there are rewards in developing younger talent."

Because proteges often feel grateful to their mentors, these relationships sometimes turn romantic. But romances that occur between mentors and proteges are as dangerous as those between bosses and subordinates. Here are some of the reasons why.

Why You Shouldn't Date Your Mentor

In a mentor relationship, the odds already are against you. Your coworkers probably are upset and jealous that your mentor chose you—and not them—to receive special treatment. You and your mentor represent a power coalition. Chances are you are attending special meetings, receiving challenging assignments, and partaking in the coaching and developmental tasks assigned by your mentor. This should be enough to capture the ire of reasonable people, and usually it does.

But should you enter into a sexual relationship with your mentor, you have granted everyone a perfect excuse to unleash their petty jealousies. They can now rationalize away his choosing you as his protege. "I never had a chance," they say. "He was just after her body, and he threw her some career assignments to get her into his bed."

Because of the jealousies that are created, the relationship is an easy target for suspicion and resentment. "What I couldn't get over was how jealous others were of me," said Mary Lee, a woman who was mentored by her boss. "They resented me for being Jim's protege. You could cut the tension in the department with a knife."

Mentor relationships are subject to the same risks as boss-subordinate relationships because often these relationships cross hierarchical levels. The power structure is as disrupted—perhaps even more so—in a mentor-protege romance.

In a May 1984 *Business Horizons* article co-authored by Kathy Kram and James Clawson, "Managing Cross-Gender Mentoring," the authors wrote:

> The risks associated with unproductive intimacy [in mentor relationships] include guilt, loss of self-confi-

dence, shame, loss of reputation among coworkers, loss of respect for others' judgment and professional objectivity, divorce or damaged marriages, disrupted careers, loss of career opportunities, loss of references, loss of focus on job demands, loss of analytic judgment, and even legal suits.

These are serious risks. The reason so much can go wrong is because so much is at stake. As a protege, you already have captured the ire and jealousy of others simply because you have been singled out as one deserving of added attention. Mentor relationships that become intimate only enhance your standing as a target for jealousy and strife.

One woman said, "My mentor was the sweetest and kindest man. I couldn't help but fall in love with him. But it was a mistake. I had to leave the company . . . because of all the gossip and problems the romance caused. He taught me a lot, and I loved him a lot, but I had to go away to do my own thing and show myself and others that I could handle the work on my own. If I had stayed, there always would have been this question that I used the relationship or he used me because of all the jealousies and problems it created."

Effective Mentor Relationships Are More Intimate Ones

But although mentor relationships should be avoided because the risks to career are magnified, mentor relationships are more likely to promote attraction than any other type of office relationship.

Think about it. For a mentor relationship to be effective, it is necessary that the protege and mentor spend time together. They must develop the relationship on a more personal level. For the protege to learn from the mentor's coaching and guidance, he or she must remain open, vulnerable, and intimate in a personal sense. This means that the conditions that spawn attraction—proximity, intensity, similarity, and opportunity—are all present in mentor-protege relationships. The close contact in mentor relationships and the mutual goals regarding the protege's success can spur intimacy, friendship, and attraction. Sometimes the natural sense of intimacy leads to romance.

In fact, professors Clawson and Kram believe that the potential for attraction is so great in these relationships that mentors should take responsibility for the level of intimacy in their developmental relationships with proteges. It is a difficult balance to negotiate, because distant mentor relationships are ineffective, but overly intimate mentor relationships present the same risks as other unequal relationships.

The case of Peggy and Bill shows how a mentor relationship can easily turn romantic and why this can be a problem.

A MENTOR-PROTEGE ROMANCE: PEGGY AND BILL

I met Peggy when she became one of my students in a night program in financial management. Sitting around during a break one day after a class on mentoring, she casually mentioned to me that her original mentor was a man to whom she had become romantically attached. She told me that in some ways, it was one of the best experiences of her life because this man had made a vital difference in her career. In other ways, her dependency on this man as a mentor had caused her great pain.

I asked her to tell me her story.

Peggy started as an editorial assistant in a small magazine publishing firm. "I was young and quite naive at the time," she said. "I thought if you did your job well, corporations were fair and eventually you would get promoted."

She waited for an opportunity to showcase her talents. After moving around in the firm to two low-level jobs, she began to despair of her chances of success. In her naivete, Peggy did not fully appreciate how many others were trying to break into publishing, or how many had more talent than she.

Peggy said, "The jobs I had were routine and not terribly exciting. I saw how busy the senior editors were—always on the phone, taking vendors and stringers to lunch at Club 24. I felt the glamour and excitement of the business—the real reason I chose this industry—were just passing me by."

Peggy moved to another low-level job in the publishing firm. But this was where she met Bill. "Bill was the managing editor of one of the smaller magazines published by the firm. He was the kind of manager who enjoyed having lunch with the members of his staff, and often walked around the office to see how work was progressing. He would roll up his shirt sleeves and jump in when he saw a problem."

According to Peggy, Bill reviewed some of her work and was very impressed. He realized she was unhappy, and made an effort to discover what was bothering her. Peggy said, "I just poured it all out—all my hopes, my fears, my disappointments. I told him some of my deepest fears, you know, that I wasn't good enough to make it in publishing. He listened, and he cared. I just knew he cared."

Bill reviewed her work and found she had potential as an editor. The problem was that her writing lacked some of the polish typically gained from experience.

"Right away, he began working with me," said Peggy. "He coached me on my writing style. He also gave me editing opportunities to polish my skills. I just loved working with him. What he did for my writing and editing skills was unbelievable! I was so grateful for his attention."

But he went one step further. He encouraged Peggy to sign up for a graduate program in journalism at night.

Peggy started her classes. Bill volunteered to coach her on her assignments. With his help, Peggy began to shine. They began meeting over lunch or dinner to discuss her homework assignments. Because her classes were at night, they found it effective to talk during lunch about her approach to a particular piece. Then Peggy would revise it quickly after hours before class.

"Our lunches were great," said Peggy. "Because Bill had an expense account, we went to all kinds of marvelous restaurants. Sometimes he would meet with a reporter first, and I would meet him for dessert. I gained ten pounds! The best part was that he would squire me around and introduce me to everybody. I met several famous authors and the vice-president of the firm."

"How did it feel to have that kind of special attention?" I asked.

"Well, everyone knew I was Bill's protege. Some people looked up to me for that reason. After a while, for example, some of the others in the office came to *me* for advice on their work. But it was a problem also, because some others were jealous."

Peggy told me of an incident that happened one day. "We were at lunch, and some employees from my department were eating in the same restaurant. They pointed and snickered at us. It was clear they suspected something more was going on. But at that time the relationship was entirely platonic."

I asked Peggy when the professional relationship turned personal. She said, "At first it was strictly business. Bill did not favor me any more than anyone else in the office. But I was a good student for his coaching, and I think that impressed him. Suddenly we were spending more and more time together. We looked for reasons—well, excuses really—to be together. Like I would bring him a piece I was working on just to have an opportunity to see him during the day."

Suddenly, Peggy realized her friendship with Bill had deepened into something more. "We were spending more and more time together in the office," she said. "We would kibbitz a lot. It took us double the time to get anything done because we had such fun just talking."

They always had been attracted to one another, but neither dared to make the first move. One day, Peggy invited Bill to her house for dinner. A short while after, they became involved in an affair.

Peggy said to me, "It was wonderful in those early stages. Here I was, with this brilliant man who had taken a personal interest in me at work. I felt so flattered. And I really needed his help. I was on Cloud Nine. Moving into the romance stage was really easy and smooth. I was so grateful to Bill that I would have done anything for him. He was the sun, the moon, the stars."

"How did coworkers react to your personal relationship with Bill?" I asked.

"It was a problem," said Peggy. "Bill was one of those special editors that everyone wanted a piece of. When he started paying so much attention to me, morale slipped. It wasn't because they suspected anything was going on. It was more because they just wanted Bill back."

Their love affair lasted two years. But Peggy eventually broke it off. "Jealousies emerged. Bill started getting grief for 'dallying with me,' as his boss put it. People in my department were already giving me a hard time. So when I finished my degree, it was time to move on. For Bill's sake and mine, I took another job in a different firm."

But the story does not stop there. Peggy told me that the "ghost of Bill" continued to haunt her. "All alone, by myself in the new job, I had to face some serious doubts about my abilities. Because Bill had helped me so much, I wasn't convinced I could do the work as an editor all by myself. I made some mistakes early on that caused a backslide, and my ego was ripped apart. But that's all part of being an editor."

Peggy and Bill have remained friends. Bill is proud of Peggy's accomplishments. Peggy said, "I will always be grateful to Bill for helping me shape up my career. And for what he did for me personally. Ending the affair was one of the hardest things I have ever done. But it was the right thing to do. I had to get on with my life."

The Power Aphrodisiac

But there may be another reason why so many proteges become attracted to their mentors—or why subordinates fall in love with their bosses. Ironically, it is the very reason why such relationships should be avoided in the first place. The reason is power.

Many people have mentioned that power—sheer power—in the office is an enticing aphrodisiac. For many people, power can be seductive. One friend of mine, who for two years has been madly attracted to her mentor but has never acted on her attraction, said to me recently, "I know exactly why I am so attracted to Harry. It's because in his job as an executive he can move mountains. I like watching him make decisions, mobilize resources, get things done. Whenever he works through a knot on a politically hot potato project, I get a rush just from working side by side with him."

Power has been defined as the ability to get things done. Although many people equate power with dominance, control, and manipulation, power can also be defined as a way to influence others to achieve a goal, or to "mobilize resources," as my friend described. Power is credibility. Power is action. And watching others take action can sometimes be sexy.

It is no wonder we feel stimulated when we are around those in power. Having an upper level executive walk into a room creates an air of tension and excitement. When he singles you out to be his protege, the excitement and adventure may spawn romance.

An executive woman in a manufacturing firm who responded to my survey said, "Women in high positions like mine are often attracted to men in high positions. The combination of power and business judgment can be a real turn-on. It's sexy as hell."

A male friend who works in the investment banking industry said, "Money and power are aphrodisiacs. Tell anyone around here you're an investment banker, and man, suddenly all these women develop crushes on you."

The aura of power that is generated by influential people makes it difficult for others to stay away. Somehow, they hope that the power of the influential person will rub off on them. They want to share in that person's power, and use it to accomplish their own goals. Deflected power is sexy.

SEDUCED BY THE POWER OF A MENTOR: DONALD AND FRANCINE

Donald and Francine are one example of the seductiveness of power, and how a mentor relationship can serve as an aphrodisiac. Donald was a highly talented and respected professor at his university, a well-known research institution of the highest caliber. He received a full professorship and was granted tenure upon the publication of his research on communication patterns in one of the most respected journals in his field. His study was considered a landmark piece of research and a classic in his field. As a result, his name became well known in academic circles.

At the time, Francine was a young graduate student interested in pursuing doctoral studies in Donald's field. She was aware of his reputation, and specifically applied to the doctoral program at his university in the hopes of working closely with him. She intended to pursue a related piece of research in her graduate studies.

Luckily, Francine was accepted as part of a class of three at Donald's institution. "I was so relieved once I was accepted," said Francine. "I had hoped for the opportunity to work with Donald for so long."

Once she matriculated at the university, Francine tried her best to take Donald's classes when they were offered. She read all of his research papers, and began a research program of her own in his area.

Francine said about Donald, "Being in class with him was an amazing experience. I mean, there he was, one of the 'great' men in my field. Students flocked to his classes just to hear his insights. He made more of a contribution to this field than ten other researchers of equal caliber. I couldn't believe I was fortunate enough to be one of the graduate students working with him."

Indeed, Donald was influential in his field. At academic conventions, people fawned over him. They arranged parties just to meet him. When Francine first met Donald, she was impressed by the intellectual caliber of the man. But after attending conventions with him and seeing how others reacted, she began to realize that she was attracted to him in a romantic way.

"His power, influence, and stature within the academic community excited me," said Francine. "I was stimulated just by being with him as one of his disciples."

When it came to work on her thesis, Francine chose a topic directly in Donald's area of research and asked him if he would chair her thesis committee. Donald graciously accepted. They began working closely together in a mentor-protege relationship on her thesis research. Donald offered many helpful suggestions, and Francine followed every one.

"He became my mentor—and my friend," said Francine, "though he was still a god to me. I was thrilled to be working with the man. And the fact that he was interested in my research was amazing. I would work nights and weekends trying to come up with interesting, insightful comments that would impress him. I doubled my productivity."

One day, after working late while performing statistical

analyses on the computer, Francine decided to let Donald know how grateful she felt to him for working with her on her thesis. "I told him—indirectly and directly—how I felt," said Francine. "At first I think he was a little embarrassed. Then I think the fact that I was interested attracted him."

They continued to work together for several months before anything happened. One day, she offered to take him to a baseball game as a token of her appreciation. He accepted her invitation. After the baseball game, they went to a local pub for drinks and conversation. They began talking about her thesis, but slowly the conversation turned to other, more personal topics.

Donald confided in Francine that his wife did not understand his dedication to his research. Francine felt she could not decline his unspoken invitation. "I could tell it was coming," said Francine. "There were a number of early signals—like I noticed him looking at me while I was working, and that he was spending more time talking about personal topics—for weeks in advance. But I had to let him make up his mind."

That night, they began a passionate romance that lasted until the day she graduated.

Francine said in retrospect, "Looking back, I really can't understand what I saw in him—sexually, I mean. He was losing his hair, looked like he dressed in the dark every morning, and had this annoying habit of biting his lip that really got to me after a while. I knew that he would never leave his wife. But there was something about his influence and power that was magic. I fell for him hook, line, and sinker."

Francine later told me she experienced some fallout as a result of her affair with Donald. "My affair with Donald tainted my professional reputation," said Francine. "It wasn't until I embarked on research totally unrelated to Donald's that I was fully accepted as a scholar."

The Ideal Scenario: Peer Relationships

Given the problems associated with mentor and boss-subordinate relationships, what is the ideal scenario for living love in the office?

Being peers in non-intersecting departments. A romance between peers brings out all the benefits of an office romance with
minimal risk. Unlike boss-subordinate or mentor romances, a
romance between peers can be good for business and the couple.

"My relationship with a colleague has worked out well,"
said one woman. "In a previous firm, I had a brief affair with my
boss that turned out to be a real mistake. In this company, there
are more relationships among peers, and I'm now in one of
them. Unlike previously, this has turned into the best situation."

Peer relationships encourage morale when love is in the air.
Motivation and productivity are increased. Teamwork and cooperation improve. There is less potential for a conflict of interest.
According to the 1988 Bureau of National Affairs report, "Most
romances between coworkers of equal rank are not disruptive to
workplace routine, unless the lovers spend too much time romancing, thus leading coworkers to believe they are not doing
their fair share of the work."

Among peers, there is no reason to worry that the power
balance of the department will become disrupted. There are few
fears of favoritism among coworkers. Coveted rewards, such as
promotions or raises, cannot be handed out among peers.

"Dating a colleague is okay," said Ashley, a twenty-seven-
year-old manager in a food-producing firm. "In fact it can have
a number of benefits. But messing around with the boss is a big
no-no. There's just too much at stake."

It is for this reason that many companies have adopted
formal or informal policies against romantic liaisons in direct
report boss-subordinate relationships. If a firm has established
any type of policy concerning office romance—and this is rare—
it most commonly states that boss-subordinate relationships are
prohibited.

In my survey of 100 executive women, peer relationships
were far more favorably received than hierarchical (boss-subordinate or mentor) relationships. Sixty-two percent found those
involved in peer relationships "easier to get along with," while
only 19 percent saw hierarchical relationships the same way.
Forty-three percent of peer relationships were considered more
productive; only 9 percent of hierarchical relationships were
characterized in the same manner.[2]

Other research suggests similar trends. The survey conducted by Carolyn Anderson and Phillip Hunsaker published in *Personnel* magazine in February 1985 found that while most people simply tolerated a romantic relationship, open approval was granted to those relationships in which the members of the couple were of equal standing.

Why Dating a Peer in Another Department Presents Little Risk

When the peer relationship occurs across different departments, there are a number of added benefits. A romance between peers in non-intersecting departments removes conflict of interest issues. Many couples with whom I have spoken who have worked for two independent departments, let's say marketing and finance, have experienced fewer problems for this reason.

One woman in my survey said, "Although I had been dating Trevor for over a year, no one in my office noticed or cared that it was an office romance, because we worked in different locations. My colleagues didn't know him, so there wasn't anything for them to question."

"We recommend finding a mate at work," said Linda, a divorce lawyer whose lover-turned-husband is a partner in the tax division of her firm. "We think we have the best of both worlds. Because this is a large firm, we are able to maintain separate identities at work. Because we are in different specialties, we do not compete. My husband is my best friend and ally in the office—and at home."

When you and your lover are trained in different specialties or professions *and* work in different departments, there is little concern. Colleagues barely realize you are involved in an office relationship. One manager who observed an office romance at his firm said, "I heard some rumors about Sandy and Pete. But because they worked in different areas, there never was a problem."

Peers in non-intersecting departments often have distinct and non-parallel career paths. If you and your lover or spouse are not competing for the same rewards, there will be greater understanding (and less conflict) should one of you become promoted over the other.

Connie, thirty-five, agrees. "When I was dating Clay, it was great. I was promoted, and he was pleased for me. He realized he was not competing against me [because] our career paths are so different."

Another woman said, "My husband is an engineer. His career track is different from mine; I'm in marketing. There are faster promotions where I am in the company, so mine haven't been such a big deal. But when he was promoted from a group of sixty in his department, we really went out and celebrated."

Lovers in non-intersecting departments who are peers really do have the ideal situation. They are able to enrich their relationship by their mutual understanding of their jobs, while at the same time minimizing power struggles and accusations of favoritism. The natural boundary between career paths allows them to balance their roles well.

For all of these reasons, love among peers can be encouraged and supported. But love among unequals—boss-subordinate or mentor relationships—should be strictly prohibited. Colleagues, the couple, and the firm suffer when relationships span organizational levels. There is too much at stake and too much to lose.

10

GAMES PEOPLE PLAY: SEXUAL POLITICS AND CORPORATE WARFARE

After leading a seminar on communication styles for executives one day, I overheard the following conversation among three highly professional, talented marketing women:

Jill, age thirty: "Did you see Joe today? I saw him at lunch with Suzanna. I think she's putting the moves on him."

Georgina, age fifty-two: "Oh yeah, she's definitely got the signs. I know a power play when I see one."

Pat, age thirty-eight: "C'mon, Georgy, that's not what it's all about."

Georgina, smiling: "You might not think so, but when you've been around as long as I have, you know how to read the signs."

Jill: "First bet it happens at the sales convention in Cleveland in two weeks."

Pat: "Bet it happens *before* then."

Jill: "You're on!"

Does this exchange sound like female locker room conversation to you? In a way it is. The only difference is that the corporate playing field of the boardroom has moved to the corporate bedroom. The new sexual revolution has changed the stakes of the game.

Innuendo, intrigue, and gossip surround office romancers whose affairs disrupt the hierarchy and power structure of a firm. Because of this risk, many couples (even those who engage in relatively "safe" peer romances) often are compelled to resort to game-playing to avoid suspicion. Preferring to keep their romances a private secret, they go to great lengths to prevent discovery—and malicious gossip. Games of secrecy, innuendo, and intrigue were played out by many of the people with whom I spoke on this subject.

In highly politicized firms, corporate politics can be likened to warfare. Anything—and anyone—may be fair game if they get in your way. Sometimes colleagues may retaliate by smearing reputations and ostracizing known romancers. And sometimes those involved in an office romance become the casualties of this new kind of war.

Game-playing goes hand in hand with office romancing because, in some firms, your romance can be used—for or against you—as a political tool. Some people risk their careers playing the games they feel they must to avoid suspicion of an office affair. Others blatantly manipulate their bosses as a way of exercising power. Still others protect their loved ones from corporate realignments and forced retirements.

Is all fair in corporate love and war? Let's see how some people play the game.

Secrecy Games

"I wouldn't have an office affair," said Nikki, a thirty-six-year-old lawyer. "I couldn't keep up with all the intrigue! I've never been a good liar."

When the politics of your firm are anti–office romance, you may go to great lengths to keep your romance a secret. One couple I met while on a consulting assignment said to me, "There's no way we would want to go public. In this company, your whole career could be at stake. Neither one of us wants to risk the consequences." In fact, they did not even want to be interviewed for this book.

Greg, a highly placed forty-six-year-old human resources executive at a conservative petroleum processing firm, said, "I have been living with Betsey for two years. No one knows. . . . We work in the same department and have the same career path in this firm. We fear recriminations if the president finds out about us."

But sometimes games of secrecy are played out because the couple fears recriminations not just from management, but from colleagues.

Ginny, a twenty-eight-year-old staff manager for an aircraft engine firm, told me that although many couples in her firm were open about their romances, she and her boyfriend purposefully chose to keep their romance to themselves. She said, "We dated on the sly—different cars to work, met at restaurants, never attended each other's company functions . . . for two years. We invented names for each other—Brian and Judy— when other colleagues asked who we were seeing. We did this for two years. At the end of the two-year period, we grew a little tired of the secrecy, but for a long time, it was really fun."

Karen, a twenty-nine-year-old retail store representative, agrees. "Secrecy can be fun. It's a big game that you play—you know, all the private eye business you see in the movies is suddenly part of your life. I wanted to avoid any gossip, so I played along."

But what few couples realize is that all this cloak-and-dagger game-playing may be futile. The Quinn survey that appeared in the March 1977 issue of *Administrative Science Quarterly* found that colleagues were aware of minor behavior changes that clued them in to a romance in their midst even before it was made public. Long lunches spent together and chatting in the hallways were dead giveaways.

In my own survey, more than one-third of the women suspected an office romance. Most believed that the couples they observed had no idea that others suspected them.[1] I can remember one such romance that I personally observed in my own office environment. During a four-month period, I observed averted glances in the hallway, heated lunch discussions when others were out of earshot, and an occasional wave or smile from a man and a woman whom I believed were attracted to one another. Sure enough, one day, I arrived at the office unusually early. Looking out my window, I saw the two getting out of the same car. Of course they were involved in an office romance! Coworkers can't miss such signals. We know when something is going on. Our antennae can sense the difference.

THE FEAR OF COMPANY RETRIBUTION: MARY AND KEN

Mary and Ken are a couple I met who were concerned about the impact their romance could have on their careers in a conservative company culture. Although they worked in different departments, Ken held an administrative position of a higher level than Mary's. He had received a graduate degree in business with a specialization in finance, and was well respected in the company for his insights and financial intuition.

Mary had graduated from a local college, with a B.A. in art history. She worked in public relations.

The company for which they both worked was known as a very strait-laced organization that did everything by the book. This was not a company where you could wear blue jeans to work. You knew, even before you set foot on their grounds, that you had better be dressed in a dark professional-looking suit with a neatly pressed tie. Their company building was austere, to say the least—shades of metallic gray with chrome around the windows.

I met Mary and Ken after they had been married for two years. One day over lunch, I asked them how they had met. They laughed. I assumed it was some sort of private joke. When they calmed down, they told me that they had met in the office, but they had kept their romance secret from others the entire time they were dating. Mary said, "Yes, we met at the office. We knew right away we wanted to see one another."

Ken said, "But on our first date we discussed our fears that our management would be upset if they knew about us. To our knowledge, at the time, no one else had become involved in a public romance in our firm. We didn't want to risk our careers for the sake of corporate politics. So we decided to keep our romance to ourselves."

"How did you manage it?" I asked.

"With great difficulty!" they laughed simultaneously. "It was a mess," added Mary. "I never felt so nervous—and yet it was such fun. We basically pretended not to know one another at work."

Ken continued, "Yeah, in the hallways, at lunch, we did not acknowledge each other's presence. We just ignored each other during the day, and then came home to each other at night. It was as if we were two different people."

Knowing that both Mary and Ken lived in the area, I wondered how they managed to date without being seen by the locals.

"Oh, that was easy," said Mary. "I'm a good cook, so mostly we just went to my place and had quiet dinners together. If we really wanted to go out somewhere, we would drive two hours to some remote place and have dinner there."

"Except for one time, it worked out," said Ken. "We went to the Olde Farmers Inne, and who did we see in the dining room but Mary's boss! Fortunately, we got out before he noticed us."

"That was a close call," said Mary. "I was shaking for an hour afterward!"

Mary and Ken told me they never came to work together, nor did they ever leave together. At company social functions, they did not acknowledge the other's presence.

"But we did have great vacations together," said Ken. "Because no one knew we were seeing each other, it was easy to take our vacations at the same time. We would go to this wonderful cabin in a remote Vermont area where no one knew us. We both felt like schizos for a while. We had two entirely separate lives."

But occasionally their work assignments did cross paths. When an article needed to be written about a packaging innovation that concerned Ken's department, Mary worried that she would need to spend time with Ken to write the report, and was concerned that people would notice their relationship.

Mary said, "I thought that people would see from the way I looked at him that we were in love. So I had to do something to avoid the situation."

Mary put off doing the report. Fortunately, just when her

boss was asking her when it would be ready, a part-time college intern surfaced and volunteered to write the article. "What a relief," sighed Mary.

Meanwhile, they decided to get married. But Mary and Ken had grown so used to pretending that their personal relationship didn't exist in the office that they could not bring themselves to tell their friends and coworkers about their impending marriage.

"How did your colleagues finally find out?" I asked.

"Well . . ." Mary and Ken dissolved into laughter. "There was one thing we hadn't counted on. My sister sent in a newspaper notice about the wedding while we were away on our honeymoon."

Ken said, "I don't know who was more surprised—our friends at work on reading the announcement in the newspaper, or us when we returned from our honeymoon to find a banner over the employee entrance that read, 'Congratulations, Mary and Ken!' "

Mary said about their decision, "I know that what we did sounds extreme, but we both felt it was absolutely necessary, given the politics of our firm. It's very cut-throat. Any little excuse can affect your career progress. So we figured, better safe than sorry."

Reputation Games

Because office romances are considered taboo in some corporations, one of the best ways to wage corporate warfare is to leak word of a secret romance. "I have seen people maliciously make up stories just to make someone else look bad," said Alice, a stockbroker in a Wall Street firm. Politically jealous peers may indeed use gossip about an office liaison—especially an extra-marital one—to their advantage. In some highly politicized firms, one of the clearest ways to best a peer is to damage his or her reputation through gossip.

One woman I know had her name removed from a promotion candidate list because rumors were flying that she was pregnant with her boss's child and would be taking a leave of absence. Another woman who was not well liked by the secretaries in her office was accused of having an extramarital affair with her boss. A third told me that rumors had spread that she was dating one of the corporate vice-presidents as a power play to get ahead. None of these rumors are true.

Few people realize that gossip is treated as a means of communication in organizations. It also provides an important release against the tedium of routine, boring work. But when gossip is used maliciously, careers can be unwittingly destroyed.

GOSSIP AND INNUENDO: FELICIA AND MATT

Felicia told me the story of her affair with Matt long after it was over. She said that although she would never get involved in an affair with a married man again, the experience taught her some valuable lessons. Matt was Felicia's boss and mentor. They succumbed to their attraction one day when they traveled to a corporate client's Midwest office.

"I'm still not sure how it happened," said Felicia. "After we completed our presentation, we returned to the hotel. We languished over dinner. Then Matt invited me upstairs. We held hands in the elevator. The moment I said yes I knew what we were about to do."

Thus began their affair. Felicia said, "I knew that Matt was devoted to his family and his wife. In fact, we had many conversations about them. I never kidded myself about his leaving his family for me. Our relationship wasn't really about that, anyway. For us, the physical relationship simply enhanced our work relationship."

"Did you want to keep your affair a secret?" I asked.

"Oh, yes, absolutely," countered Felicia. "It just didn't work out that way for us."

"How did you handle the secrecy, then?" I asked.

"When we were in our home office, it was business as usual. We did not see each other. But we had lunch every day. I think even then people suspected something," said Felicia. "Matt went home to his family every night. I even dated other men."

"So when did you get together?" I asked.

"It was when we were away from the office. In our business, there's a lot of travel, so we were away from the office twice a month or more. After a while, sleeping together became standard practice when we were on the road. But it was sort of a game. We arranged separate hotel rooms each time. With clients we were the picture of decorum. You would think we were total strangers brought together to work on this project for the first time. So I don't know how word leaked out about us."

"When did you first find out your affair was no longer a secret?" I asked Felicia.

"It was because of Matt's promotion. One day his boss hinted that he was up for a new job. In this firm, a personnel committee has to approve any internal job changes, so it was a matter of time before all the paperwork was completed. But two weeks later, after the committee had met, Matt's promotion had been withdrawn. When he asked his boss why, he got a lot of [ambiguous] reasons out of him. Through further probing of contacts on the committee, we discovered that some people knew about the affair."

"So what did you do?" I wanted to know.

"We immediately broke it off. But the damage had been done. People were saying they could no longer trust Matt's judgment. One person in particular, in fact—one of Matt's more ambitious peers. God knows what they were saying about me. That's why we both left the company. The gossip was too destructive."

Logistics Games

I reported earlier that a _Men's Health_ survey in Fall 1987 showed some surprising statistics: that among 444 readers, over 50 percent had been sexually propositioned by someone at work; a quarter had sex in their place of work; and another 18 percent had sex with a coworker during work hours. The question is How does this happen?

Some couples, unlike Felicia and Matt, play brazen sex games in the office. Perhaps they wish to be discovered. I heard a number of titillating stories in my research. I'm not sure to what extent some of my sources fictionalized their anecdotes, but they certainly make for juicy gossip.

One woman, an editor at a publishing house, said, "When I had a boss who played around blatantly with my young secretary, we never could figure out what they did behind that closed door—since he had no office couch—until we realized the truth, which I blush to tell."

Another woman told me that a highly placed man she worked for was found or seen by someone with one of his young female employees on the conference room table.

A third reported, "I caught my boss with his zipper unzipped coming out of a female colleague's office one day. The woman had left her shoes under that same desk. I can only imagine what they were doing in there!"

A few others: A human resources manager told me that a man in his firm had been caught using the company's automatic messaging system to place sexy messages on the lines of the firm's most attractive and highly placed women. A woman and man enjoying a tryst on the man's desk were caught by security guards routinely patrolling the floors. A couple was discovered *in flagrante* on an unoccupied floor of their office building during lunch hour.

Sometimes couples are forced to play games of logistics as a means of concealing their affair. Others do it for excitement and adventure.

A VIDEOTAPED OFFICE AFFAIR: DAN AND SELINA

The case of Dan and Selina illustrates how logistics can backfire. I heard about this example through a friend who told me he had "this great story" for me to include in this book.

Dan first met Selina when both started working for the same sales firm. They quietly became involved in an extramarital affair. Said my source on this case, "No one knew at the time. A few of us suspected, but there really was nothing on which to base our suspicions. It was business as usual between them."

But later, the couple began flaunting their affair in the office. "They adopted a habit of staying late in the office after hours. After everyone had left, Dan and Selina made good use of the company's exercise room in the basement of their building as a place of rendezvous. They had regular trysts together on

Monday and Wednesday evenings. I know, because once I saw them going downstairs together when I was working late."

But Dan and Selina neglected to realize one very important fact: Their office building was equipped with a new, high-tech security system—complete with video cameras. "The cameras tracked all the floors, including the basement," said my friend. "Their nighttime activities were recorded on more than one occasion by security personnel. Can you imagine? Their affair actually was recorded! And they never knew it."

When it appeared that the nighttime trysts were occurring on a regular basis, building security personnel decided they had no choice but to alert management about the situation. The couple was informed of the company's knowledge of their antics. The affair ended shortly thereafter. But, of course, gossip about the affair spread like wildfire throughout the company. "For three days, this was the topic of great interest and conversation—in hallways, behind closed office doors, in the lunchroom and lavatories. The common joke was, 'Will the tapes be out on VHS or Beta?' " said my source, laughing.

Advancement Games

Dan and Selina suffered for their dalliance. Their reputations in the firm were ruined after news leaked out about the videotaped affair. But such antics seem mild in comparison to games that exploit sex for advancement.

Sexploitation is alive and well in some corporate corridors of America. Because romances between bosses and subordinates raise questions of power, these relationships sometimes involve manipulation in a way that peer relationships do not. An executive in the pharmaceuticals industry commented, "In my industry, there are a lot more men than women, and I have seen some women use this to their advantage to receive favorable treatment in raises and assignments."

A magazine editor said, "That kind of thing goes on all the time! I have been in this business a long time, and I have seen some of the games people play to protect or maintain their power. Some women are not at all above using their sexual wiles to get ahead. I have been the victim of one of those power plays. It was uncomfortable at the time."

Zandra, a thirty-four-year-old marketing representative, found herself in one such situation. "Dick and Jane were fooling around on the side, but they sure didn't fool us. He took her everywhere, gave her the easy stuff, and drooled all over her desk. We were madder than hell and told his boss."

For some women—and men—sexploitation may be the new corporate game to beat out the competition. Some people believe that if you sleep with your boss, you definitely will have an edge. Innocent tidbits of information during pillow talk sessions may become invaluable in the game of corporate politics. This is the material of which many Hollywood movies are made.

But does it occur in real life? Maybe. We all were exposed to a recent news story in which American armed services personnel, on two-year duty in Moscow, actually sold American espionage secrets to the Russian women they were dating—who turned out to be spies. The men involved were young and in search of companionship, and the Russian women were ready to comply.

If such incidents are happening on a worldwide basis, we can infer that something similar is probably happening in the corporate boardroom. Now it is the corporate bedroom in which favors such as promotions, money, favorable task assignments, plum opportunities for travel, and other corporate perquisites are being exchanged.

But what happens to those women and men who resort to this? I believe that women and men who exercise sexploitation to get ahead ultimately lose. Colleagues are smart. They know what is going on. Given an opportunity, they will retaliate in full force in their own game of corporate warfare.

FOILED BY SLEEPING HER WAY TO THE TOP: ALEXANDRA AND FRED

Let me give you an example of sexploitation—and how coworkers will retaliate if given the opportunity. I learned about this case from a source who claims he saw it all happen from the first day Alexandra came to work at his firm, a soft drink manufacturer. My source, whom I will call Paul for the purposes of this story, is a human resources director for this firm.

According to Paul, "The problem with this incident was that it was such a tragedy. Fred was and is a nice, all-around guy, with a comfortable family life. But he was ruined by Alexandra's machinations, and his career will never recover."

Fred was considered an average but not outstanding manager. Fred had earned his stripes in the company by being responsible for one of the key departments that brought innovative marketing campaigns to the marketplace in the early 1970s. He was known as a "people developer" within the company, having served as a mentor to many younger employees.

Alexandra was something else. Tough, dark, attractive, strong, decisive, regal—she had a distinctive bearing. "But there was something about her that many people felt they could not trust," said Paul. "The facade she wore was easily chipped. Once you got beneath the surface, there was nothing more than tough, driving ambition in her character—and a penchant for power."

Stories about Alexandra abounded in the company. According to Paul, it was said that she managed to take away another coworker's project by carefully manipulating her boss. Another tale rumored that she deftly extricated herself from the same project when it started to go down the tubes.

Alexandra decided that she wanted to be part of Fred's new management development program. She was convinced that this assignment would launch her career in the appropriate direction. Said Paul, "Alexandra had been assigned to Fred's division, and had been given a project that required her to interact frequently with managers at Fred's level of the company. But when she was assigned to Fred's division, he was in the middle of a midlife crisis. Alexandra decided to take advantage of this. She purposefully set out to seduce him."

Alexandra made certain that every time she met with Fred to report on her project, she wore clothing that was suggestive. "It was unbelievable what she would wear," said Paul. "Red, suggestive little numbers, cut low in front or in the back—with red shoes. She purposefully set out to attract Fred, I know it. She arranged a lot of meetings with him at five P.M. and they worked on after hours. It was in the cards."

According to Paul, this went on for several months. Fred told Paul that they finally slept together the night of an after-hours retirement party when his wife was away visiting family.

"I was there that night, and I could tell something was going on," said Paul. "At the time I thought they already had slept together."

They conducted their romance in secret at first. In exchange for the secrecy (Fred was married with two children, and did not want to upset his home life), Alexandra made it clear what she wanted: a seat on the task force and her name added to the high potential list. To ensure her success, Alexandra made Fred desire her—so much so that he could no longer concentrate on his work.

Paul said, "I could see how Fred couldn't resist her. She teased him with her clothes. She winked at him in lascivious ways. She talked 'double talk' so that he would get excited from her presence. It was something to see."

However, their behavior toward one another tipped off their coworkers very quickly. Long lunches together outside of the office, meetings behind closed doors, notes passed to each other in the hallway, and Fred's surreptitious visits to retail stores to buy many expensive presents (ostensibly for his wife) caused the gossip mills to flourish.

According to my source, "I remember one time I was working late, so was Fred. Suddenly Alexandra waltzed in to Fred's office, after hours, with her arms full of packages from Saks. She thanked Fred for letting her go off on a shopping spree, and said something about he would receive his reward in due time. They didn't know I was still working, and they didn't know that I overheard them."

Fred gave in. He became increasingly dependent upon Alexandra, and she grew to have more and more influence over him. "He fell madly, completely, fully in love with Alexandra," said Paul. "He decided that he was willing to risk his comfortable home life—and his career—for her. He told his wife about the affair. He moved out of his home."

Fred fought long and hard to overcome the objections of others to putting Alexandra's name on the high potential list. He appointed her to the task force anyway, and assigned her the most visible and challenging assignments.

Colleagues understandably were upset. Their reactions grew increasingly negative. Even though the romance had still not been made public, everyone in the office knew what was going on.

Paul said, "When Fred appointed Alexandra to the task force, it was his fatal mistake. It's one thing to have an affair. It's another to let yourself be used as a pawn in someone else's scheme."

Alexandra was not well liked. Her appointment caused her colleagues to feel an injustice had been done to them. My source said, "We were all seething. I mean, I didn't care about the task force myself. But there was this other guy who was really good, interested, and deserved the appointment. We were upset."

Her colleagues decided to take subtle action. They talked about the romance whenever Alexandra and Fred left the room. They made jokes about Fred's sexual performance. Paul told me about a graffiti cartoon in the ladies' room that showed their anger. It depicted Fred as a dog, on a leash held by Alexandra. Others began to feel it was Alexandra, and not Fred, who was running the office. They feared her influence over him, and worried what she would do to them, given her newly assumed power.

Paul said, "The joking and insults grew into concerted action. Some people actually dropped hints about the romance where they could be heard by Fred's boss. Others made Alexandra look bad—I remember there was this report she had due that suddenly was 'misplaced.' "

Alexandra's peers started taking long coffee breaks and equally long lunches to challenge Fred. Members of the task force belittled Alexandra's remarks, and challenged Fred's authority as the chairman. My source continued, "The whole situation had gotten out of hand. Nothing was getting done in the office."

Morale among coworkers hit an all-time low. For the first time in years, the department did not meet its budget nor its quotas, and other departments in the company began complaining about the lack of efficiency and cooperation that they found when dealing with Fred's unit.

Ironically, after Fred left his wife, Alexandra dropped him

once she achieved her goals. "Basically, she went after a better prey," said Paul. "She soon became involved in a hot and heavy romance with the division president."

But there is a twist to this story. According to Paul, the tables were turned on Alexandra one day when the division president, after tiring of her, transferred her to a deadbeat job in another division of the company. She eventually left the firm. "But it was a small comfort to Fred to discover, years later, that Alexandra had received her comeuppance," said Paul. "By then, his reputation already had suffered. Fred was looked upon as a chump for having been taken in by Alexandra's charms. I don't think his career will ever recover."

Corporate Games

Another type of game-playing concerns the politics of realignment. In this day and age of corporate takeovers, downsizing, and reorganizations, many people fear for their jobs. Corporate warfare may sometimes involve job security.

When power positions shift within a firm, such as during a corporate reorganization, everything becomes off-balance. In such situations, mentors protect their proteges, and lovers protect each other. Sometimes the resulting organizational charts resemble an emotional checkerboard more than a series of logical business decisions. Organizational uncertainty leads to political maneuvering to protect turf.[2]

Ken, an investment banker, believes that an office romance actually can improve your job security in a firm. He further believes that this should be considered a benefit of office romance. "Twice, I have seen women who were having an affair with their bosses protected against firings," said Ken. "In neither case was there any other reason except the affair. When the October crash hit, and so many people like me were out on the street, these women were riding high. I think if you're a woman in a highly politicized environment, it's the best thing you can do for your career [to have an office romance]."

Beth, a thirty-five-year-old sales representative, disagrees. "I don't think having an office affair affords you any extra protection. Only being good at your work does. An office affair may be a reason for dismissal when shakeups are happening."

There may be some truth to this perspective. One woman I know told me that, as a personnel representative, it was her assignment to go out and "dig up the dirt" on people prior to a layoff. "This way, we had something to really hold against them. Can you believe they asked me to do this? I was supposed to be the eyes and ears for the division president—to find out who was fooling around with whom so he could get his way if needed. I felt like I had dropped onto the set of 'Dallas' or some other soap opera."

Because the politics of a firm may be likened to corporate warfare, some people pull out all the stops—and all the information—to advance their careers. In this day and age, with career ambitions so cut-throat, this should not be surprising.

"When my boss started dating Kathleen, everything suddenly became political," said Tara, thirty-three. "Our business must run like a clock, we have high pressure deadlines. He became lackadaisical about some things and spent all his time cavorting with Kathleen. She got off scot-free, and we were angry at both of them."

Any kind of favoritism in an office situation simply isn't businesslike. But sometimes people play the corporate games of romance just to see how far they can go.

A GERRYMANDERED DIVISION: STAN AND MAURA

One of my students, Shirley, told me the story of Stan and Maura. Since Stan is Shirley's boss, she was able to observe the long-term development of this romance.

The affair between Maura, a division president, and Stan, the manager of one of the company's most profitable districts, began three years ago. "I know when it started," said Shirley. "It was right after I returned to work from maternity leave. Something had happened while I was gone. One day, I saw Stan stop by Maura's office late in the day. Night fell, and when I walked out to the parking lot, I could see through the window-shades that she was sitting in his lap."

The lovers carried on in blissful ignorance for several

months. But one day Shirley spotted them together at an out-of-town department store. "It was pretty hard to pretend nothing was going on at that point," said Shirley. "But we all continued to act as if nothing had happened."

A year ago, a major corporate reorganization took place. "They wanted to downsize all the districts—including Stan's. Everyone thought that was stupid because things were working so well. But we had to satisfy them somehow."

Maura interceded at headquarters on behalf of Stan. She managed to keep his district intact. Not only that, but she got him another district so he could increase his empire.

"We all laughed at the time when we heard the news," said Shirley. "We knew what was going on. The two districts did not make sense combined. Stan had no experience with the work that was done in the other district. It was a classic case of gerrymandering. But my job was saved as a result. At that point I realized that yes, office romance can indeed have some benefits!"

But Maura found she had to pay dearly for her intervention. Rumors ran throughout the firm that she had protected her lover. When the upper levels heard the rumors, they decided that Maura's relationship with Stan had rendered her ineffective. No one would trust her judgment. She left the firm.

"Stan suddenly was sent away on a field job," said Shirley. "I don't know if he and Maura still see each other. I know he is thinking of leaving the firm. The new division president came in and separated the two districts. It was pretty weird around here for a while."

Why Lovers Are Compelled to Protect Themselves

Why do lovers in the office go to such great lengths to protect the secrecy of their affairs? Why would Maura risk her own career to protect Stan? Despite the businesslike setting, or maybe because of it, people find they welcome the warmth that a love relationship can bring. They relish the time spent alone with a lover as a calming respite from corporate shenanigans.

Many studies of dating and romantic relationships suggest

that the degree to which we are drawn to someone else is influenced by the extent to which we become dependent on that person to satisfy our needs.[3] We begin to need him or her to fulfill our dreams. If money is a factor, we choose a partner who can provide us with sufficient monetary resources to maintain a particular style of living. If we seek social companionship, we search for a partner who can meet our needs for social support and affection. If we are uncomfortable making decisions, we search for a partner we can trust to make appropriate decisions for us.

But our dependency makes us vulnerable by giving others power over us. According to researcher Richard Emerson, a sociologist at the University of Northern Colorado who published an article called "Power-Dependence Relations" in the *American Sociological Review* in 1962, dependency is the twin of power. If you have more invested than the other, you may have more to lose. Your feelings render you more vulnerable and powerless.

This is what people fear in a romance. If we love too much, we place ourselves in a position where we can be manipulated. Once that happens, we will go to any length to protect the stability of our relationship, including game-playing that risks our careers. This is what happened to Fred with Alexandra. According to Paul, my source on that case, "Fred really needed Alexandra in his life at that time. He was questioning the meaning of life with his midlife crisis. She came along and manipulated his crisis."

Lovers will protect one another if they are dependent on each other for the mutual strength of their relationship. It was for this reason that Mary and Greg jealously guarded their privacy, and Maura went to great lengths to protect Stan.

Love, power, vulnerability, and dependency are all intertwined. If the feelings run sufficiently deep, the lovers will play whatever games they must to keep each other happy.

What to Do if You're a Victim of Sexual Politics

Sometimes the games lovers play to protect one another and make each other happy have troubling consequences for others in the firm. You may become an unwilling victim of these political games.

What should you do if you find yourself bested by a romantic power play? Many skilled corporate survivors learn to return dirty politics in kind.

In the social sciences, social exchange theory has been widely advocated as a model that explains others' reactions to inequitable situations.[4] This theory says if we believe we have been treated unfairly, we feel justified in restoring the balance of power by participating in similar actions. This is how colleagues often rationalize "an eye for an eye and a tooth for a tooth" behavior when office romances become disruptive. When game-playing upsets the power balance and corporate alignments of the firm, colleagues become threatened and they take action against the couple. The first order of business is to break down the power coalition forged by the romance.

Peter Blau, a sociologist at Columbia University who wrote a book entitled *Exchange and Power in Social Life* (Wiley Press, 1964), believes that coalitions provoke a range of reactions from social disapproval to outright hostility. Colleagues retaliate against office romances that disrupt the delicate political balance of the firm as a way to restore justice and equity.

This is what happened to Alexandra and Fred. Coworkers did whatever they could to malign Alexandra and let Fred know he was a chump to be fooled by her charms. Alexandra had found an unethical means of getting visibility, and had beaten out more deserving candidates for the task force position. Her peers wouldn't take this for long, which eventually caused the situation to deteriorate. "We just couldn't stand it any longer," said Paul, my source for the Alexandra and Fred romance. "We had to do something."

Sometimes, as in this case, concerns about the misuse of the relationship are very real. There is a natural tendency if you are involved in an office relationship to protect or favor your lover. You may not grant him or her an automatic promotion, but you may look the other way when he or she walks in late after a hot date with you the night before.

Promotions, raises, time off, favorable task assignments, traveling, and other perquisites sometimes are exchanged in a love relationship between bosses and subordinates, or mentors and proteges. So what should you do if a colleague of yours is having an affair with your boss—and reaping unfair rewards?

When peers realize that an unfair situation has developed, they usually will take action. If telling the boss is required to restore equity, coworkers will do so. If they decide that unfair competition is causing one lover to favor the other, they, too, will respond with dirty politics. Sabotage of the couple's work, sniping about the affair, or even outright blackmail will be exercised to restore justice and a sense of equity to the office environment.

"There was this sleazy guy who would do anything to get ahead, even sleep with the boss's daughter," said one woman who worked for a small family-run firm. "We knew he was no good. He was lousy at his job but got to keep it because he was dating the boss's daughter. What we did—well, we just made things a bit more difficult for him. We made sure Sally [the daughter] knew when he was flirting with some of the other women in the firm. We worked in concert to get him out of the firm and her life. We sure weren't going to let him wind up as our new boss someday."

Peers become gravely upset when the game-playing sparks charges of usurped power. The Quinn survey showed that if coworkers suspect the relationship is causing a change in the power balance in the office, they will retaliate against the couple. According to Quinn:

> [Peers] may try to undermine or sabotage one or both of the participants. . . . For example, members of a steno pool stole files and hid parts of projects that one romantically involved secretary was working on. In another case subordinates leaked damaging information about the work of their boss to a regulatory agency. . . . Other strategies included blackmail, ostracism, and quitting. In one case, a romantically involved manager began to reprimand a subordinate for inadequate work. The subordinate interrupted and threatened to tell the man's wife about the manager's romantic involvement.

In the Quinn survey, approximately 28 percent complained to a superior about the relationship, 22 percent argued about what should be done, 13 percent tried to undermine the couple, 10 percent quit or left the firm, 6 percent sabotaged the couple's work, 5 percent ostracized the couple, and 4 percent threatened to—or actually did—blackmail the couple.

Because of this, sexploitation may *not* be a surefire way to the top of your corporation. It probably is the fastest way to ruin your credibility and truncate your career advancement.

One woman, anticipating a need to guard herself against a power play that happened when her boss started dating a coworker *and* ordered the coworker to monitor her work, said, "I wasn't about to stand for that. If he thought he could use me as a pawn in his scheme, or if she thought she could get away usurping my authority, they were wrong. I immediately went to my boss's boss and told him what was going on. They were called in for a discussion, and the other woman suddenly was transferred to another department."

Ken, the man who told me about several corporate realignments caused by lovers' protecting themselves, once reacted negatively. "This woman was being protected by her lover, and we knew about the relationship. It was easy to block her power because all we did was make sure she looked bad. Reports were lost, deadlines were missed. She was rendered incapable to do her job."

The Last Word

The central point that I learned from my research was that *coworkers always have the last word.* They play a game of their own with those romancers who offend their corporate sensibilities. Although the couple may *think* that their secret has gone unnoticed, savvy colleagues usually know something is going on, and they will find a way to turn the tables on the offenders. Whenever corporate realignments become gerrymandered for the sake of an office love, peers find a way of rendering the focal manager "ineffective."

But coworkers feel little need to break apart *productive* office romance coalitions. Said one woman who observed a positive office romance, "We are so happy that Charles and Jeana found one another. Her support has really modified his management style to the point that we no longer hate coming into the office. There's no way we would do anything but encourage this romance!"

Others who have seen the positive side of office romance agree. "When an office romance is having a positive effect in the office, there is no need to do anything to undermine the couple," said one executive woman in the cosmetics industry. "But should a power play take place, watch out! I'll be there with my nails sharpened." This is what happened to Maura and Stan, to Bruce, to Alexandra, to Felicia and Matt, and to many of the others included in this chapter. Their coworkers ultimately had the last word.

Perhaps all is fair in love and war after all.

PART FIVE

THE PASSION AND THE PAIN: WHO GETS HURT?

11

EXTRAMARITAL AFFAIRS

One of the things I learned in my research was that coworkers generally are uncomfortable dealing with someone who is having an extramarital office affair.

Nathan, a personnel executive whom I met while consulting, asked me if my research dealt with extramarital office affairs. I asked him why he was interested. "Since I've been in this job, I swear there has been a rise in the number of extramarital affairs in this firm," he said. "What worries me is that there must be four others for every one that I hear about."

Nathan's personnel job involved employee counseling. He often is placed in a position of hearing confidential information and making referrals to qualified therapists for employees with specific needs.

I asked Nathan why he thought this was so. He said, "I am convinced that the increase of women in executive positions will be the downturn of the modern family. With so many women around, there is a greater likelihood of adultery. I see it all the time now, much more than before."

I pointed out to Nathan that extramarital affairs do not always involve executive women, and that this could be interpreted as a sexist statement. He smiled and said, "Well, maybe

189

it's sexist, but I really think it is true. With more women in the workplace, there is bound to be more relationships of all kinds— singles, marrieds, gay, May-September romances, and whatever other combinations you can think of. Because of this, the propensity for extramarital affairs will increase."

I thought about his comment later in the day, and realized he may have a point. *Because the workplace promotes attraction, extramarital affairs are bound to increase.* Yet extramarital affairs, because of their illicit nature, are beset with complications. Not only do extramarital romancers face ordinary risks to career advancement, but because extramarital affairs pose questions of ethics, morality, and judgment, it is more likely they will be considered disruptive.

Gay affairs in the workplace also present an additional level of complexity. Because so many gay couples fear retribution from their employers should their sexual preferences become known, many gay couples keep their romances private. Because society retains antiquated views of gay love, most gay workplace romances remain in the closet.

How people conduct their own lives is, of course, their own business. Nowhere is the "gray" area about office romances grayer than in this arena. But extramarital affairs and some gay relationships present complex moral, ethical, and legal dilemmas that managers must consider. These relationships only will increase as the new sexual revolution takes hold in the workplace.

Extramarital Affairs Are More Common Than You Think

Extramarital affairs have been around since the dawn of time. We all have heard the stories about secretaries and their bosses, and about the new modern mistress. But today extramarital affairs may be even more widespread than you think. When Alfred Kinsey and colleagues began publishing their landmark findings on sexual behavior forty years ago, their statistics on extramarital affairs took most people by surprise. Kinsey's data indicated that one of every two husbands had engaged in an extramarital affair. One of every four married women had done the same.

Shere Hite's controversial book *Women in Love: A Cultural Revolution in Progress* (Alfred A. Knopf, 1987) presented even more surprising statistics. Her survey indicated approximately 70 percent of women married five years or less had participated in an adulterous affair. Even though her research was widely criticized for its sample bias, other reports suggest similarly scandalous statistics.

The current educated guess on marital infidelity by sex researcher Anthony P. Thompson (in his February 1983 *Journal of Sex Research* article, "Extramarital Sex: A Review of the Literature") is at least 55 percent for married men, and the figure for women is rapidly approaching the same level. Keep in mind that these statistics are considered to be conservative. Data on extramarital affairs is understandably difficult to estimate with any reasonable degree of accuracy.[1]

Personally, I find these results—even with the bias considered—to be somewhat amazing. If it is true that one out of every three marriages will end in divorce, this may illustrate one of the reasons why.

Why an Extramarital Affair?

Why would someone become tempted by an extramarital office affair? As you would expect, it is difficult to obtain data on this subject directly from the romancers themselves.

Dr. Jeffrey Zimmerman, of Connecticut Psychological Associates in Hartford, believes that extramarital office affairs are on the rise. He has counseled many couples dealing with the crisis of an extramarital affair. "People become tempted by office affairs," said Dr. Zimmerman, "for the same reasons as they would in other contexts outside the office. If they are lacking satisfaction in their marriages, they may seek companionship elsewhere."

According to Dr. Phyllis Hopkins, a private therapist in Fairfield, Connecticut, who has treated clients involved in extramarital office affairs, "Office affairs have a forbidden quality. Their illicit nature can be stimulating. But the guilt that people must work through is far more significant [in an office affair].

And the additional complications of an office relationship—where everyone knows everyone else—can be severe."

Most people told me they think office affairs usually begin as flings—temporary liaisons in which the participants inadvertently become involved. If the affair progresses further, the couple may have to deal with the depth of their attraction. At this point, a decision must be made about the character, strength, and goals of the relationship.

One woman reported, "I don't think it is planned in most cases, and I don't think people can help themselves sometimes—no matter how much they believe in the sanctity of marriage. People are only human, some marriages are not made in heaven, and sometimes the affair is a way of supplementing or complementing the marriage."

Another woman told me privately after hearing a lecture on office romance, "My affair in the office is public knowledge, so I don't mind telling you what happened. It wasn't something planned. . . . It happened while my husband and I were separated, and we are now divorced. . . . But it did me a lot of good. It helped me to realize the sorry state of my marriage."

But Rachel, forty-one, told me that her affair was her worst mistake. "I'm down on office affairs because I had one. I got caught up in the glamour of it all and forgot about what was important to me. My affair cost me my husband and my children. All I have left is my work."

Pamela, a forty-nine-year-old manufacturing executive, is another woman burned by an office affair. "I became so caught up in the passion I forgot what had meaning for me. I couldn't handle work, my marriage, an affair, and my children growing up all at once. I suppose that's why I became involved. . . . But it ruined my life. I am now only beginning to pick up the pieces."

The temptation to become involved often is planted in the seeds of a bad marriage. Because love is irrational, many people do not realize the consequences of their actions—both in the office and at home—until it is too late. "As people grow a little older and realize they're only passing through this once, when you begin to wonder 'Is this all there is to life?', they may become tempted by an office affair. If the marriage has gone sour, the temptation becomes action," said one woman.

"Even if a person gets some very valuable things from a marriage and has no desire to overturn it, but longs deeply for the well-being that the lover is able to inspire, an extramarital affair becomes more likely," said a publishing assistant. "After all, people are only human, and the workplace provides the right ambience for romance."

This certainly is true. Because the workplace is conducive to attraction and intimacy, the likelihood of extramarital affairs is bound to increase. More temptations will ensue as a result of the new sexual revolution. And there will be more pain and sorrow for jilted wives and husbands as a consequence.

AN EXTRAMARITAL AFFAIR: SAMANTHA AND PAT

My friend Elizabeth told me the story of Samantha and Pat, two married lovers who engaged in an extramarital affair. They met while working for the same division of a manufacturing firm in the South. Samantha held a job as safety captain, and Pat was a plant engineer.

According to Elizabeth, Samantha and Pat were both married at the time they first met. Because this was a small town plant, coworkers knew Samantha and Pat's respective spouses quite well. "Pat's in-laws and niece also worked for the same plant in different areas," said Elizabeth. "The company followed a corporate policy that supported the hiring of relatives, so a number of married couples were employed at the firm."

The manufacturing plant had several safety problems, and Samantha was frequently called away from her home at night to inspect machinery and recommend alternatives for its safe operation. Her job was demanding and quite intense. Pat, as one of the chief engineers responsible for plant operations, usually was called to work with Samantha side-by-side. Over the years, they became close friends.

Elizabeth said, "Working under extreme pressure while handling safety crises made them really close. Samantha and Pat were both fond of recounting stories of, 'Do you remember when . . .' in front of new recruits. Everyone knew they were the experts. Frequently they were called away to consult with other plants in the area.

"Because of their odd work hours and their close working

relationship, Samantha and Pat ate a lot of dinners together rather than at home. Once a month, they were required to travel together to report to the company headquarters. On weekends when a problem arose, I honestly think they saw more of each other than their families!"

Over time, Samantha's marriage began to crumble. Her husband wanted to move to the Northeast to accept a new job, but she had refused. Her children experienced problems with drug abuse. Samantha confided her troubles to Pat as a friend.

Elizabeth said, "I could tell the relationship had taken on new dimensions when Samantha stopped confiding in me. Suddenly Pat was her number one confidant. She no longer needed me in that role."

After a difficult argument with both her husband and children one night, Samantha traveled with Pat to a nearby plant to check out a safety problem. That night, they made love. "She told me what had happened months later," said Elizabeth. "They made a mutual agreement to separate the affair from their home life. Pat was committed to his marriage and young family, and Samantha was uncertain about whether she wanted to stay in her marriage and work out her problems. I think the affair was mostly a convenience for both of them. Samantha needed something else in her life at the time, because of her family problems. She was questioning her life, her purpose, her marriage—she needed some added support."

Coworkers began to suspect that an affair had blossomed between them, but they tried their best to ignore the situation. Because this was a small plant, colleagues were very sensitive to subtle changes in each other's behavior. They earnestly hoped that nothing was going on, but began to notice a few differences. "It became obvious when Samantha and Pat no longer sat together at lunch," said Elizabeth. "They avoided one another. Many of their conversations took place in private areas or stairwells." Because they were known as a "team" within the plant, these changes in their behavior seemed unusual.

"They still worked together, but they almost couldn't look at each other," said Elizabeth.

One weekend, a major safety problem occurred at the plant. Samantha and Pat were called in to mediate. In the stairwell after the crisis was over, Samantha and Pat congratulated each other with a kiss. Little did they know that three of their coworkers were standing at the top of the stairwell, watching their embrace. "Sally [another coworker] told me all about it the next day. There was such gossip—it spread like wildfire throughout the plant," said Elizabeth. "Everyone knew what was going on. It was our own version of the *National Enquirer.*"

Some of Samantha and Pat's coworkers were indignant. Others felt they should mind their own business. Still others believed that they should confront the couple with their information. "There were all these debates in the office," said Elizabeth. "Should we or shouldn't we let them know what we knew? This was about the time Sam told me the whole story, so I let her know the word was out."

By this time, however, the affair between Samantha and Pat had cooled. "Samantha had decided that she wanted to work out the problems in her marriage with her husband, and Pat had returned to his wife," said Elizabeth. "The affair had ended. Ironically, the kiss in the stairwell was for old time's sake, according to Sam."

But coworkers did not know this. Because Pat's relatives were well known in the company, word got around about the affair. His niece heard the news, and promptly told her other relatives. The news, of course, got back to his wife.

"Two nights later, Pat discovered that he had been locked out of his own house by his wife," said Elizabeth. "She refused to hear his explanation. Her mind was made up. She wanted a divorce."

Later, Pat was able to repair the damage done to his marriage. But Samantha's marriage was unable to be reclaimed. A year later, she and her husband divorced. She is now working at a different plant in the Midwest. "Samantha was hurt by the affair far more deeply than Pat," said Elizabeth. "I sat up with her many nights comforting her pain. She lost her husband and her family. But now she's starting a new life and I'm happy for her."

Gossip about Extramarital Affairs Can Be Devastating

Because adulterous affairs are considered a form of marital misconduct, they provide wonderful material for gossipers. Questions such as "Does her husband know?" or "Are they only interested in sex, or something more?" become the subject of endless hallway debates.

Most of the people with whom I spoke steadfastly argued against adulterous affairs. Even with today's more liberalized sexual mores, adulterous behavior still is not widely sanctioned. The recent media events surrounding Gary Hart's presidential campaign and his rendezvous with Donna Rice suggest that extramarital affairs still remain controversial.

But because of this, most married lovers steadfastly guard their privacy. Rather than risking disruption to their home lives, they prefer to conduct the liaison secretly, quietly, and with minimal interference.

Ironically, as I reported earlier, few office romances—especially extramarital ones—remain under wraps for long. In my survey, 36 percent said they were aware of an office affair that the couple believed was their private secret. An additional 40 percent said that the romance was known to some but not to all.

For example, I once heard about a married man whose wife also worked for the same firm but in a different department. This man was famous for his extramarital exploits—some conducted right under his wife's nose. Rumors about his rendezvous with other women in broom closets, on top of desks after five o'clock, and during lunchtime trysts spread throughout the company. To this day I cannot understand how his wife could have been oblivious to the gossip.

Once the affair has become public knowledge, coworkers are presented with special problems. Should they confront the couple to let them know their secret is out? Or should they ignore the affair in the hopes that it will soon run its course? In the example I just related, colleagues openly wondered if they should directly tell the wife in question about her husband's many exploits. This became the subject of tantalizing gossip.

"What are we supposed to do?" asked the employee who

told me this story. "Ignore him? Tell her? Make a joke and hope she catches on? The whole mess has put us in a difficult situation."

Gossipers want to know four things: the state of the romance, whether the spouses know, who said what to whom, and what the projected outcome of the relationship may be. Often they maintain they *need* to know this information to understand how to treat the spouse when he or she arrives at the office.

And many colleagues seem to *enjoy* the gossip that an office affair brings. It breaks up the humdrum routine and allows employees to take their minds off their workday responsibilities. Sometimes others can have fun with an office affair. For example, I know of one case in which colleagues in an advertising firm actually took $100 bets on whether an extramarital affair between a partner and a graphics artist would last more than six months!

Personally, I am thankful for those gossip mongers who were willing to share details of romances they had observed for my research on this book. But I certainly would not want to be the subject of such juicy tales!

CORPORATE CASUALTIES: ANNA AND DENNIS

The story of Anna and Dennis illustrates how an extramarital affair can open up the floodgates of gossip. Dennis was a division manager of an automotive firm. Anna was one of his direct reports. They had met at work.

I asked Anna how the affair began. "Pretty typically, I guess," said Anna. "Dennis was my mentor in a sense. He helped me out of several jams. I grew to know him, to like him, and one day I realized that we looked at each other differently. I started to care more about how I was dressed in the morning. One weekend when we both had to work in the office it suddenly happened."

"Did anyone know?" I asked.

"Not at the time," said Anna. "We did not want anyone to find out. But they did, eventually. That's what caused all the trouble."

"What trouble?" I wanted to know.

"Well, it only was a short, one-month affair. But Jeffrey, Dennis's boss's boss, somehow got wind of it. To this day I don't know how, because we were very discreet. Anyway, Dennis was up for a promotion at the time. Somehow his name was removed from the list."

"Did this Jeffrey have anything to do with it?" I asked.

"I think so," said Anna. "He was in a position to influence the decision. I overheard him once talking about how he no longer could trust Dennis's judgment. So I really think he was the culprit. It didn't help that his wife was a good friend of Dennis's wife. So it fits."

"Did your spouses ever find out?" I asked.

"My husband doesn't know because there was nothing to tell. I didn't want to upset him over nothing. But Dennis's wife did find out and was very hurt. Dennis got the raw end of the deal. His career was plateaued and his wife never forgave him. All because of a short, one-month dalliance."

Working with Married Coworkers Having Affairs

Anna may have thought that her affair was "nothing" at the time. But remember how I said earlier that coworkers always have the last word? This dictum also applies to extramarital affairs. When colleagues are displeased with an extramarital relationship in their midst, it shows. This could be why Jeffrey allegedly acted to break up the affair.

One woman told me, "Probably one of the most difficult experiences I have ever had to endure is when my best friend decided to have an affair with a man in our office. We had worked together for several years, and suddenly they were involved in an affair. . . . At the same time her husband, also a friend of mine, came to work for the company in a different department. I had to look him in the eye and make excuses for my friend when she was away from her desk, and I had to socialize with both of them as if nothing had ever happened."

Another woman, who worked in the pharmaceuticals industry, said, "I was good friends with this man with whom I had lunch four times a week. For a while I didn't know what was going on, but on Fridays, he rendezvoused with his female boss. The problem was, after I learned about the affair I couldn't deal with his wife. She worked in a department that worked closely with mine, so I saw her frequently."

In my survey, I received a number of comments from colleagues expressing displeasure at married liaisons. One woman who worked in the apparel industry said, "In my last position as a vice-president, my head designer was having an affair with our vice-president of sales. Both were married. She used working weekends as an alibi. . . . I'm all for romance, but when one or more parties is married, it's very uncomfortable. Especially if others at work have to socialize with the spouses involved."

These are messy ethical situations. What should coworkers do? Often, they are placed in an uncomfortable position of lying—or omitting crucial pieces of information—when they are in touch with the spouse. They lead a double life to protect the coworker having the affair. Their implicit condoning of the affair makes them feel like partners in crime. As the woman I quoted earlier said, "The whole affair . . . made me sick to my stomach. I hated my friend for what she was doing, and I hated myself for not telling her husband. He was the one I felt sorry for."

How Coworkers Learn to Tolerate Extramarital Affairs

No matter how strongly colleagues feel about an extramarital affair, they must tolerate it. To do so, they pretend they "see no evil, hear no evil, speak no evil" about the affair—especially when the spouse is around.

Levels of tolerance toward extramarital affairs seem to depend on three factors: whether the affair is discreet, the motives of the couple having the affair, and the level of conservatism in the company culture.

In my odyssey to gain information for this chapter, I talked with many people who claimed that they were aware of an extramarital affair in their companies, but that it did not bother them. "It's not really my business," said a partner in a small accounting firm. "I wouldn't do it. But it's a free country. As long as they're discreet it doesn't bother me."

Others gave me an earful about how extramarital affairs cause flagrant disregard for workplace professionalism. One employee with whom I spoke told me the story of an illicit affair that had gotten out of hand in his office. He said, "One member of the couple was recently separated; the other was still married. They often held hands at meetings, played footsie under the table, and frequently were seen with their arms around each other." According to my source, coworkers grew uncomfortable with their open displays of affection. Their discomfort caused them to write an anonymous letter to the personnel department, which called the couple in for a discussion about their actions.

Others are more tolerant of extramarital affairs if they understand, or can empathize with, the motives of the couple. In one case reported to me, a man who had been married for twelve years, and whose wife had been committed to a state mental hospital, began an affair with a woman in his small real estate office. The office employees were genuinely pleased that their boss had found some happiness in his life, and they were supportive of the affair.

But few colleagues are tolerant of extramarital affairs if they work for a company that frowns on illicit activities. For example, witness the recent events surrounding Jim Bakker's demise as the president of his highly publicized religious organization, the PTL Ministry. Accusations of homosexuality, adultery, and other improprieties led to his dismissal. Similar events caused the Reverend Jimmy Swaggart to be removed from his post temporarily.

"In this company, even going to lunch with your male boss can cause rumors to surface," said one executive woman who works for a large-scale family business. "The family founders still believe in the strong family unit, and they want their employees to act as they do. Who knows what would happen to me—a woman—if I fooled around?"

Corporate Reactions to Extramarital Affairs

The official corporate response to illicit affairs seems to be, "None of our business—unless work performance or morale is affected." I could not find anyone to tell me of a situation in which a gay affair caused reprisals. But in a poll of corporate executives, I discovered that in many cases extramarital affairs compel management action.

Several executives told me action was necessary if colleagues sent anonymous letters to officers saying that an adulterous affair was taking place in their department. One executive said, "The one situation . . . that causes the worst kind of morale problems is the affair between married employees. Usually that's when I get letters. It's almost as if coworkers are trying to sabotage the relationship because they are uncomfortable with it in their department."

Managing extramarital affairs presents particular problems. In an (unpublished) BFS Psychological Associates survey of 112 executives conducted by Mortimer Feinberg and Aaron Levenstein (cited in the *Wall Street Journal* on November 29, 1982), many respondents expressed concern about illicit affairs between married employees, especially when such affairs occurred between supervisors and subordinates.

Seventy-six respondents said they had been admonished by their superiors to "observe caution," and fifty said warnings were issued to discontinue such relationships. Twelve said the relationship was penalized by a denial of promotion; twenty indicated that other actions had been taken. In many of the cases, charges that sexual involvements had led to favoritism proved correct.

One personnel manager said, "In this company, there are some older guys who really take advantage of their power and play around with some of the younger girls on the side. For some reason, they forget that these affairs can damage their marriages, not to mention their jobs. We have had to take action—including one dismissal—against extramarital affairs that had become disruptive."

Extramarital affairs have been used as grounds for termination in some firms. In most of these cases, however, work performance also had been demonstratedly poor. As one executive said, "Fooling around on the side sometimes can be interpreted as a sign of poor judgment. The inference is that if this guy—or lady—is messing up in their personal life, what kinds of poor business judgments will they make? Romance between singles is one thing, but extramarital affairs are a different animal. Sometimes it can be used as an excuse not to promote someone, to truncate their career path."

A Word of Caution

In my opinion (and it is only my opinion), marriage is a covenant that deserves respect. Office romances are sufficiently complex without added legal, moral, and ethical retributions. The risks of damage to career advancement, charges of impropriety, and workplace disruption are greater with illicit complications. So why bother with an extramarital affair?

Legally, employers are within their rights to terminate employees for improper behavior. It is also less likely that the potential benefits of an office romance will be realized through an extramarital affair. Because extramarital and gay affairs present questions of ethics, morality, and judgment, it is more likely that they will be considered disruptive. There may be a greater likelihood that others will retaliate against the affair by acts of sabotage, reports of infidelity to spouses, or discussions with upper management.

Of course, extramarital relationships rarely are premeditated. Usually it just happens. If the idea for an affair comes at a time when the person is questioning other aspects of his or her life, the temptation may be difficult to resist. Increases in affairs that "just happen" may be one of the unwelcome aspects of the new sexual revolution. But it makes you wonder, as one woman in my survey put it, "What ever happened to faith and morals in the workplace?" After hearing some of the stories on extramarital affairs, sexual harassment, and sexploitation, I wondered the same.

12

VICTIMS AND CASUALTIES: THE INJURED SPOUSE

One day I received an anonymous letter from a man who had read about my research and wanted to give me a piece of his mind.

> Dear Professor,
> I think your research is somewhat irresponsible because you have not talked about the damage an extramarital affair can do to a person's self-esteem and that person's marriage. My wife had an affair with her boss for two years that I just discovered. We have spent several days crying and trying to decide what to do. . . . She tells me the affair ended several months ago, and now she is hurting at work, but this is minor in comparison to what the affair has done to our marriage. I'm not sure if we can pick up the pieces, and she's not sure she can continue to work at her firm. Why aren't you focusing on the damage an extramarital affair can do and how this should be stopped?
>
> Sincerely,
> An Injured Spouse

I kept thinking about what this man had said. The more I considered his perspective, the more I realized I needed to study the new casualty of the modern sexual revolution—the injured spouse.

So I gathered some of my case material together and began to look at it in a new light. This time, I focused on the impact an extramarital affair has on its primary victims, neglected husbands and wives.

Husbands and Wives

Spouses are the casualties of extramarital affairs. Like most victims, they feel unjustly treated. Many blame the modern workplace, as well as their wandering spouses, for their misfortunes.

A staff psychologist at a chemical company with whom I spoke about this subject said, "The husbands and wives are the victims. Employees come for counseling when they begin to feel guilty about their actions. Resolving that sense of guilt usually has implications for the marriage, even if the affair is kept a closely guarded secret from the spouse."

One woman who requested anonymity said, "I think women today must worry more about affairs. My husband was involved with one of the analysts in his office. . . . It was a nightmare that I hope no other friend of mine will ever have to go through."

Another woman said, "The affair . . . my husband had with his secretary almost tore up our family. We slept in separate beds for two years afterward because I refused to believe that it was over. Even though now she is married to someone else, I'm still not sure. The trust we had is gone."

Husbands and wives are the unwilling victims of love in the office. With the modern workplace becoming so sexy, it is no wonder that many more spouses are worried about how long their marriage commitments will last.

Even for the most straight-and-narrow spouse, office affairs are likely to be tempting. This is particularly true for those who work in professions that require long hours and much time spent away from home.

One friend of mine who worked for a consulting firm said, "In this business, it is difficult to get away from affairs. Marriages break up here almost on a monthly basis. Because we have so much traveling to do, affairs happen out of loneliness or opportunity. And to top it off, because we're away from home so much, sometimes our wives *think* we must be having affairs. I can't tell you the number of times my own wife has questioned me."

Husbands and wives who have spouses in demanding professions—such as doctors, consultants, Wall Street lawyers, or investment counselors—grow accustomed to the specter of extramarital affairs. As one wife said, "You learn to grin and bear it. Either you get out, or you go along and play the game."

THE INJURED SPOUSE: BARBARA

I met Barbara at a meeting of executive women where I presented the results of my survey on office romance. She took me aside during the break and began telling me about the havoc an extramarital affair was wreaking on her marriage to her husband, Hal.

Barbara said, "For the past ten years of marriage, my husband has had an extramarital relationship. I don't know why I am still married! This was a coworker relationship which passed, but then after a while, the relationship started up again. Now I don't know what to do. I'm so hurt and betrayed. I came here tonight to see if I could get a better handle on my feelings."

"How can I help you?" I asked Barbara.

"Sometimes I feel like no one can help me. I have been to therapy," said Barbara as her voice trailed off, filled with pain. "What I have learned is that I have to come to terms [with this] after nineteen years of much happiness. The last ten years have been very rocky. But it would be a lot easier if I didn't love my husband so much."

Sensing her pain, I ventured a delicate question. "Have you ever thought of dissolving the marriage?"

"Constantly!" said Barbara. "Even though I accepted my husband back, it took years off me to do so. . . . And it was traumatic to work through all the guilt he had. I mean, I could understand his attraction for her, but why did he have to go ahead and engage in an affair? I'm still angry. For months thereafter, I dreaded when he left for work in the morning, and I dreaded his not coming home at the end of the day. Every time he was late, I figured that he was seeing her again. We had a lot of stuff to work through."

"It sounds to me that you are still working through some of the problems," I ventured.

"Oh, yes, constantly, just constantly," said Barbara. "But I thought I had when I went out and had my own affair with my boss. It equalized things. It was just a one-night stand at a convention, one of those silly things that you regret later. But I couldn't wait to get home and tell my husband what I'd done."

"You thought that having an affair might equalize the guilt in your relationship with your husband?" I asked.

"Yes, I did," said Barbara. "And it worked for a while. But in my husband's job, he travels a lot, and there are many opportunities for him to get involved again. Every time he has to go somewhere, I cry. I just know he is having another affair. Then I stop myself, and think things through, and realize it's just my imagination."

There was a silence. Then Barbara continued, "I have no answers as yet, but I am finally thinking of _my_ life, and future alone. . . . Right now I leave it in God's hands."

I wished her the best of luck. But later, when I received that letter from the man who wanted me to study the effect of extramarital affairs, I remembered her pain.

The Extramarital Crisis: The Spouse's Perspective

Barbara clearly was reeling from the emotional and behavioral changes in her marriage produced by her husband's betrayal. Her feelings and behaviors are consistent with those of others who have experienced similar pain. According to expert Anthony P. Thompson, a sex researcher and author of the article "Extramarital Sexual Crisis: Common Themes and Therapy Implications" in the Winter 1984 _Journal of Sex and Marital Therapy_, there is often a need to know endless details about the affair. "Many spouses exert pressure to know everything. This process is stressful for both partners as queries and disclosures are likely to hit upon areas which are most sensitive and threatening to the married couple."

Barbara certainly felt this pressure. "Every day I would badger my hubsand about her—what she wore, how she looked, what she said and did. Even though now I know it's over, I can't help myself."

Maggie Scarf, the well-known researcher and author, took an emotional approach to describing the crisis precipitated by an extramarital affair in her book, *Intimate Partners: Patterns in Love and Marriage* (Random House, 1987):

> The crisis generated in the marriage, upon the discovery of a partner's extramarital activity, is—like other crises—one characterized by intense psychological strain and profound emotional disequilibrium. Many individuals find it extremely difficult to concentrate, and even to think; they ruminate, and are distracted by thoughts of the affair and the betrayal. . . . We may, in this culture, have experienced a revolution in our sexual mores, but most spouses continue to feel intensely afflicted and distressed by a partner's violation of the boundaries around the marital relationship.

For some, the extramarital crisis becomes an issue of power. The love and dependency balance of the relationship is upset—and may be broken forever.

In chapter 10, I discussed how emotional dependency forms the basis for a power struggle within relationships. According to sociologist Richard Emerson, dependency is a joint function of your investment in the relationship and your alternatives. The partner who has engaged in an adulterous affair has become all-powerful, because she or he has found someone else from whom to gain gratification.

Scarf agrees with this analysis. In her book *Intimate Partners*, she adds:

> In the wake of the affair's revelation, the comparative status of the two marital partners inevitably changes. The partner who has been involved extramaritally is,

to some degree, the one in the more powerful position. For while his spouse feels staggered, helplessly enraged, overwhelmed, and the like, he feels—amid whatever guilt feelings he may be experiencing—victorious and attractive. His sense of self-esteem may have been enhanced by the relationship, making him feel more likable and confident, while his partner's self-concept will, as a result of the affair's revelation, inevitably be deflated and diminished. The faithful spouse is thus, because she feels hurt, one down and inadequate, at a power disadvantage in the relationship.

Barbara identified with this feeling. She said, "It felt like this woman had gone through my drawers and knew all my dirty laundry. I feel entirely, emotionally vanquished. Even having my own affair has not entirely restored my hurt feelings."

The emotional struggles faced by those coping with the crisis of an extramarital affair vary in intensity depending on the strength of the marriage and the degree of investment of both partners. How invested we are in a relationship determines our dependency, and conversely, the relative power that can be exercised by each spouse in the marriage.

Barbara said, "I still feel like I am at a disadvantage in this marriage because no matter how hard I try to pick up the pieces, I know I am more in love with him than he ever will be with me. I always will be the loser."

The Concerns of Injured Spouses

Not only did Barbara have to cope with the ordinary crisis of betrayal, and questions of self-esteem and power within her marriage, but she had to cope with these feelings *ad infinitum* because office affairs never end. Like Barbara, most spouses never outgrow the specter of the affair, even once power struggles within the marriage return to normal and each partner has renewed his or her commitments to the marriage.

According to Dr. Jeffrey Zimmerman, of the Connecticut Psychological Group in Hartford, who has counseled many couples, "What makes extramarital affairs in the office so difficult is that once they're over, they're never really over. The spouse may wonder whether or not the affair is still going on, and the guilty party may continue to feel a pull toward the third party if they continue to work closely together."

Many spouses feel threatened by the close proximity an office situation affords once the affair has ended. Said one fifty-two-year-old woman, Margaret, "What has made all of this so difficult is that I will never be certain that the affairs are really over. Especially after three of them. I know he is still working with one of the women, and I can't believe that he still does not have feelings for her. . . . It's an impossible situation. How am I supposed to live with this anguish?"

Anjelica, a forty-eight-year-old real estate broker, said, "My husband has had three affairs with women in his office. I don't know why I stay with him. . . . Partly I understand why he does what he does, but the rest of me is pure anger. We've been to counseling. . . . I am insanely jealous of the women of his office [because] of his history."

It is difficult to overcome the effects of an extramarital affair when you know your spouse continues to see his or her ex-lover day after day at the office. Jealousy seems a mild emotion compared to the rage and terror many jilted wives experience.

"I had to hold myself back . . . from tearing her eyes out," said one woman whose husband had a two-year love affair with a colleague. "Once I found out, I wanted no part of him. I couldn't live with him—knowing that he would continue to see her on some basis at the office."

Many jilted spouses require as a condition of reconciliation that the husband or wife find another job. "I didn't care what it cost us," said one jilted wife. "I wanted him out of there. Even if he had to take a pay cut and if the children's education had to suffer. There was no way I would take him back otherwise."

The May-December Affair

In addition to these complications, what many wives fear is the May-December romance. An ad executive said, "I know of one marriage between a very senior older gentleman in this business who fell in love with a copywriter in her twenties. He left a long-term marriage that involved two adult children to marry the copywriter, who could be his granddaughter agewise."

May-December romances often occur between younger women and older men. Men who are older and more seasoned corporate executives often are considered attractive by younger women because of the power they wield. "I know she was after my husband only because she was attracted to his stature as a vice-president," said one jilted wife. "She saw my husband as the perfect target."

May-December romances also occur because men in the middle of a midlife crisis are vulnerable to the attentions of a younger woman. This is what happened in the Alexandra and Fred romance reported in chapter 10.

Said one woman, "Younger woman–older man romances are going on in business all the time. In some cases the men don't leave their wives, but in others they do. It's a wife's worst fear because the husband is so vulnerable and the young woman is so tempting. It causes wives to doubt their attractiveness, lose their self-esteem, and reject the entire life structure they have built."

Today's Modern Mistress

But the new sexual revolution has birthed another new phenomenon: the modern mistress.

In the past, a mistress was a woman who allowed herself to be "kept" by a richer, often more powerful executive. These women presented themselves as a comfortable alternative to a dull and boring marriage. In exchange for sexual favors, they requested an apartment, nice clothes, a car, and a food allowance. The man's generosity influenced the style in which his mistress could live.

But today, with many more women working and pursuing careers of their own, this definition of mistressing has become antiquated. Today's modern mistress is more likely to purchase expensive fur coats for herself. She probably owns her own co-op in the city.

"I know that what I'm doing probably sounds wrong," said one woman who refused to be identified. "But I'm not a mistress in the old sense. I have my own job and my own life. Just because I'm seeing a married man doesn't necessarily make me a mistress."

But even though mistressing may have changed, the effects remain the same. A mistress is a mistress regardless of who is paying the bills. She may remain a man's paramour for an extended period of time. This is what most wives—and perhaps even some husbands—fear.

A MISTRESS OF HER TIME: SALLYANNE

Sallyanne is a willing mistress of a married man. I heard about her from one of my students who served as my source on this case. According to my student, Becky, Sallyanne is a junior partner in a fast-paced, highly respected law firm in Boston. She works a ten- or twelve-hour schedule each day, and frequently must work weekends. Her case load is extremely heavy. In addition to normal research work and meetings with clients, many of her work hours are spent in different Massachusetts courts settling claims and legal motions.

Becky described Sallyanne as a workaholic. "I have never seen someone love her job so much. Even if she didn't have to, she would work weekends simply because she gets such a thrill out of her work." Becky claims that there is an additional reason why Sallyanne enjoys her work so much. Recently, she confided to her best friend that she was having an affair with one of the partners in the law firm.

According to Becky, "Sallyanne claims that there really isn't much to this affair. Her lover has problems at home because his wife doesn't understand why he must spend so much time at the office. . . . On her end, she says that with her schedule she really doesn't have time to find someone her own age to socialize with, and she's not ready for a commitment with a man. The affair suits her fine."

On a recent visit to Boston, Becky met her friend's lover. She said, "They really have a very respectable schedule. About twice a week, they get together between court appearances and client meetings. They go right back to work after their rendez-vous. He buys her presents, every so often, but she buys things for him, too. It's not as if she's a kept woman or anything. But she jokes around about having become a mistress."

Sallyanne has her own life, her own job, and her own source of funds. She purchases presents for her lover, just as he does for her. Their affair is somewhat known—and accepted—in their office. But her lover's wife is unaware of their situation. Business goes on as usual—both in the firm and at home.

Jilted Lovers Are Casualties, Too

But sometimes affairs are not as simple as Sallyanne's would seem. There is an additional source of pain—that experienced by the jilted office lover once her colleague has decided to return to his wife.

One woman said, "There were several worst things about having an affair with my boss that I will always remember. But one of the very worst was that because it involved my married boss, we had to keep everything quiet. No one knew about our affair. But when it ended, I had no one to talk to. All my friends worked in the same office, so I couldn't turn to them. College friends were long gone. I never felt so alone in my life."

Because extramarital affairs often are conducted in secret, the pain experienced by the jilted lover must be handled in silence. Even if the relationship is known to coworkers, few will offer support. Most will be relieved that the relationship has ended. One man who works in a computer firm said, "I was never so happy as when my boss ended his affair with his secretary. Until then, I had to watch what I said around her. We were all pleased."

But nonetheless there is a special pain and loneliness when an extramarital affair runs its course. The pain felt by the jilted lover is exacerbated because the work context provides added opportunities to see the former paramour. One woman, a comp-troller for a small firm, told me that when her lover decided to return to his wife, she couldn't cope with the dissolution of the affair. She visited him every day in his office, begging forgiveness. She used coworkers as a way of finding out how the reconciliation with his wife was going. "Anytime there was a hint of continuing problems in the marriage," said this woman, "I made sure I was available. I wanted him back desperately. The trouble was I was all alone with my pain. No one in the office cared because they already thought I was the scarlet woman."

In another case reported to me, a woman who was desperately interested in a married man with whom she had had a one-night stand made life miserable for him in the office. She constantly sat down with him at lunch and met him at his car after work. When she finally got the message that the affair simply was a fling to her married paramour, she took all the air out of his tires while his car was parked in the company parking lot.

Jilted lovers must suffer in silence. They question their self-esteem and self-worth for having allowed themselves to be placed in such a vulnerable position. Sometimes there is an added feeling of guilt that jilted lovers must reconcile. Finally, jilted lovers must cope with the experience of pain that anyone feels when an important love relationship ends—but with little support for their actions from disapproving others.

How Hurt Spouses—and Lovers—Can Learn to Cope

What if you are a victim of an extramarital office affair? If you are a spouse—or a lover—hurt by an office tryst, what should you do?

Many spouses have found strength in support networks as a way to cope with their pain. "I never realized how widespread affairs are," said one woman who has endured a spouse's affair. "I thought I was the only one whose husband cheated on the side. But once I confided in my best friend, I discovered her husband had an affair three years ago. And then she told me about another friend in her office whose husband is currently messing around with his partner! Now the three of us get together for lunch once a month for our own private therapy session."

But many injured spouses—and jilted office lovers—prefer

to keep news of the affair a private secret. "I never told anyone except you," wrote one woman on my survey. "I am glad I had this chance. I did not realize how difficult it has been carrying all of this around inside me. Thank you for the opportunity."

There are many excellent, professionally supervised support groups that serve marriages in crisis. There also are support groups for people undergoing severe emotional crises, and those groups would welcome jilted office lovers. Rather than carrying around all the hurt feelings, you may be better off attending one of these sessions. Getting your problems and your fears off your chest is the first step in cleansing yourself from pain.

Dr. Phyllis Hopkins, a therapist in Fairfield, Connecticut, who has counseled many women in crisis, agrees. "The best thing a spouse can do is to go into therapy to better understand the hurt feelings. The spouse needs to understand what went wrong and why. Affairs don't happen overnight."

Dr. Jeffrey Zimmerman, a psychologist with Connecticut Psychological Associates, echoes Hopkins' statement: "Don't keep it in—let it out. There are many good therapists who can help an injured spouse. Ideally, both members of the couple should be brought in for marriage counseling."

How you cope with an extramarital affair, whether you are an injured spouse or a colleague, is strictly up to you. Professional therapy is one important option. And there may be comfort in realizing that you are not alone in your fears. The increase in extramarital casualties may be one of the unwelcome consequences of the new sexual revolution.

I often wondered how the man who wrote to me dealt with his marital crisis. I have written this chapter for him.

13

LOVE GONE WRONG: THE BREAKUP

As the song lyric says, "Breaking up is hard to do." But nowhere is it more difficult than in the office.

Cathy, a forty-six-year-old graphic artist, told me about her affair with a man in her publishing firm. He was married. When he decided to return to his wife, she couldn't cope. "I never thought the ending of the affair could turn me into such a worthless human being," said Cathy. "I was inconsolable. Every time I looked at him I was reminded of what we had, and what we lost. It got to the point when I couldn't stand seeing him in the office."

"What did you do?" I asked.

"Everything," said Cathy. "I tried to get him back. I visited him every day in his office. I begged for his forgiveness. I wanted another chance. But he wouldn't hear me."

"That must have been difficult for you," I ventured.

"It was impossible," said Cathy. "I was a mess. But I didn't give up. I spied on him with his wife from my car. I would follow him home, park across the street, and watch them through the kitchen window. I even was going to send his wife an anonymous note about the affair, but, fortunately, I never did. I must have been out of my mind."

"How did you manage to work together in the office?" I asked.

"I refused to attend meetings where my lover would be present. And then I would break down and cry in the middle of a hallway. But eventually, I got over the affair and returned to my normal, rational self. Now I can't understand how I could have behaved that way."

The dissolution of a relationship always is a painful experience. Rarely does someone *not* get hurt. Either the hurt wife or lover becomes a casualty of the affair.

But, if Cathy's experience is any guide, breaking up a love affair with someone with whom you work closely can be next to impossible.

Gina, twenty-eight, reported, "Breaking up [with my boss] was one of the most difficult and painful experiences I ever had to endure. The work context added additional problems; he used to be my mentor. Now I'm alone at home and unprotected in the office."

Sheila, one of the women I interviewed for this book, said about her breakup with Sam, "Usually if my love life is a problem, I can escape into my work, and when work is awful I can take away some of the stresses through my love life. But when the two are linked, that's not possible."

Being forced to see your past lover at work on a daily basis, as if nothing has happened, can be excruciatingly painful. The stress and tension experienced by those coping with broken love affairs in the office sometimes can be overwhelming. As one woman said, "I have watched friends of mine cope with breakups, and it's taught me an important lesson. Their work performance went down and their personal lives were a mess. The constant contact [in the office] was much too much to take."

According to Dr. Phyllis Hopkins, "If the relationship does not work out, dealing with the trauma of the broken relationship and at the same time coping with the demands of a job can be extremely stressful. Making decisions about what to reveal, what to do, who to tell, and should one of you leave add additional complications."

Dr. Jeffrey Zimmerman agrees. "An office breakup is that much more difficult because the boundaries and roles are less well defined. The lack of separateness and the interweaving of personal and professional roles provides an added layer of complexity not present in non-work relationships. You must continue to work with the former lover and may still retain feelings for that person. It is that much more difficult to make a clean break."

Why Office Breakups Are So Complicated

When your office love affair comes to an end, there are many problems to consider. Can you survive, day after day, seeing your ex-lover in the same office? Will he be a constant reminder of lost love? Can you handle the hushed stares of coworkers as they watch you watching him? Will you be able to cope with the pity in their eyes?

Cathy found she could not. "Eventually I had to leave the firm," she said, "because there were so many reminders. I became ineffective in my job."

Because we cannot turn off our feelings and emotions as easily as we turn off the kitchen faucet, broken love affairs can be messy. Personal and professional lives collide when a breakup occurs. It is difficult to relearn how to view your coworker solely in the context of his or her former professional role. The memories die hard.

As one man who works in a prominent Silicon Valley firm said, "Most people are unable to differentiate between the net present value of happiness during the relationship and the net future worth of the pain later when the relationship breaks up." As another woman put it, "I wouldn't do it again."

Couples must confront several major complications in dissolving an office affair:

• *Dealing with the change in role relationships from lover back to colleague*

Love affairs in the office are never really *over* in the same sense as non-work relationships. Once you stop seeing each other on a personal level, your work relationship must continue. This requires that you switch roles several times—from your original position as colleagues, to colleague/lover, and then back to your original colleague role.[1]

But the process of making a smooth readjustment back to a collegial level can be problematic. As one woman who had been through a recent breakup said, "I usually am successful keeping my feelings close to the vest. But it is very difficult to function in a meeting with him and not feel heartbreak. I want to comfort him, to have him comfort me. I want to return to the way things were."

Another woman said, "When we broke up, I missed him on every level. Waking up with him in the morning, having coffee with him in the office, finishing reports together at night."

The productivity benefits of working and loving together also are lost when the affair ends. A retail consultant said, "Sometimes I wonder if we should have continued to have our affair—if only for occasional one-night stands. We worked so well together, we were a real team. When we stopped seeing each other, my work performance went down the tubes. Together we were great."

• *Coping with your own low sense of self-worth and self-esteem*
When a lover dumps you, you feel rejected. You feel unloved. You feel unworthy. As a result, your self-esteem can go right down the tube. And sometimes if you allow it, your work performance will slide down that same tube as well.

One woman I know quite well was undergoing a difficult split from a man who worked in her firm. She told her manager that because she was having a difficult time coping with the dissolution, she did not know how she could handle additional work responsibilities. Her self-esteem was so low that she rejected a high visibility opportunity that undoubtedly would have garnered her a promotion in a few years. She simply couldn't cope.

When the emotional stress and tension that follow a breakup spill over into the work setting, productivity suffers. Motivation declines. At the very least, lowered self-esteem often leads the participants to question their competencies, skills, and ambitions.

Peggy, the woman who had a relationship with her mentor, Bill, which I discussed in chapter 9, echoed this feeling. "When Bill and I ended our relationship, I questioned my competence, my qualifications in my work. Even though I knew I had accomplished so much on my own, he was my mentor—and my friend. After a while, I grew stifled . . . but breaking up with him was one of the hardest things I ever had to do."

• *Handling pity*

Once when I gave a talk on this subject to a group of women, one participant pulled me aside during a break. She told me she had just ended an affair with a colleague in her department. She said, "You know, what you didn't talk about much is the exact thing I'm having to deal with right now. What I can't stand, what is really driving me wild, is the pity. I can get along all right, I knew that the romance wouldn't last no matter how hard we tried to make it work. But their *pity* is what I can't take."

We appreciate it when people sympathize with our troubles. but we find it difficult when their pity is a constant reminder. Colleagues may express pity because they do not know how else to react. Should they pretend that it is business as usual? That the relationship never happened? Should they help the couple deal with their pain? The first alternative denies reality; the second is uncomfortable. Colleagues can only respond with pity, empathy, and concern.

One person who had seen an office relationship end recently said, "It is so uncomfortable and awkward. No one knows how to react to them anymore. If I make a suggestion to go to lunch with one of them, and the ex-lover comes along, what am I supposed to do?"

• *Anticipating sexual harassment*

A final complication is the potential for sexual harassment. Suppose you decide that you want to break off the affair, and your lover disagrees? You may find yourself dealing with a very serious problem. Breakups bring out the worst in people. In my survey, eight different situations of harassment after a breakup were reported. Each person described feelings of guilt, anger, and resentment about the affair. Each person said they would never, ever, get involved in an office romance again.

Said one woman, "My breakup . . . turned out to be a nightmare [because] of sexual harassment. He refused to end the relationship . . . and used the office as a way of rekindling the romance. I couldn't avoid him in the office, so I had to work with him while I feared him and what he would do to me. He continually stopped by my office, called me on the phone all day, and was waiting by my car at night."

Some people believe that all's fair in love and war. They use the office situation as the setting to continue what has become an unproductive relationship. But what they don't realize is that this type of behavior constitutes harassment.

Jilted female lovers may harass men just as men harass women. As one man reported in a phone interview, "I took this secretary out—once. She wouldn't leave me alone after that. She told everyone in the office she loved me, that she wanted to marry me. Once she came into my office when I was working late, and took off her top! I couldn't believe it."

Sometimes, a charge of harassment is used as a way for the jilted lover to get back at the offender. In one case reported to me, a male boss and a female subordinate had an affair. When it was over, the woman brought the man up on charges of sexual harassment. But it wasn't true. The man maintained that the affair was a "business mistake," but once it was over, he did not harass her. Witnesses proved his claim.

With these complications, it is no wonder so many people believe the risks of breaking up are one reason to avoid office romances in general. Breaking up a relationship is generally difficult. In an office setting it is that much more complex. Even when the romance is long gone, the work relationship must live on.

The Stages of Dissolution

As couples break off their once active relationships, they experience a grieving process not unlike the stages of denial, anger, depression, and acceptance described by Dr. Elizabeth Kubler-Ross in her famous book _On Death and Dying_ (Macmillan, 1967).[2] More recently, Dr. Barbara DeAngelis, a Los Angeles psychologist and author of the book _How to Make Love All the Time_ (Rawson Associates, 1987), believes that relationships go through four stages of recovery.

In *Stage One: Tearing Apart,* which lasts from two weeks to two months, you realize that the relationship is over. You mourn the loss of the relationship by crying or feeling sad. You may experience symptoms of depression, hopelessness, and helplessness. Work performance may decline. You also may experience some of the physiological signs of stress, such as loss of appetite and headaches. You may be tempted to return to your former partner.

In *Stage Two: The Adjustment,* which lasts from two to six months, you learn to adjust to your new life without your partner. You catch yourself beginning to care about your future. You no longer feel like a victim. You can talk about your former lover without feeling such intense pain, or without crying at the drop of a hat. You gain a clearer perspective.

In *Stage Three: Healing,* which lasts from six months to one year, you see your life returning to normal. You may become interested in someone else. You can talk rationally to your former lover. Your work performance improves. You learn from the experience and move on.

In *Stage Four: Recovery,* which lasts from one to two years, the transition of recovery begins. You begin to establish a new social structure—new friends, new relationships. You become able to put your relationship behind you—in the past, where it belongs. You may even become good friends.

Most failed relationships, in the office or out of it, follow this pattern of recovery. It may take a long time to fully recover, but the struggle to do so always is worth it.

AN ANATOMY OF A BREAKUP: JERI AND GENE

The tale of Jeri and Gene shows the pain, anguish, and concerns of couples who dissolve an office affair. Their breakup went through a series of predictable stages.

Jeri hired Gene in the marketing department to work on a special project. Although they were attracted to each other from the beginning, they did not become involved in an office romance until after two years of working together. I asked Jeri how it began.

"We were on the road en route to a trade show. Many

things led up to the beginning of the romance. It didn't just happen overnight. Gene had been promoted to my level and had transferred to a different department. But while we were traveling, we had a lot of private time together to get to know each other better. Our relationship evolved naturally."

Both were single, but Gene was involved in a live-in, committed relationship with another woman. Their mutual passion, goals, and interests caused Gene to realize that he had more in common with Jeri than his live-in partner. He broke off the live-in relationship.

"The breakup was very painful," said Jeri. "I didn't realize how painful at the time. He really loved her, and that overshadowed his relationship with me."

Said Jeri, "I wanted to move in with him right away. But Gene wanted some time to himself. I should have realized that he would be sensitive about a live-in arrangement, since he had just gone through a difficult time. He needed to be free before getting more deeply involved. That was my mistake. But by then I already was madly in love with him."

Gene, however, remained unsure. He had no idea how his feelings for Jeri would develop. He wanted to continue to see her, but he offered no guarantees. "I was disappointed that he did not return the same feelings for me that I had for him," said Jeri. "But I thought at the time that he would come around. We had so much in common."

They continued their relationship for a full year. At the end of a year, on Jeri's birthday, Gene was promoted. "The promotion was a turning point for us," said Jeri. "Gene decided to take stock of his life. He decided he wanted out."

That night, he talked frankly with Jeri about his feelings. They agreed to dissolve the relationship. "I was dumbfounded," said Jeri. "I had thought things were going along smoothly, and that we soon would be living together. But he had a number of concerns that he had never discussed with me until that point. It all poured out of him that night. I was stunned."

But they still had to work together. Gene's position, even though it was a different department, required him to work closely with Jeri on planning initiatives. More than twice a month they attended meetings together. Several times a month they were expected to share information, determine deadlines, and establish objectives.

I asked Jeri how she handled working together with Gene after the breakup. "When the breakup first occurred, I wasn't sure if I could even look at him, let alone continue to work with him," Jeri said. "Every morning I would get up and miss him. I would look for his car in the parking lot. I hoped that the day would come when he would realize his mistake and come back to me."

As time passed, Jeri grew depressed. She said, "There was a full week I called in sick so that I wouldn't have to see him. I wasn't interested in my work. I stopped caring."

After a few months, Jeri realized she was ready to get back to work. When friends invited her to dinner, she accepted their invitations. She said, "The day when I didn't look for his car in the parking lot was a major victory. I knew things were getting better."

A crisis occurred one day when Jeri noticed that Gene was paying special attention to another woman in the office. "There was this financial analyst who hung around him a lot, and I could tell he was getting interested. She was making herself so available there was no way he wouldn't be. I did everything I could to keep them apart. I even enlisted the help of my best friend in the office to alert me to when she was hanging around."

Jeri grew depressed again. But one day, when her boss offered her the opportunity to tackle another special project, she leaped at the offer. She said, "When I got home that night, I looked at myself in the mirror and said, 'What have you done? You don't feel like doing this extra work.' But now I know why. I needed the extra work as a way to heal myself."

Jeri plunged into the project. The work required her to interact with many different departments to gather information about their planning needs. She loved the distraction the project afforded. She said, "I was always having lunch with someone new, learning about their departmental needs. I would wish Gene would see me meeting over lunch with every last man in that company."

But she still needed time to heal. When her best friend tried to match her up with another friend on a double date, she rebelled. She went along but refused to have a good time. "I was a real bitch," said Jeri. "I don't know what that poor guy ever thought of me. It was horrible. But the experience showed me I still wasn't ready to let go of Gene."

Because her special project was taking so much of her time, she was forced to delegate much of her monthly planning work to a subordinate. "At first, I'm sure that everyone was talking behind my back that I couldn't deal with Gene any longer. But actually, that wasn't true. That was right about the time I was feeling better about the breakup."

A few months later, Jeri learned from a friend that Gene was involved with another woman. I asked her how she coped with this new information.

"I was surprised by my reaction. I expected to be upset, angry, crying all the time. But I wasn't. I really was okay."

Shortly thereafter, Jeri went on a date of her own. She said, "I knew, when I was able to accept Gene as a work colleague, and not look at him as a former lover, that I was fully recovered. We are now good buddies in the office again. The situation is not ideal—sometimes there is still pain—but I'm involved with someone and so is he and it's okay for both of us now."

Why Relationships Turn Sour

It is hard to predict the relative success or failure of a romantic relationship. So many different factors can contribute to its demise. But work colleagues often dissolve their relationships for the same basic reasons as couples outside of the office: because of a mismatch of motives and goals.

In their February 1985 *Personnel* magazine survey, Anderson and Hunsaker found most office relationships had four motives: love, job, ego, power.

Love motives influence those who become sincerely involved in a relationship at work. Usually their interest in the relationship is long-term, and the relationship may end in marriage or some defined commitment. *Job motives* impel those who become involved in an office romance as a way to advance their professional goals. *Ego motives* impel those who become involved in an office romance as a way to gain personal rewards such as excitement, satisfaction, adventure, and sexual experiences. *Power motives* prompt those who pursue a romantic relationship as a way to achieve deflected power, contacts, and advancement.[3]

In their survey, approximately 30 percent of the men and 38 percent of the women were thought to be in love; 37 percent of the women were judged as seeking ego rewards, while 40 percent of the men fell into this category; and more women than men were seen as seeking increased power (16 percent for the women, 12 percent for the men). Very few romances were characterized by job motives.

When the couple's motives are misaligned, the romance will come to an early demise. For example, if one member of the couple falls in love, but the other is simply having a quickie extramarital affair, the relationship is bound to fail. Cathy, whose story I recounted at the beginning of this chapter, agrees. "If only I had known that my lover was simply interested in a fling," she said, "I never would have let myself get so involved. Now I've learned my lesson."

Goals are another matter. If one coworker is interested in a permanent commitment and the other is interested in a short-run fling, the relationship will soon become unstable. Jeri said to me about her office breakup, "If I had been paying attention, I would have seen the early warning signs. I wanted more out of the relationship than he was willing to give. I was more interested in a long-term relationship. He was only interested in getting over his former lover and moving on."

Jeri's investment in her relationship with Gene was high. She was interested in a long-term, love-motivated relationship. Gene's motives and goals were quite different. He needed a short-term relationship to smooth over his hurt feelings from the dissolution of his live-in love, and strengthen his ego and self-esteem. Because their motives and goals were misaligned, they soon discovered they were incompatible.

But because many couples recognize that they must sustain their work relationship at any cost to their personal one, some couples "play ostrich" and pretend that the relationship is as strong as ever. Long after the bloom of love is over they continue to see each other *because* they must work together. "I know it sounds silly now," said Sheila about her office breakup with Sam, "but Sam and I realized we were incompatible very early on. But we just didn't want to deal with the ending."

MISMATCHED MOTIVES AND GOALS: KIRK AND SARA

Kirk and Sara are a classic case of mismatched motives and goals. This is a case with which I am personally familiar, having observed and watched the dynamics of the relationship that led to its eventual demise.

Kirk was an ambitious man who was ready to take on the best that life could offer. Outgoing, creative, extroverted, he made you feel like you were one of the gang from the moment you met him. Very sports-oriented, he always was ready to get a group together for a quick game of touch football after work. You always knew that on Fridays at five o'clock, Kirk would be seated at the bar of his favorite hangout.

I asked Kirk how he first met Sara. "I had arranged a quick game of touch football after work," he said, "and there she was. Blonde, tall, and beautiful. I was transfixed."

But there was one problem. Sara was engaged. At thirty years old, she followed her fiance out to the West Coast. They were living together in a house they jointly bought prior to their upcoming marriage.

Kirk and Sara became close friends but not lovers. They found they had a lot in common.

"I coaxed her to attend the Friday night sessions after football at the local bar. She usually agreed, mostly because her fiance, Larry, suddenly had developed a habit of missing dinner and returning home late at night."

At first, Sara assumed that her fiance, Larry, was working late. At least, that's what Larry said he was doing. But later Sara discovered that Larry was seeing other women—many other women.

Kirk said, "You know, I couldn't believe this guy. Day after day, night after night, he was giving her the same excuse. It seemed suspicious."

Sara confronted Larry, who welcomed the exchange. He confessed his exploits with women, and told her he was uncertain about their marriage. Sara was hurt and upset at first, but after two weeks of crying and pain, she was ready to forgive and forget.

"I couldn't believe it when she told me she was going back to him," said Kirk. "She had been so hurt by his deception. But love is blind, I guess."

Sara and Larry made up. Larry tried his best to be faithful. But he couldn't. Finally, Larry said he wanted out of the relationship. Sara was left holding the bag. Unaccustomed to being without a man and hurt by Larry's rejection, Sara turned to Kirk. "I had been Sara's friend and counselor all along, and I cared deeply for her. I wanted to soothe her pain," said Kirk. "It was a difficult and complicated situation."

They started dating. Their romance quickly bloomed. The more they saw of one other, the more they liked. "Things were going well for us," said Kirk. "But Sara remained confused about her true feelings for me. And because of her history with Larry, I remained unconvinced about the sincerity of her feelings for me as well. But neither one of us was willing to admit our concerns at the time. We just laughed it up and had a good time together."

Sara and Kirk held different jobs in the company in which they worked (a high-technology firm in Texas), but the nature of their jobs forced them to interact closely on a variety of projects. Their work took them to meetings throughout the world.

At the office they were inseparable. "We had lunch together each day, met our clients together, arrived at work together, and left for home each day arm in arm," said Kirk. "We played tennis, racquetball, went skiing, bicycling, and took vacations together. We had a great time."

Meanwhile, Larry, Sara's ex-fiance, decided that he wanted Sara back. She began meeting Larry for dinner while Kirk was away on assignment. One day, when he returned from a business trip, she told him that she and Larry had become re-engaged.

I asked Kirk how he felt about Sara's decision.

"Well, of course, I was hurt. I couldn't believe that she would return to such a destructive relationship."

"How did you deal with Sara at work?" I wanted to know.

"It was very difficult, very painful, to meet her at work each day after we had broken up," said Kirk. "I would see her coming into the office after Larry had dropped her off—happy and glowing. And I was supposed to make like I didn't care. Suddenly, we had to return to being coworkers when we already had been together. And it was hard."

But the soap opera continues. Larry, despite his vow of fidelity, just couldn't do it. He continued to see other women, and once again, broke off the relationship with Sara. This time Sara was resolute. She figured she was better off without this man after all.

"So we started up our relationship again," said Kirk. "But this time, I was suspicious of Sara's every move. I watched her like a hawk—probably too much so, but I had been hurt once and didn't want to be that hurt again."

"What did you do?" I asked.

"Lots of things. I listened to her phone calls; I accompanied her to lunch; and I dropped by her office unexpectedly throughout the day," said Kirk. "I did what I had to do."

Sara felt uncomfortable with Kirk's distrust. To rebel against his suspicions, she began to flaunt her relationships with other men. She made a point to have drinks with other men, played tennis with her ex-fiance, and held parties in which there were several other men present. Her behavior, in turn, caused Kirk to doubt Sara's commitment to him in the relationship.

Kirk said, in retrospect, "Now I can see what was going on, but at the time, I just didn't know. Maybe it's just my nature to be suspicious, but I want a woman to care only for me. With Sara, I was never sure."

After more events like these, Kirk and Sara ended their on-again, off-again relationship. "There were many reasons why," said Kirk. "In the end we just found we were incompatible."

Because Sara's motives and goals for the relationship were different from Kirk's, I believe this romance was a time-bomb waiting to explode. As Kirk admitted, "The relationship . . . was doomed from the start."

INAPPROPRIATE BALANCE OF ROLES: PHILIP AND MELISSA

There is another reason why romances sometimes fail that is specific to office relationships. Occasionally a workplace romance will fail because the couple is unable to appropriately balance their personal and professional roles in the office. Philip and Melissa are one such case.

Philip, an accomplished, action-oriented, fortyish, attractive man, had been hired as a strategic planner in the soft-drink business. He loved his job, and was very good at it. In what was a remarkably short period of time, he managed to help the upper level executives see that the company needed to be steered in a new direction. He was responsible for several company acquisitions to fulfill this goal.

Melissa was a highly trained professional organizational development consultant. Surprisingly, however, she was deaf, dumb, and blind when it concerned the emotional subtext of her personal life. Melissa's job involved developing internal training programs, identifying high potential candidates, and establishing cooperative working relationships between departments. She, too, did her job well.

I heard about this case when a friend told me that she knew of a woman who had recently undergone an office breakup. According to my source, Terry, "Melissa adopted a habit of walking into Philip's office unannounced. She thought nothing of interrupting his meetings. She often waited to go to lunch with him. She left love letters and sentimental cards on his desk, and on one occasion, sent him a dozen balloons."

I asked Terry about Philip. "He never sought out Melissa in the office. He felt he could gain her opinions on work issues over the dinner table at home. He also felt concerned when Melissa wanted to openly attend business/social functions with him. Philip resented Melissa's constant presence."

Melissa, on the other hand, was completely unaware of the depth of Philip's discomfort. When I talked with Melissa, she said, "I couldn't understand Philip's behavior. There we were, everyone knew that we were involved with each other, it was no problem or anything, but he acted as if I was some sort of a monster. He just couldn't stand to see me at work; it was as if he were cheating on a wife or something. I remember one time when a corporate dinner was being held. I wanted to go. He said no. It caused a major fight, because I couldn't understand why he had turned to stone on me. We probably should have broken off the relationship right there and then."

According to Terry, Philip didn't quite know how to tell Melissa directly to spend less time with him in the office. He feared hurting her feelings. As a result, he found that Melissa's attentions were interfering with his work performance. He couldn't concentrate on his work.

Melissa said, "I had no idea the kind of tension he was under until I heard some discussion that his name was being removed from consideration for a promotion. I couldn't believe my ears. Philip had been such a star in the company. But he was really freaked out by our relationship. He wanted me with him, but he didn't want anyone to see I was there. He wanted people to know we were involved, but he didn't want anyone to hear it from me. He had all these rules, restrictions, guidelines, and concerns."

I asked Melissa if she had any difficulties managing the personal versus professional boundaries of the relationship. But her problem was the opposite of Philip's: She wanted to be with him at all times.

Said Melissa, "It's true, I guess, that I had my own problem about personal and professional roles. I was crazy for Philip. I thought he was great. I wanted to be with him at all times. I really loved him and wanted to share every part of every day with him. Because I was in love, I wanted to shout it from the rooftops. I wanted everyone else to know that we were in love, that he loved me. So I did. That just aggravated Philip all the more."

They eventually broke up. I learned from Terry that Melissa was grievously hurt. She really fell apart.

"Melissa was a lost child in the office," said Terry. "She badgered Philip. She called his secretary to find out where he was during the day, offered to work on projects that would bring her closer to contact with him, and made a pest of herself with his coworkers. She sometimes joined him for lunch without his approval. It was heartbreaking to watch."

Eventually Melissa recovered. When I asked Melissa about the breakup, she said, "I guess I mishandled things. If I had realized that he was uncomfortable earlier, I might have done things differently. But how was I to know?"

Melissa left the firm and now runs a personnel office in a major Fortune 500 company. Terry tells me that Philip is now involved in another romance. But this time, the woman with whom he is involved has no ties whatsoever to the office environment. Hardly surprising, wouldn't you say?

Pain Is a Function of the Depth of the Relationship

It is often easier to play Monday morning quarterback and assess what went wrong in retrospect. I'm sure if Kirk knew that Sara only considered him a passing fancy he never would have considered regenerating the relationship the second time around. If Melissa had realized Philip could not handle an office romance she might have acted quite differently.

One thing is clear, however. The degree of pain you will experience in a breakup is a direct function of the depth of feeling in the relationship. Passionate love affairs that endure for a long period of time are far more difficult to overcome than a one-night stand. Dissolved flings have less of an impact upon the total organization than a messy breakup among highly placed executives.

According to the 1988 Bureau of National Affairs report: "Broken love affairs differ from sexual liaisons that end. In the latter case, coworkers sometimes can resume their former roles as working colleagues. In the former case, often one of the partners in a broken love affair ends up leaving because of the discomfort involved in seeing the other person each day."

Let's look at three different cases of failed relationships of different duration:

- *The fling*

Jody and Richard met at a district managers' meeting for their company. Both were married. The sexual attraction between them was electric. They arranged to have lunch. Directly after lunch, they booked a hotel room nearby. For the next several weeks, Jody and Richard rendezvoused at the hotel at least twice a week.

Jody said about their relationship, "From the time we got involved, we knew it wouldn't last. We both had stable marriages but we were interested in each other at the same time. Life is very complicated sometimes. Once we satisfied our passions, the affair simply ended. I still see Richard in the company from time to time, but our relationship is quite platonic. In fact, his kids attend the same school as mine, and one day my husband met his wife. It's very civilized."

• _The active affair_

Brenda and Sean are financial analysts in the same office. They have been involved in an on-again, off-again romance for over two years. Brenda said, "I really love Sean. The problem in our relationship was that he doesn't want to commit to a more permanent relationship. I broke off with a former boyfriend to be with Sean, so when I realized that he wasn't ready, it caused problems for us. At first everything was rosy, but then we broke up—not once, but three separate times. Each time I swore I would never get involved with him again. Seeing him in the office, especially when he was dating one of the secretaries and I had to watch them together, was horrible. But now that we're back together, things are okay again."

Brenda continued: "I can't tell you what it felt like to be dumped and then to see the man you love take up with someone else in the same office. The pain was excruciating—because I really loved him. I still do; that's why we're back together. I decided life is better off with him in it, despite his problems with commitment. Right now, things are good. I'm trying not to think about the future to avoid the pain."

• _The divorce_

Patricia and Michael were once married. They started working for the same company, an insurance firm, right after completing undergraduate degrees in business. Patricia was promoted—twice—while Michael remained at entry level. The competition in their relationship caused their divorce.

Patricia said, "It was a very messy divorce. Michael held all this resentment against me for getting promoted ahead of him to the second level. Each time I was promoted he told me it was only because I was a woman. He accused me of sleeping with the boss to get ahead. For two years I tried to hold the relationship together. I did everything I could. But what was I supposed to do, sacrifice my career for my marriage?

"For me, the divorce was the worst experience of my life. I used to love him a lot, and my pain was overwhelming. I couldn't function. I thought about moving to another company, but I realized I would still be at a higher level. Our home life was impossible. Thank God we didn't have any kids. I used to tell my friends that I felt beaten to a bloody pulp by the wreck of my marriage at the cost of my career. That's how I still feel."

Divorce in the Office

Married couples in the office face a difficult situation. Even though their marriage is over, they must continue to work together and function as if nothing is wrong. But working closely with your spouse after your marriage is over can be untenable.

Said one woman who recently observed a case of corporate divorce in her office, "I don't know how they can continue working together after having been through such an experience. This couple I know had a civil, almost too civil, recent divorce. But to look at them working together, you never would know they once were married."

Another woman who had been through a corporate divorce herself said, "When the divorce was recent and my emotions were raw, the only way I coped was by thinking of myself as an actress playing the role of a work colleague in the presence of my ex-husband. I had to act my way through the pain."

Most of us can sympathize. There is enough pain associated with an office breakup, but a divorce presents different emotions. It is for this reason that one ex-spouse often makes the decision to leave the firm or department—to minimize the pain.

In one case with which I am familiar, the divorce was caused by the woman's rapid rise in the management hierarchy. Her husband retaliated by flirting with his wife's female subordinates. One of those flirtations turned into a torrid affair. The affair split loyalties in the office and the subsequent divorce was acrimonious—not just for the couple, but for work colleagues. Later the wife transferred to another division to avoid scenes in the office with her ex-husband.

Another story I heard concerned a husband and wife team who created and managed their own small-scale management consulting firm. When the firm was just an entrepreneurial start-up, the marriage was strong; when the firm became successful, the marriage weakened. Because the husband and wife could not agree on central business decisions, the firm began to falter. The separation and subsequent divorce grew ugly. During the separation, the wife stole key clients and employees away from the original firm she helped build to set up her own fledgling rival firm. As part of the divorce settlement, the wife's rival business was subsequently dissolved.

Corporate divorces at the upper-executive level by couples who own and manage a firm can have far-reaching implications for business practice. In one now famous case of a trendy clothing manufacturer couple, their separation split loyalties in the firm and caused tensions in the office. The wife, a chief designer for the firm, wanted to make the firm more socially responsible and chic; the husband, the president and chief executive officer, advocated a plan of quick expansion. The couple's incompatible goals caused the business to falter. Colleagues in the firm began to play wife against husband, and loyalties within the firm were split. Finally, through a reorganization and reevaluation of the entire business, compatible corporate goals were reached that brought the business back on course.

But sometimes corporate divorces may have absolutely no effect—or only a minimal effect—on the inner workings of business practice. In another now famous case in the publishing world, when the marriage of two highly placed executives began to falter, it was business as usual at the firm. Colleagues at their firm were impressed—and amazed—at how little the marital breakup affected their work relationship.

Another case shows how effectively divorce in the office can be handled. A couple who met, married, and divorced at the same small business maintained that their divorce had nothing to do with their work. They didn't confide in colleagues and told only their supervisors when the marriage ended. Their supervisors handled the breakup in a professional manner, allowing the couple to go on with business as usual.

The scenes played out when a divorce in the office occurs have many endings. Some couples manage to handle their personal problems outside of the office; others use the workplace as a battleground for displays of power and revenge. If the couple handles their conduct—and their problems—professionally, life can go on and business can move ahead with minimal disruption.

More Than One Office Relationship

But there is another complicated situation that deserves mention. People who date more than one coworker often find their office exploits create workplace soap operas like that of some divorces.

Brenda, one of the women I spoke of earlier, is an example of someone who had to suffer through this type of pain. Because Sean was unwilling to make a commitment, he dated several others in the same office. Brenda said, "Every time I saw him with that secretary, I wanted to smash her face to pieces. And then I wanted to turn around and belt him a couple."

One man I know, Dan, has a reputation for dating anything in a skirt in his office. Dan is a true ladies' man. While living with Lynn for six months, he began dating Donna on the sly. Donna and Dan were an item for about eight months and talked of marriage, but during a major office fight they broke off the relationship. Dan then turned to Sally, a secretary in the same office. They later dissolved their relationship.

By this point, the office relationships had grown so inbred that Dan's actions had become the butt of several jokes. Anytime he was in a meeting with a woman, the others in the office chided her to "Watch out for Dan!" Worse, his three former girlfriends got together and spread malicious gossip about his sexual performance. The situation grew so untenable that Dan eventually transferred to another company.

Dating several people in the same office—especially a small

office like the one where Dan was employed—is trouble. Break-ups between coworkers cause resentment, anger, and upheaval. When the behavior persists, and other relationships are formed, the cycle escalates.

Colleague Reactions to Office Breakups

Of course, the breakup of a juicy office romance is wonderful material for the gossip mill. Often the breakup causes coworkers to choose sides. "His" and "Hers" camps are founded.

Colleagues feel they have two choices: to align themselves with one member of the couple, or to stay out of the breakup altogether. "What were we supposed to do?" asked one bewildered coworker who had observed a failed office romance. "The woman is a personal friend, so I feel I have to be on her side for support. But I would rather stay out of it because it's really none of my business."

Many coworkers have complained to me about how uncomfortable and awkward a breakup made them feel. One source said, "There was this couple—highly placed in the company—who were fighting all the time. When one would walk into a meeting where the other was present, you could cut the tension with a knife. They were always at each other's throat. If you said you agreed with one position in a meeting, suddenly you were on 'His' side. Or 'Hers'." The meetings were never rational."

Another colleague said about the same situation, "This couple is unbelievable. We can't get anything done. But sometimes it is a good thing. I know if I want to get [her] to go along with my proposal, all I have to do is talk to her ahead of time. She fights better than he—she wins more often. So if I get her on my side, I can get my way."

Especially for those who have supported the romance, the tendency to fall into respective camps is seductive. One workplace relationship with which I am familiar even made me feel as if I should take sides. I felt sympathy for both persons involved, but I listened to—and participated in—discussions about who was right and who was wrong and why the relationship failed.

A supervisor in a manufacturing firm said, "The worst part about office affairs is the breakup. . . . I have had to mediate three different cases of broken office romances, and each one turned out badly. I'm beginning to wonder if I should get a degree in psychology just to help me do my job."

Coping with an Office Breakup

What everyone wants to know is, "How can I handle a failed office romance? What can I do to minimize some of the complications?"

I recommend that you develop a *contingency plan* in case of a breakup. Recognize that not all lovers ride off into the sunset. Realize that there may be some serious complications ahead. Plan for them—just in case.

A written contingency plan may look something like this:

Sample Contingency Plan

I, (your name), agreed to respect my lover, (his or her name), at all times in our relationship together. (His or her name) agrees to show the same respect toward me.

We recognize that our relationship will be complicated. We have dual roles to fulfill—coworkers and lovers.

Should our personal relationship dissolve, we would like to part as friends to the greatest extent possible.

We would also like to preserve the professionalism of our work relationship.

Therefore, we agree to do the following:
1. To be sensitive toward one another regarding our feelings about the breakup
2. To continue to act professionally with each other as well as with colleagues
3. To avoid emotional scenes in the office

4. To agree, if necessary, to minimize our professional contact should that become bothersome to one partner and
5. To consider a mutual decision about a transfer for _____ if necessary

You may think that writing a contingency plan is asking the impossible—especially during the early stages of your relationship. But do it anyway. The more you are able to discuss rationally and objectively how you will handle the breakup, the more you will be able to guard against failure.

Breaking Up Is Hard to Do

The new sexual revolution requires that you be prepared for the inevitable. In this day and age of corporate takeovers, cutthroat career ambitions, and office divorces, you need to be aware of all the angles. Whether you are considering an office romance or are the colleague of someone who is, you have a stake in how the relationship ends.

When an office relationship meets its demise, colleagues worry that a failed relationship will mean diminished office productivity. Managers wonder if they should take concerted action to forestall morale problems. For many of these reasons, the management of failed office relationships is delicate.

Said one manager, "Katy, one of my best people, has been moping around ever since her breakup with Bruce. I just don't know what to do with them. . . . The situation is causing havoc in my department."

Another executive said, "Everyone is walking around on eggshells because there is this couple in my district who no longer are on speaking terms. What am I supposed to do? Fire them because they are having a personal problem?"

Breaking up indeed is hard to do. But what many people fail to realize is that an office breakup has far-reaching consequences. This is all the more reason to carefully consider a potential romance in the office—all the positives and the negatives—before you become involved.

$\mathbb{P}$ART $\mathbb{S}$IX

WHAT MANAGEMENT (AND COUPLES) SHOULD KNOW AND DO

14

MANAGING OFFICE ROMANCE

How *should* office romances be managed? Executives across the country are asking for help to resolve this question.

I polled over forty executives to discover their answers. Much to my surprise, I found there were few to be had.

One manager with whom I spoke summed it up like this: "Damn if I know what to do about affairs! I'm not the company psychologist! Our policies and practices change all the time. I'm just trying to run my organization as efficiently and effectively as possible."

He then related to me a story about a recent situation in which a woman boss had an affair with one of her married male subordinates, and then dumped him for a relationship with her boss: "The disruption she has caused with her antics has been unfathomable," said this manager. "But she is one of the best district managers we have. I'm not about to say anything to her about office decorum. What she does on her own personal time is, of course, her business. But I really think I should have, given the level of problems she has caused."

Clearly, he was frustrated with my question—and with the problem. The new sexual revolution has changed office decorum to the point where most managers simply do not know what to

241

do. But something *must* be done. With office romance on the rise, managers no longer can politely look the other way when a supervisor starts dating a subordinate. Bosses cannot ignore sexploitation in their midst.

Most corporations are confused as to which way to turn— whether to lay down a strict policy prohibiting fraternization, or to adopt norms that encourage love in the workplace. Because this is a gray area for corporate policy-making that may conflict with employee rights of privacy, many managers have adopted a broad range of attitudes, opinions, and mandates on this subject. In fact, many found ways to dodge the question. "Office romance? I wouldn't touch it with a ten-foot pole!" said one manager of public relations in a manufacturing firm.

A vice-president of personnel in a sports manufacturing firm said, "In this company, there is a great respect for privacy. No one will pay much attention to this kind of problem because it is considered an issue of employee privacy."

"I can't speak for this topic in this firm—we change our minds so often it really is being treated on an individualized basis," said a manager of human relations in the aerospace industry.

But as I managed to get some of the executives with whom I spoke to open up a bit about the policies and practices toward office romance in their firms, I came to an important conclusion. *Office romance has sparked a subtle change in management philosophies about personal relationships at work.* Corporate attitudes, beliefs, and values about the management of human resources— and about love in the office—are changing. The new sexual revolution has forced managers to address the implications and consequences of office romance.

How the New Sexual Revolution Has Affected Management Attitudes

At the present time, two management strategies have evolved to meet the challenges of the new sexual revolution: Open up the doors and embrace office romancers of all types (married, single, gay, or otherwise); or steadfastly work against— and attempt to prevent—attraction at work.

Many financial, insurance, and accounting firms, especially those with more conservative cultures, have developed informal rules or policies that discourage close working relationships between married or unmarried romancers. For example, at Arthur Andersen and Co., a well-known Big Eight accounting firm, there is a strict rule that prohibits partners from marrying other employees. If this occurs, one member of the couple must leave. According to Gene Herman, a managing partner for human resources, "We have a general policy at Arthur Andersen and Co. that the firm will do what serves the interests of its employees and the firm by making reasonable accommodations elsewhere in the firm if warranted."

A similar policy has been adopted by Price-Waterhouse, another Big Eight accounting firm. According to Richard Kearns, human resource managing partner, "It is the policy of our firm to permit employment of relatives and staff members in the firm and in the same practice unit, except that a relative of a partner, other than a spouse, may not be employed in the same practice unit or geographic location. For the purposes of this policy, a relative is defined as a spouse, all dependent persons, and the following non-dependent persons and their spouses: child, brother, sister, parent, grandparent, or parent-in-law."[1]

There are often solid reasons to adopt strict policies against nepotism in financial firms. Collusion may disrupt the financial integrity of the firm. Conflicts of interest may develop if the couple works in the same department. Highly confidential information could be compromised.

At CBT, a prominent northeastern bank, part of the Bank of New England, security reasons sometimes may prohibit married couples or relatives in the firm from working together. Assistant Vice-President Susan Dineen said, "There are good security reasons—for example, regarding auditing practices—why married couples are discouraged from working together. When my husband and I were first married, we were pioneers in this area. We were told we would need to be separated, so we moved to different bank locations in the state. Now the rules are more flexible, but married couples still may not work for the same department where a conflict of interest is involved. Our current policy reads, 'Employees related by blood or marriage are discouraged from working in the same area of the bank. Situations where relatives do work together in the same area will be reviewed.' "

If a direct reporting relationship is involved, many firms actively will become confrontational. Terminations are not unheard of in many firms when romances become disruptive. For that matter, sexploitation is not sanctioned anywhere in the corporate world.

Catherine Rein, senior vice-president for human resources at the Metropolitan Life Insurance Company, says, "No formal policy concerning dating relationships exists, but we do not permit people who are married, especially at the officer level, to work together or report up the same chain of management hierarchy. We do not have an anti-nepotism policy—married couples and relatives are employed by the firm—but we prefer to separate them from even the appearance of conflict of interest situations as much as possible."

Direct report relationships _should_ be discouraged. Not only can the power structure be disrupted, but the greatest potential for sexual harassment occurs in boss-subordinate relationships. In the classic example of United Parcel Service (UPS), the company established a widely known policy against fraternization and nepotism. New employees are asked whether or not any relatives work for the company. Office romancing is strongly discouraged, because, according to a source in the 1988 Bureau of National Affairs report, management fears "the appearance of favoritism."

In a now famous lawsuit, _Crozier vs. UPS,_ a manager was fired for inappropriate work behavior. The manager, Crozier, contended that the real reason behind his termination was an extramarital affair he had with a lower level employee. The California Court of Appeals upheld the original UPS decision.

But other firms, those with action-oriented, innovative cultures, may openly support—or at least not discourage—office romance. Apple Computer, a Silicon Valley company, is a good example. Debbie Biondolillo, human resource director, said, "We do not have a formal corporate policy against romance among employees. We do not try to control or monitor these situations."

Paul Jurata, another Apple employee, said, "At Apple,

there is an unspoken attitude that says that if you get involved with another person at Apple, that person will be aware of your work, and sensitive to the demands and pressures of your work . . . so romancing in the office may even be good for business. Because people work so many long hard hours around here, you also have few opportunities to meet anyone else. . . . The company benefits enormously when two employees are involved."

Susan Vieira, a product manager, agrees. She said, "At Apple there are social events that bring employees together. There are lots of couples, and it's no big deal. If romance is not officially encouraged, at least it is not discouraged. When I first came to work here, I was told to be careful about what I said— not to say anything off-guard about someone—because [that person] could be someone's lover or spouse and you may not know it!"

Other companies, like Apple, also have embraced the new sexual revolution. According to Gwendolyn Tucker, a senior product manager at Tymnet-McDonnell Douglas, who had previously worked for Calma and Racal-Vadic, two prominent Silicon Valley firms, said, "Attitudes are so liberal out here that my inclination is that romancing in the office is pretty commonplace. . . . Although my original motto was 'Don't date the people you work with,' it is so much easier to develop friendships and meet people at work that I have now been involved in two office romances in different firms. In fact, at my last company, there were twelve romances that I knew of, and probably many more I didn't know about."

In Silicon Valley, office romance may be unofficially encouraged as a means of retention. According to one employee who works at Sun Microsystems, "I get the feeling out here sometimes that firms would prefer for you to get involved with someone in your own firm—keep it in the family. Romancing an employee of a competitor firm might cause much more serious concerns about confidentiality."

This is exactly what happened in the case of Gina Rulon-Miller, a former employee of IBM, who started dating Mark Blum, an account manager at IBM who moved to a competitor. Despite the fact that she was an award-winning marketing manager in a division office in San Francisco, she was ordered to forget about Blum or be demoted. She pressed a wrongful discharge suit and won a $200,000 award when the court found in her favor.

Of course, not all Silicon Valley firms are a haven for romance. But because corporate cultures in Silicon Valley espouse action-oriented, fact-paced, creative, and high-pressure norms, there is a greater tendency toward open behavior.

Most other companies fall somewhere in the middle. A 1985 _Fortune_ magazine survey sent to human resources managers at 220 Fortune 500 companies showed that 94 percent said they had not developed formal policies regarding personal/romantic relationships. Over one-third said their companies tried to overlook such relationships, and a fifth said they felt such problems would resolve themselves.[2]

For example, at General Electric, no formal policy prohibiting office romance exists. According to Bruce Bunch, manager of media relations, "The only common-sense practice we have is not having people who are directly related working for one another in a situation where, for example, a husband is making decisions on his wife's performance appraisal and salary recommendations. Otherwise, any problems are treated as a work performance problem."

John Matz, a vice-president for employee services and development at Champion International, a Stamford, Connecticut-based firm, said, "At Champion there is no official policy that even remotely relates to this issue. We have a practice of frowning upon husbands and wives working in the same department; however, there is a strong norm here not to interfere in the privacy of employees' personal lives."

My own recent survey showed similar results. Among the managers I polled at forty corporations across the nation, representing such diverse firms as American Telephone and Telegraph, Pepsico, Hewlett-Packard, Sun Microsystems, Xerox, General Electric, Champion International, Southern New England Telephone, Cable News Network, Sun Company, and many others, the most common response was that if they had any policy at all, it was that office romance needed to be treated on an individual basis. In general, many corporations are reluctant to develop strict written policies regarding office romance. Most firms recognize this is a gray area and prefer not to intervene.

Coping with the Issue of Employee Privacy

Most executives have adopted middle-of-the-road attitudes out of respect for employee privacy. Because of this, they prefer to let the romance run its course—as long as it doesn't affect business. Certainly, employee privacy *should* be respected. If corporations were playing Big Brother all the time, most of us would feel resentful and angry at the interruptions in our personal lives. After all, your personal life *is* your own private business.

But what happens when the romance *does* affect business? Alexandra and Fred (in chapter 10) are a case in point. Because that romance was allowed to run its course, the reputation of a solid, well-liked, once respected manager was lost. Even more destructive effects occurred with Bruce and Sandra (in chapter 8). Their romance turned into sexual harassment. If management had turned a blind eye on Anne and Gregory's romance (chapter 5), the firm's reputation would have been seriously compromised.

Should persons like Alexandra simply be allowed to exploit a romance for personal gain? Certainly not. Should Anne and Gregory be allowed to defiantly forsake their work? Definitely not. Should Bruce be allowed to harass Sandra without management sanctions? Absolutely not. Something must be done.

Margaret Mead, in an April 1978 *Redbook* magazine article, advocated strong management action in the form of "incest taboos" for modern corporations. In her article she pleaded, "What we need, in fact, are new taboos that are appropriate to the new society we are struggling to create—taboos that will operate within the work setting as once they operated within the household. Neither men nor women should expect that sex can be used either to victimize women who need to keep their jobs or to keep women from advancement or to help men advance their own careers. A taboo enjoins. We need one that says clearly and unequivocally, 'You don't make passes at or sleep with the people you work with.' "

Corporate incest taboos may be unrealistic with the proliferation of office romance at all levels of the modern corporation. Such taboos also would ignore the positive aspects an office romance may bring. But too many managers do too little too late. They put their heads in the sand and prefer to pretend—or hope—a suspected romance will simply run its course. Or they apply one particular policy for one case and an entirely different set of rules for another. Usually, by the time they take action, disruptive effects already will have occurred, and work group morale will have reached an all-time low.

Why Office Romances Should Be Managed

According to Tony Leighton, who published an article entitled "When Love Walks In" in the May 1984 _Canadian Business Journal,_ an executive love affair can be "managed" just like any other personnel dilemma. He further believes that for the sake of the lovers, and for the company itself, it _should_ be managed.

But few managers seem to agree. According to the Robert Quinn survey reprinted in the March 1977 _Administrative Science Quarterly,_ more than half of the managers took no action, ignored the romance, or felt the problem would resolve itself. Over one-third did not want to risk taking any action, and another third said they did not know what to do.

My own survey showed similar trends. Of the ninety-four cases reported, 64 percent said that no action was taken at all. Only 10 percent said that management forced a transfer or dismissal of one party; an equivalent number said that management issued reprimands and warnings. One-quarter of the respondents said one party willingly transferred or left the company.

Informal practices in the absence of written policy guidelines can be dangerous. Detrimental situations may be overlooked because there are no formal guidelines concerning how they should be approached. Second, it can be easy to guess wrong. What you think is current practice suddenly may no longer pertain.

Informal practices also can be misapplied. The informal norms that pertain to one case of a boss-subordinate romance may not be appropriate for *your* romance with a peer in another department clear across the company. Or what is used as an informal practice for men may be different from that used for women.

Firms that have no official policy or practice may be doing themselves and their employees serious damage. But there are some situations in which non-intervention may be equally damaging—or more so—than strict action. Managers need to identify these situations and rectify them as quickly as possible.

Three considerations legitimately should drive management action:

- Whether the involvement concerns a direct reporting relationship
- Whether the involvement concerns an extramarital affair
- Whether the involvement concerns a potential conflict of interest

DIRECT BOSS-SUBORDINATE REPORTING RELATIONSHIPS

Employers are concerned about relationships that occur between bosses and subordinates in direct reporting relationships, and understandably so. Sexploitation can be devastating to morale. Coworkers are less willing to be productive if promotions are defined not by what you do, but with whom you are sleeping at the time. A source in the insurance industry said, "We never would want to have anyone in this situation directly reporting to one another. There is too much at stake. For their sakes, as well as for the corporation, we prefer to separate boss-subordinate couples as soon as we know what is going on."

If disruption occurs, morale is bound to suffer. Coworkers may act out by a decline in their performance. Exceedingly long coffee breaks, personal calls, and arriving to work late all are subtle forms of employee sabotage. Even if the couple *does* conduct themselves in a professional manner, coworkers fear the *potential* for damage in the relationship and worry that something will happen. Direct reporting relationships also involve the greatest potential for sexual harassment.

Paul Upham, a vice-president for human resources at Donnelley Marketing, said, "There are some situations—especially those that could victimize a lower level subordinate—in which managers are shirking their duties if they do not take action. That is why we have a sexual harassment policy."

CONFLICT OF INTEREST PROBLEMS

Managers also are warranted in taking action when a conflict of interest may hamper the work performance of the couple. In situations where the possibility for collusion exists, managers would be remiss in their responsibilities if they did not separate the couple. Security problems that occur in banks or investment firms are a good example. According to a source in the banking industry, "It is understandable why my firm has adopted a policy of separation. There are real possibilities for security leaks—for example, embezzlement in a branch office—as a result of collusion. To prevent this, the company is right in taking a stand."

This means that when peers work for the same department in a potential conflict-of-interest situation, or for intersecting departments with confidential interaction, managers should intervene in the romance. Managers of personnel departments across the nation face this situation.

According to one personnel department officer, "I have a rule that says that the members of my department may not get involved with anyone else in the firm. We deal with a lot of confidential information here, so office relationships may cause a serious breach of confidentiality."

Catherine Rein, senior vice-president for human resources at Metropolitan Life Insurance Company, said, "We have a policy that married couples may not work together, for their sake as well as ours. This way we prevent uncomfortable conflicts from happening."

EXTRAMARITAL AFFAIRS

Extramarital affairs also carry potential for disruption. There are moral, ethical, and legal issues at stake when an extramarital affair is involved. When managers turn a blind eye, they may neglect serious disruptions in morale.

According to Bruce Bunch, manager of media relations at General Electric, "If an extramarital affair or any other type of personal relationship were to be disruptive in some way so that work performance was adversely affected, we at G.E. would treat it simply as a work performance problem. The manager of the couple would discuss the problem as part of a normal performance review discussion. But the focus would be on work performance, not on the affair."

Because this is such a delicate area, I believe that the informal practice advocated by this General Electric manager is the most enlightened approach anyone could expect. Discussing the affair—as an affair—may infringe on employee rights of privacy. But if work performance is affected, it is appropriate to discuss the problem as such.

The Decision to Terminate

Many companies, if they believe sufficient disruption has occurred, will terminate an employee under the employment-at-will doctrine. But who should leave? How should corporations make this decision? In her September 1983 *Harvard Business Review* article on the subject, Eliza Collins recommended that the lower level member of the relationship should voluntarily leave the company, since the lower level member traditionally would be considered less valuable to the organization.

I strongly disagree with this idea. By suggesting that the lower level participant should be the one to leave, organizations make a potentially erroneous assumption regarding the lower level member's capabilities. Who is to say that the lower level member will not outshine the higher level member at a later date?

As the saying goes, managers tend to be promoted to the

level of their own incompetence. How can hierarchical level be used as an open-ended criterion on which to judge the value of particular organization members?

Second, it takes two to tango. To punish one party blindly is to do a disservice to the other. Some managers may believe that transferring one party or letting go of one of the members is a fair solution, but this is not so. Work group members will recognize the inequity this solution presents, and rail against it. At least I hope they will.

Third, the solution of letting the lower level member go is likely to be injurious to women as a group. Because most women have entered the workforce later than men, and have had difficulty ascending the managerial ranks, it is proportionally more likely that women will be in the lower level position more frequently than men.

The 1985 *Personnel* magazine survey conducted by Anderson and Hunsaker supports this contention. Almost two-thirds of the romances they studied involved a man in a higher position than the woman. Only 8 percent involved a woman as the boss. Therefore, dismissing the lower level member means that women will be punished more often for their affairs.

But some firms have adopted a different strategy. At one company that has strict policies against fraternization, a secretary and a partner fell in love. They conducted their relationship in secret, but once they decided to get married, they made their relationship public. Management at the firm made it clear that one member would need to quit or be transferred to another location. But whom did they transfer? The higher ranking member of the couple—the partner. They felt the secretary was so valuable to the firm that they could not bear to lose her.

Performance as the Criterion for Action

To fire people simply because they have become involved in an office romance and there is *potential* for damage to the work group neglects the fact that some of the romances, including some reported in this book, indeed have positive effects. To ignore the romance altogether neglects another possibility—that the romance may indeed have a negative effect on the work group, and that the situation deserves management attention.

I think the best way to cut through all the dilemmas easily is to consider the problem in standard human resource terms— as with a situation of drug or alcohol abuse. Whether two people are involved in a hot and heavy romance should *not* be the issue of concern; whether the romance is affecting the couple's performance on the job *is* a management concern.

According to the earlier-cited survey conducted by Professor Gary N. Powell, of the University of Connecticut, in 1986, future MBAs seem to agree with this general theme. The 102 MBA students in his survey (reported in the July 1986 issue of *Business Horizons*) agreed that companies ought to adopt a policy of tolerance—as long as the romance does not affect productivity. They also felt sex-oriented behavior between supervisors and subordinates ought to be discouraged because of the potential for harassment. Coworker relationships were considered more acceptable.

Therefore, office productivity should be the guideline that determines management action—not the presence of a romance itself. *When worker performance is affected, management should take action.* If worker performance remains unaffected, there is little reason to act.

When Intervention Is Necessary

When pressed into action, managers should consider using a range of disciplinary actions to cope with unproductive office romancers.[3]

For minor offenses:
- Informal discussion and/or counseling for both members of the couple regarding the implications of their actions on the work group
- Formal warnings if job performance is adversely affected by the romance

- Participative discussions regarding transfers for one or both members of the couple if job performance remains adversely affected or if work group morale continues to suffer

For more severe offenses:
- Formal warnings and disclosure of the problems the romance has caused
- Direct transfer of the more marketable party if a conflict of interest becomes evident or sexploitation is suspected
- Termination if there is *reasonable certainty* of a serious violation of workplace professionalism (such as sex traded for promotion)

In situations where no disruption occurs, no action is warranted. Remember, office romances can be beneficial and may have many positive effects on productivity, motivation, creativity, and innovation. Peer relationships are less likely to cause concern. In such circumstances, employees can be allowed to police themselves.

Employees deserve the courtesy of being informed of the implications of their romance if it is having an undesirable effect on coworkers. They also deserve fair warning if conservative values in the culture cause management to view the romance negatively.

Professor Gary N. Powell, of the University of Connecticut, adds a few helpful suggestions. He believes that companies should make counseling available to all the individuals involved—the couple, their managers, and coworkers who may have been disrupted by the romance. Managers should be trained how to recognize the detrimental effects of a romance, and the conditions under which action may be required. He also suggests that coworkers need a neutral third party to whom they can go to report incidents of exploitation without fear of reprisal. Their boss may not always be the best choice in this matter for a variety of reasons.

Dr. Powell also recommends that the couple should be presented with two options: Either they may cool the relationship and demonstrate to coworkers that it has been cooled by their workplace behavior, or they may accept being transferred to equivalent positions elsewhere in the company. Either one or both participants could be transferred, depending on the situation.

I believe that if counseling is made available, the couple may be able to make a more effective *choice* about whom should be transferred, if anyone. When a transfer becomes necessary because of a conflict of interest, managers should consider putting both members of the couple on a transfer list, and make the decision on the basis of who gets transferred *first*. Whichever member of the couple is more marketable is more likely to move quickly. Decisions about transfers, in my opinion, should be made on the basis of marketability rather than level.

Of course, sexual harassment is a different matter. If harassment occurs, management should take strict and immediate action. Dismissals are warranted if harassment occurs (as in the case of Bruce and Sandra) or if there is a reasonable certainty that power has been traded for sex (as in the case of Alexandra and Fred). If this should become necessary, the lower level member should *not* be made to suffer for the higher level member's lack of responsibility. When the person who has committed the greater offense receives the greater punishment, the appearance of an equitable decision will help to restore the morale of the work group.

A Sample Corporate Policy

What might a corporate policy on office romance—as opposed to one on sexual harassment—look like? How can you establish a corporate policy for *your* firm? A corporate policy on office romance should:

- Recognize that romance is a natural by-product of close working relationships
- Distinguish romance from nepotism and harassment
- State that *performance* is the primary factor that would compel management to take action

- Specify the situations which may cause workplace disruption, such as romance between bosses and subordinates in direct reporting relationships, possibilities of collusion within departments, and/or conflict of interest across departments
- Identify the steps that management would use to monitor and review romantic relationships under each of these circumstances

The policy also should:

- Clarify that the same rules and actions will be applied consistently across the organization, regardless of gender or level
- Recognize that employees are entitled to their own privacy, and that romance between two employees is a private and personal matter that occurs outside of normal business hours
- Acknowledge that not every situation will have deleterious or negative effects, and that action will be brought to bear only regarding those romances that have an adverse effect on business practice

I believe that definitive action should be taken with regard to direct reporting boss-subordinate relationships because of the complications that may ensue. Sexual harassment is most likely to occur in such relationships, and charges of favoritism or exploitation are equally likely to be levied. There is too much at stake for management _not_ to monitor and review such relationships on a routine basis.

My most urgent message is that employers need to realize that they do not need to lose good performers simply because employees are involved in an office romance. Their involvement is _not_ the issue. Disruptive effects on the performance of the couple or the work group _are_.

Some Final Words

Sexual attraction, and the conditions that facilitate it in the workplace, will not suddenly disappear. Managers must recognize that changing sexual mores have created a new responsibility—the management of office romance. Each manager must carefully diagnose the effect a romance is having on *performance* to determine an appropriate solution. In most cases, none may be required.

In the modern corporation, there is no place for heavy-handed management techniques or corporate mandates against romance. The proclivity toward attraction in the workplace is too great. Ignoring the situation is not an effective solution. Nor are informal practices or norms the answer.

Corporate policymakers must make room in their busy agendas to establish a minimum set of broad-based ground rules on this subject. This way, each manager can determine the most appropriate solution for the good of the firm, the couple, and the other employees involved.

15

LIVING LOVE IN THE OFFICE

No matter what the odds, no matter how great the risk, office romance is here to stay. The new sexual revolution has changed office decorum. Colleagues routinely date, have flings, fall in and out of love, marry, and even divorce—and business goes on as usual.

One conclusion is clear. My research shows that the conventional wisdom that suggests "Don't fool around in your own backyard!" is unfairly exaggerated. Office romances *can* be beneficial. My survey results, discussions with managers, and case research all show that under certain *limited* conditions, romance may improve morale, strengthen motivation, improve work relationships, and enhance teamwork and cooperation.

But my research also identified a number of problems and risks associated with engaging in an office romance. Workplace romances are made more difficult when:

- The romance involves a relationship of unequal power
- An extramarital affair takes place
- The corporate culture discourages romance

Restrictive corporate cultures force romancers to go underground. Romances between bosses and subordinates, or mentors and proteges, may create the potential for sexploitation or harassment. Extramarital affairs cause concern, worry, and gossip among coworkers.

If these problem scenarios are avoided, I believe that the benefits may indeed outweigh the risks. What could be better than meeting your lover at work every day, and using the sexual energy you generate to enhance your work performance? There is some truth to the saying that when love is in the air, people feel happier and more satisfied. They also may be more motivated. Creativity, innovation, and excitement surround those involved in an office romance. What more could a manager ask?

The problem is, when the power balance of boss-subordinate relationships are unfairly manipulated, or when hurt spouses become casualties of extramarital office affairs, we remember the sensationalism of these stories. This causes many people to focus on the negatives more than the positives of office romance. We forget there are a number of advantages.

Most of the benefits are realized when the relationship involves *peers in non-intersecting departments* in companies that do not discourage personal relationships at work. This is the ideal scenario. When colleagues at the same level but with unique career paths fall in love in the same company, all of the good—and little of the bad—is experienced.

It is up to the person involved to make a fully *informed* decision before going ahead and plunging into an ill-considered office romance. We each have new responsibilities to ourselves, to our colleagues, and to our firms as a consequence of the new sexual revolution in the workplace. You must weigh carefully all the risks and benefits, all the advantages and disadvantages—about your firm, the individual whom you are considering, and the opportunities presented—before proceeding.

Guidelines for Successful Office Romances

What guidelines might be helpful for those considering an office romance? Here are some suggestions:

• *Be aware of office norms about romance before acting.*
The degree of risk assumed is directly related to a company's cultural norms and attitudes toward office romance. Be aware that previous histories of other corporate romances will affect

coworker attitudes toward personal involvements. If past romances were met with success, office norms are probably lenient on this subject. If the past romances were met with coworker animosity, keep in mind this will be a hurdle to overcome.

If no precedent exists for romance in an office, then their behaviors and reactions will be carefully monitored by other coworkers and the boss. Lovers will truly feel as if they are living in a fishbowl.

If lovers are uncomfortable with this, they may want to seriously consider whether or not to discontinue the relationship. The level of discomfort may affect personal attitudes toward a partner.

• *Evaluate the potential risks to career advancement.*

Love sometimes can make a person vulnerable—to hurt, pain, and, in the case of an office romance, added career risks in conservative firms. Many couples blindly fall in love at work only to realize later that their careers may be threatened by gossip, innuendo, and risks to reputation.

These risks should not be minimized, especially for those who work in conservative firms. The perils of office romancing should be carefully considered by both members of the couple before proceeding. If one member of the couple is unwilling to risk his or her career for the sake of love (or even a fling), the other should carefully consider whether to go ahead. Movement forward should continue only if both members of the couple are willing to take a risk on love that may (or may not) have career implications.

• *Don't mess around with a boss—or mentor.*

This rule should be inviolate. Hierarchical relationships—or any relationship where there is power inequity—can be exploited or manipulated. Sex can be traded for promotion. But it is only those with power who can recommend career assignments, promotions, raises, and favorable projects; peers cannot do so.

It is for this reason that boss-subordinate or mentor relationships should be strictly avoided. Office romances between unequals affect office morale negatively. Jealousy, favoritism, petty strife, and lost objectivity cause anger and dissatisfaction. Anyone who enters into a relationship with someone above them in the corporate hierarchy becomes a target for gossip.

Even the appearance of favoritism in such relationships can be deadly to office morale. Furthermore, a participant's competence and self-esteem may be forever jeopardized because he or she always may wonder, "Could I have achieved success on my own?"

Sexploitation is unconscionable in an office environment. So is harassment. Any misuse of power causes unpleasantness and dissatisfaction. Coworkers will not tolerate any misuse of power. They always will have the last word.

• *Maintain strict boundaries between personal and professional roles.*

Couples who draw strict boundaries between their personal and professional roles in the office seem to have the greatest chance of success with office relationships. It is for this reason that I recommend relationships with colleagues in different departments. Romances in the same department may be too close for comfort. Many problems disappear when there is a natural boundary between departments.

Even if lovers work for the same department or small office, they must learn to maintain strict boundaries between work and personal lives. Make a pact that business is business, and refuse to discuss domestic problems at work, such as dealing with child care or housework.

In the office, successful partners treat their lovers with more reserve than they treat others, and interact on a professional level at all times. They are careful not to constantly lunch together. If they must attend a corporate dinner or social function, they make certain to circulate with other guests. Those couples who prioritize their professional roles in the office and place their romantic concerns second seem to have the greatest chance of success.

• *Clarify at the start exactly what you want from the relationship.*

Romantic relationships at work can easily become troublesome if the lovers have different motives for the relationship. The more potential lovers clarify at the start of the relationship their motives and goals (is this a fling or something more?), the better their chance of success.

To avoid surprises, potential lovers should use the work environment as a way to pick up cues about their partner's level of commitment. Is he or she often seen with other members of the opposite sex? Does he or she have a reputation for office affairs?

Successful office lovers allow their partners the time and space to make up their minds about the relationship. Better safe than sorry when it comes to work relationships.

• *Identify the possible areas in which partners may become competitive.*

Career competition can sometimes be the downfall of successful peer romances. Because the office environment is competitive, lovers can sometimes feel left out when one partner is promoted before the other. Size up the situation and be realistic about career options. Develop a long-term career plan for both partners. Neither person should give up career goals for the other.

Successful couples who avoid competition go one step further. They identify alternatives should one partner's career trail off into the sunset. They develop contingency plans and find non-competitive ways to fulfill career goals. One partner, for example, may return to school once his or her career becomes plateaued. Or another may start a new entrepreneurial venture. If partners are on a collision course, they should get off. Someone will have to give in. Compromises are necessary in any personal relationship, but in office romance, they are essential.

• *Anticipate possible conflict-of-interest situations.*

Office lovers must learn to respect the confidentiality of any private information that partners share. Do not gossip. The code of professional ethics should not be broken.

When a conflict of interest arises, each partner must recognize and respect the other's viewpoint. Successful couples realize that it is most productive to agree to disagree. They leave a potential conflict alone until it is resolved by appropriate channels.

Because conflicts of interest are an important concern to the company, management must be assured that couples will not allow conflicts of interest to disrupt the normal information flow of business decisions. If conflict of interest issues continue to arise, one member of the couple should consider a transfer to obviate future conflicts.

- *Be sensitive to the reactions of colleagues and management.*

Coworkers are concerned that the romance will cause them to constantly work with the couple as a team, rather than as individuals. They worry that the partners will engage in pillow talk about them. They fear the ending of the romance, and the prospect of being forced to choose sides.

Coworkers and managers need reassurance that many of the problems and pitfalls they fear will not come to pass. At the start of the relationship, lovers should clarify the boundaries of their relationship with coworkers and address the issue of communication channels. They must make it known that they will not be information conduits, forever forwarding messages to a partner.

Lovers also should follow normal office routine. If there is an informal norm that everyone has lunch together, or has drinks together after work, they must continue to do so.

Finally, couples should respect the boss's concerns. Ideally, office lovers should try to improve job performance, if possible, to dispel any concerns the boss may have. They must make sure that their romance demonstrates all the benefits—and none of the disadvantages—that a boss may anticipate.

- *Remember that the romance will not remain a secret for long.*

Few workplace romances remain a secret. But it may be prudent to maintain a closely guarded relationship in the early stages of a romance. Problems occur, however, when couples persist in believing their romance *remains* a secret. They never do. If they think theirs is the exception, it is the first sign of trouble. This is especially true for extramarital affairs.

The duplicity that extramarital affairs create by the need for secrecy causes many problems. Coworkers find themselves caught in a moral and ethical bind. Managers are uncomfortable and may choose to step in to "set the record straight." So extramarital affairs in particular are vulnerable to gossip.

- *Discuss "contingency plans" at the start of the romance.*

I cannot emphasize how important this is. Planning is helpful in any romance, but advance planning seems crucial for the success of a workplace romance. Partners who will continue to see each other on a professional basis even if the relationship ends badly need the protection advance planning affords. Lovers also need to be prepared if management decides to take action and requests a transfer for one of the partners once the romance becomes public knowledge.

Planning ahead will go a long way toward easing the complexities of an office romance. In fact, planning may be *the* key to success.

Final Conclusions

I said at the beginning of this book that its purpose would be to educate people about the pros and cons of office romance. My research shows that it is *not* true in every case that careers are threatened, reputations ruined, or damage done to professional relationships. It is true, as popular opinion suggests, that there are a number of risks and disadvantages to a poorly conducted, unprofessional, or explorative office romance. This cannot be denied. But it is equally true that some romances, under certain limited conditions, can be quite beneficial—in terms of corporate morale, employee motivation, and departmental productivity.

My research shows clearly that most of the benefits are realized when the relationship involves freely attached peers in non-intersecting departments in companies that do not discourage personal relationships at work. The success of a romance depends on an employee's willingness to maximize the benefits and minimize the risks by avoiding the problem scenarios described in this book.

The new sexual revolution has forced us to reevaluate our perceptions, attitudes, and judgments about personal relationships at work. I hope this book will help all concerned to understand the issues, dilemmas, perils, and benefits of this new modern corporate phenomenon—love in the office.

RESOURCE SECTION

Chapter Notes

C H A P T E R   O N E

1. Academic case research usually involves detailed transcripts of facts and quotations that represent a specific genre of field research. I hesitate to call all of the examples recounted in this book "cases," because many are simply stories that I heard as I continued my research. Some are examples, others are anecdotes, still others are cases in the true sense of the research genre. Many are composites included for purposes of illustration. I encourage you to keep this in mind as you read through the chapters.

C H A P T E R   T W O

1. Sixty-three percent represents the combined indices of two questions in the survey. Twenty-six percent responded that office romances were "very common," and 37 percent said office romances were "becoming more and more commonplace."

2. The survey conducted by professors Carolyn Anderson and Phillip Hunsaker at the University of San Diego showed proximity also was an important antecedent of attraction. The authors write, "Sheer proximity—apart from any information it may provide about another and apart from any rewards or punishments that the other may administer—encourages attraction. Increasing contact increases the probability that a male/female interaction will go beyond a work relationship."

3. The book written by Professors Berscheid and Walster, *Interpersonal Attraction* (Reading, Mass.: Addison-Wesley, 1969), does not directly list

265

intensity as a factor in attraction. However, the intensity brought about by stress and the intensity of competition are discussed. It is in this sense that I am referring to it here.

CHAPTER THREE

1. The law (Section 703 of Title VII of the 1964 Civil Rights Act) on sexual harassment is very specific. The statute from which it is derived prohibits discrimination on the basis of sex in employment and provides legal authority for the guidelines listed here.

2. These stages have been generated through content analysis of my sample cases. However, I cannot speak for the generalizability of my findings; these stages may only suit the relationships I studied.

3. Further discussion on roles is recorded in Katz, R., and Kahn, R., _The Social Psychology of Organizations_ (New York: Wiley Press, 1966). Additionally, most psychology and organizational behavior textbooks yield the same information.

CHAPTER FOUR

1. In my survey, there were mixed results for productivity. Although 29 percent did say productivity increased, an additional 23 percent said that participants became less productive. Other surveys (Anderson and Hunsaker, Quinn) also show similar patterns. The negative effects on productivity declines are explained in the next chapter.

2. Similarly, keep in mind that conflicts also can be _created_ by office romance—especially if a breakup ensues. The next chapter discusses these implications.

3. These actors appeared on a recent _Donahue_ show, taped in 1987, in which they publicly proclaimed their work relationships enhanced their personal relationships on the set. Each of these actors also has been widely quoted in the media.

CHAPTER FIVE

1. A sample contigency plan and more information about breaking up an office romance are included in chapter 13.

2. See note 1, chapter four.

3. The results were: for those who attributed perceived or expected risks who said "work performance may decline," 55 percent; for those who rated actual cases in their work environment who said the participants were "less productive," 23 percent.

CHAPTER SIX

1. Information on this firm was provided in the Bureau of National Affairs report, 1988, as a case study.

2. See the Bureau of National Affairs report, "Corporate Affairs," for a complete description of this case.

3. Actual results when the cross-tabulations were complete: Of those who characterized their firms as reactive, 48 percent were kept secret. Only 28 percent of those who worked in more creative or liberal environments felt compelled to do so. Note: These results do not appear on the survey located in this resource section because they represent cross-tabulations of the data when analyzed.

4. Actual results: Sixty-eight percent said the risks were greater for women than for men; 24 percent said the benefits and risks were equal regardless of sex. These results also represent cross-tabulations that do not appear directly on the survey.

CHAPTER SEVEN

1. Ms. Harragan's book was written at a time when women felt compelled to battle their way to the top. Much of her extreme language is intended to have an impact that was appropriate at that time.

2. Specific results: Ten percent were "more difficult to get along with," 23 percent were "less productive," and for 36 percent, favoritism was shown. Additionally, 41 percent were "easier to get along with," and 29 percent were "more productive."

3. These statistics were quoted in Ann Morrison, Randall White, and Ellen Van Velsor, *Breaking the Glass Ceiling: Can Women Reach the Top of America's Corporations* (Reading, Mass.: Addison-Wesley, 1987).

4. Dr. Kanter's work applies broadly here. She was the first to note that women's lack of progress in the management ranks is a direct result of their powerlessness more than of their gender. The management styles of women, often accused of bossiness or territorialism, also are a consequence of powerlessness. For further reference, please read *Men and Women of the Corporation* (New York: Basic Books, 1977) or her *Harvard Business Review* article, "Power Failures in Management Circuits," 57(4).

CHAPTER EIGHT

1. For those who evaluated boss-subordinate relationships, a total of 79 percent evaluated them as "more difficult," "unproductive," "resented the relationship," or showed "favoritism." Only 21 percent of peer relationships were similarly evaluated. As examples, only 19 percent of boss-subordinate relationships were rated as "easier to get along with" as compared to 62 percent of peer relationships. Forty-three percent of peer relationships were considered to be more productive, while only 9 percent of boss-subordinate relationships reported similar results.

2. Source on this material is my *Academy of Management Review* article, "The Power Dynamics of Organizational Romances." The article was published in October 1986, volume 11(4).

3. Attribution theory, and its consequences for male and female behavior, is highly controversial. Other researchers have found non-similar results. For a full discussion, see Deaux, K., and Enswiller, T. (1974), "Explanation of Successful Performance on Sex-linked Tasks: What Is Skill for the Male Is Luck for the Female," *Journal of Personality and Social Psychology*, 29, 80–85; Feather, N., and Simon, J. (1975), "Reactions to Male and Female Success and Failure in Sex-Linked Occupations: Impressions of Personality, Causal Attributions, and the Perceived Likelihood of Different Consequences," *Journal of Personality and Social Psychology*, 31, 20–31; Feldman-Summers, S., and Kiesler, S. (1974), "Those Who Are Number Two Try Harder: The Effect of Sex on Attributions of Causality," *Journal of Personality and Social Psychology*, 30, 846–855; and Garland, N., and Price, K. (1977), "Attitudes Toward Women in Management and Attributes for Their Success and Failure in Management Positions," *Journal of Applied Psychology*, 62, 29–33.

CHAPTER NINE

1. According to Dr. Kram in her article, "Phases of the Mentor Relationship," which appeared in the *Academy of Management Review*, 26(4) in 1983, career functions include sponsorship, exposure and visibility, coaching protection, and challenging assignments. Psychosocial functions include role modeling, acceptance and confirmation, counseling, and friendship activities.

2. Results for peers were overwhelmingly more favorable for any survey result studied. In my case research, I observed that the most favorable comments came from peers in non-intersecting departments.

CHAPTER TEN

1. Actual results: Thirty-six percent suspected refers to the survey result that reads, "The couple thought no one knew but we did."

2. See Gerald Salancik and Jeffrey Pfeffer, "The Bases and Uses of Power: The Case of a University," *Administrative Science Quarterly*, 19, 1974, 453–73; and Hickson, D.J., Hinings, C.R., Lee, C.A., Schneck, R.E., and Pennings, J.M., "A Strategic Contingencies Theory of Intraorganizational Power," *Administrative Science Quarterly*, 16, 1971, 216–29, both of which sources refer to political behavior and uncertainty reduction.

3. For further discussion regarding the rewards and sources exchanged in dating and marriage relationships, see Cornelia Safilos-Rothschild's *Love and Sex Roles* (Englewood Cliffs, New Jersey: Prentice-Hall, 1977). Another source that is quite revealing is Susan Sprecher's article, "Sex Differences in Bases of Power in Dating Relationships," which appeared in *Sex Roles*, 12(4) in 1985, pages 449–461.

4. Theories of social exchange, notably by Adams, J.S., "Inequity in Social Exchange," in L. Berkowitz (ed.), *Advances in Experimental Social*

Psychology (vol. 2) (New York: Academic Press, 1965), and Festinger's original theory of cognitive dissonance in "Informal Social Communication," *Psychological Review*, 57, 1950, form the basis for these comments. I believe these theories are as applicable today as they were in their time.

CHAPTER ELEVEN

1. These results were reported in Maggie Scarf's book, *Intimate Partners: Patterns in Love and Marriage* (New York: Random House, 1987). She has included a sensitive chapter entitled "Marital Infidelity" that I recommend to anyone who would like to read more about the impact extramarital affairs may have on a marriage.

CHAPTER THIRTEEN

1. Further discussion on roles is recorded in Katz, R., and Kahn, R., *The Social Psychology of Organizations* (New York: Wiley Press, 1966). Additionally, most psychology and organizational behavior textbooks yield the same information.

2. Many researchers have modeled stages of grief, depression, and anguish on Elizabeth Kubler-Ross's earlier work on the grieving process in her book, *On Death and Dying* (New York: Macmillan, 1967). Dr. DeAngelis's work is the most recent and direct observation of the stages of dissolution, so it is used here.

3. Robert Quinn's 1977 *Administrative Science Quarterly* survey, "Coping with Cupid: The Formation, Impact, and Management of Romantic Relationships in Organizations," vol. 22, pages 30–45, also discusses motives for attraction. The motives he identifies are job motives, ego motives, and love motives. He further categorizes relationships on the basis of these motives: true love, utilitarian, and fling.

CHAPTER FOURTEEN

1. I am not singling out these highly respected accounting firms to demonstrate in any way that they are backward or behind the times. Rather, I commend these firms because their attitudes, policies, and procedures are appropriate, given the confidentiality of material they protect and the likelihood of conflicts of interest presented in financial firms.

2. This survey appeared in the Bureau of National Affairs report, *Corporate Affairs: Office Romance, Nepotism, and Harassment* (1988).

3. Gary Powell and I have recently co-authored an article expressing our joint views on the management of office romance. Tentatively titled "Organizational Romances: Dealing with Power/Dependency Issues," it has been submitted for publication.

CHAPTER FIFTEEN

1. Please understand that I am neither encouraging nor discouraging office romance. I have written this book to educate people about the issues. It is the reader's responsibility to analyze the dimensions of the problem in his or her own work environment and make a decision.

APPENDIX B:

Bibliography

Adams, J. S. "Inequity in Social Exchange." In *Advances in Experimental Social Psychology* vol. 2, edited by L. Berkowitz. New York: Academic Press, 1965.

Anderson, C., and Hunsaker, P. "Why There's Romancing at the Office and Why It's Everyone's Problem." *Personnel.* February 1985. 57–63.

Berscheid, E., and Walster, E. *Interpersonal Attraction.* Reading, Mass.: Addison-Wesley, 1969.

Blau, P. *Exchange and Power in Social Life.* London: Wiley Press, 1964.

Bradford, D., Sargent, A., and Sprague, M. "Executive Man and Woman: The Issue of Sexuality." In *Bringing Women into Management,* edited by F. Gordon and M. Strober. New York: McGraw-Hill, 1975.

Bunker, B., and Seashore, E. "Power, Collusion, Intimacy-Sexuality, Support." In *Beyond Sex Roles,* edited by A. Sargent. New York: West Publishing, 1977.

Bureau of National Affairs, Inc. *Corporate Affairs: Nepotism, Office Romance, and Sexual Harassment.* Washington, D.C., 1988.

Clawson, J., and Kram, K. "Managing Cross-Gender Mentoring." *Business Horizons.* May–June 1984, 22–32.

Collins, E. "Managers and Lovers." *Harvard Business Review.* September–October 1983, 142–153.

271

Crary, M. "Managing Attraction and Intimacy at Work." *Organizational Dynamics.* Spring 1987, 26–41.

Cunningham, M., with Fran Schumer. *Powerplay: What Really Happened at Bendix.* New York: Linden Press/Simon and Schuster, 1983.

Deal, T. E., and Kennedy, A. A. *Corporate Cultures: The Rites and Rituals of Corporate Life.* Reading, Mass.: Addison-Wesley, 1982.

Deaux, K., and Enswiller, T. "Explanation of Successful Performance on Sex-linked Tasks: What Is Skill for the Male Is Luck for the Female." *Journal of Personality and Social Psychology.* 29 (1974):80–85.

DeAngelis, Barbara. *How to Make Love All the Time: Secrets for Making Love Work* New York: Rawson Associates/Macmillan, 1987.

Driscoll, J., and Bova, R. "The Sexual Side of Enterprise." *Management Review.* 69(7) (1980):51–62.

Emerson, R. "Power-Dependence Relations." *American Sociological Review.* 27 (1962):33–41.

Feather, N., and Simon, J. "Reactions to Male and Female Success and Failure in Sex-Linked Occupations: Impressions of Personality, Causal Attributions, and the Perceived Likelihood of Different Consequences." *Journal of Personality and Social Psychology,* 31 (January 1975):20–31.

Feinberg, M., and Levenstein, A. "Sex and Romance in the Office and Plant." From an unpublished study from BFS Psychological Associates, New York, New York. Cited in *The Wall Street Journal,* November 29, 1982:26.

Feldman-Summers, S., and Kiesler, S. "Those Who Are Number Two Try Harder: The Effect of Sex on Attributions of Causality." *Journal of Personality and Social Psychology.* 30 (1974):846–855.

Festinger, L. "Informal Social Communication." *Psychological Review,* 57 (1950).

Garland, N., and Price, K. "Attitudes toward Women in Management and Attributes for Their Success and Failures in Management Positions." *Journal of Applied Psychology.* 62 (1977):29–33.

Goodman, E. "When Love Enters the Executive Suite." *Boston Globe.* September 27, 1983.

Harragan, Betty L. *Games Mother Never Taught You.* New York: Warner Books, 1977.

Hart, L. B., and Dalke, J. D. *The Sexes at Work: Improving Work*

Relationships Between Men and Women. Englewood Cliffs, NJ: Prentice-Hall.

Hickson, D. J.; Hinings, C. R.; Lee, C. A.; Schneck, R. E.; and Pennings, J. M. "A Strategic Contingencies Theory of Intraorganizational Power." *Administrative Science Quarterly.* 16 (1971):216–29.

Hite, S. *Women in Love: A Cultural Revolution in Progress.* New York: Alfred A. Knopf, 1987.

Horn, P., and Horn, J. *Sex in the Office: Power and Passion in the Workplace.* Reading, Mass.: Addison-Wesley, 1982.

Jaccoby, S. "Business Affairs." *The New York Times Magazine,* November 29, 1987:53, 87–89.

Jacobs, B. "Sex in the Office." *Industry Week.* February 9, 1981:32–38.

Jamison, K. "Managing Sexual Attraction in the Workplace." *Personnel Administrator.* August 1983:45–50.

Kanter, R. *Men and Women of the Corporation.* New York: Basic Books, 1977.

————. "Power Failures in Management Circuits." *Harvard Business Review.* 57(4) (July/August 1979):65–75.

Katz, R., and Kahn, R. *The Social Psychology of Organizations.* New York: John Wiley, 1966.

Kram, K. "Phases of the Mentor Relationship." *Academy of Management Journal.* 26(4) (December 1983): 608–625.

Leighton, T. "When Love Walks In." *Canadian Business Journal.* May 1984:78–83.

McLaughlin, F., and Ford, R. C. "Should Cupid Come to the Workplace?" *Personnel Administrator.* October 1987.

Mainiero, L. "The Power Dynamics of Organizational Romances." *Academy of Management Review.* 11(4) (1986):750–762.

Mead, M. "A Proposal: We Need Taboos on Sex at Work." *Redbook.* April 1978:31–38.

Morrison, A. M.; White, R. P.; Van Velsor, E. *Breaking the Glass Ceiling: Can Women Reach the Top of America's Largest Corporations?* Reading, Mass.: Addison-Wesley, 1988.

Nass, G. D.; Libby, R. W.; and Fisher, M. *Sexual Choices.* Belmont, Cal: Wadsworth Press, 1981.

Neugarten, D., and Shafritz, J., eds. *Sexuality in Organizations.* Oak Park, Ill: Moore Publishing Co., 1980.

Peplau, L. "Power in Dating Relationships." In *Women: A Feminist*

Perspective, edited by J. Freeman. Palo Alto: Mayfield Press, 1978.

Powell, G. "What Do Tomorrow's Managers Think about Sexual Intimacy in the Workplace?" *Business Horizons.* 29(4) (July/August 1986):32–33.

————. *Women and Men in Management: The New Dynamics.* Newbury Park, Cal: Sage Publications, 1988.

Powell, G. N., and Butterfield, D. A. "The 'Good Manager': Masculine or Androgynous?" *Academy of Management Journal,* 22(2) June 1979:395–403.

Quinn, R. "Coping with Cupid: The Formation, Impact, and Management of Romantic Relationships in Organizations. *Administrative Science Quarterly.* 22 (March 1977):30–45.

Quinn, R., and Lees, P. "Attraction and Harassment: Dynamics of Sexual Politics in the Workplace." *Organizational Dynamics.* Autumn 1984: 35–46.

Safilos-Rothschild, C. *Love and Sex Roles.* Englewood Cliffs, NJ: Prentice-Hall, 1977.

Salancik, G. A., and Pfeffer, J. "The Bases and Uses of Power: The Case of a University." *Administrative Science Quarterly.* 19 (1974):453–473.

Scarf, M. *Intimate Partners: Patterns in Love and Marriage.* New York: Random House, 1987.

Schultz, T. "In Defense of the Office Romance." *Savvy.* May 1982: 54–64.

Spellman, D., and Crary, M. "Intimacy Versus Distance: A Case of Male-Female Attraction at Work." *Organizational Behavior Teaching Review.* (1984) 72–85.

Sprecher, S. "Sex Differences in Bases of Power in Dating Relationships." *Sex Roles.* 12(4) (1985):449–461.

Spruell, G. "Daytime Drama: Love in the Office." *Training and Development Journal.* February 1985:20–33.

Staff Reporters of *Business Week.* "Romance in the Workplace: Corporate Rules for the Game of Love." *Business Week.* June 18, 1984:70–72.

Staff Reporters of *Fortune.* "Managing by Mystique at Tandem Computers." *Fortune.* June 28, 1982:84–91.

Staff Reporters of *Newsweek.* "Love in the Office." *Newsweek.* February 15, 1988:48–52.

Staff Reporters of *New York.* "Dick and Joni: The Blockbuster Row

That's Rocking Best-Sellerdom." *New York*. December 14, 1987:60–68.

Staff Reporters of the *New York Post*. "The Best Dating Service? Try the Workplace." *New York Post*. February 12, 1988.

Staff Reporters of the *Wall Street Journal*. "Flagging Spirit: Esprit's Fortunes Sag as Couple at the Helm Battle over Its Image." *Wall Street Journal*. March 16, 1988:1, 17.

Thompson, A. P. "Extramarital Sex: A Review of the Research Literature." *The Journal of Sex Research*. 19 (February 1983):1–22.

——————. "Extramarital Sexual Crisis: Common Themes and Therapy Implications." *Journal of Sex and Marital Therapy*. 10 (Winter 1984): 239–254.

Thompson, J. *Organizations in Action*. New York: McGraw-Hill, 1967.

Westhoff, L. "What to Do about Corporate Romance." *Management Review*. February 1987:50–55.

——————. *Corporate Romance*. New York: Time/Life Books, 1986.

APPENDIX C:
Primary Survey Sources

The American Society for Personnel Administration (ASPA) Survey (1987):
> McLaughlin, F., and Ford, R. C. "Should Cupid Come to the Workplace?" *Personnel Administrator*. October 1987.

The Anderson and Hunsaker Survey (1985):
> Anderson, C., and Hunsaker, P. "Why There's Romancing at the Office and Why It's Everyone's Problem." *Personnel*. February 1985: 57–63.

The Bureau of National Affairs Report (1988):
> Bureau of National Affairs, Inc. *Corporate Affairs: Nepotism, Office Romance, and Sexual Harassment*. Washington, D.C., 1988.

The *Business Week* Survey (1984):
> Staff Reporters of *Business Week*. "Romance in the Workplace: Corporate Rules for the Game of Love." *Business Week*. June 18, 1984.

The Feinberg and Levenstein Survey (1982):
> Unpublished survey by BFS Psychological Associates of New York, cited in *The Wall Street Journal*. November 29, 1982:26.

The Fortune 500 Survey (1985):
> Swartz, R. A. Fortune 500 Survey, cited in the Bureau of National Affairs report, *Corporate Affairs: Nepotism, Office Romance, and*

Sexual Harassment. A BNA Special Report. Washington, D.C., 1988.

The *Men's Health* Survey (1987):

Staff Reporters of *Men's Health.* "Desire under the Desk." *Men's Health.* Fall 1987.

The *Newsweek* Survey (1988):

Staff Reporters of *Newsweek.* "Love in the Office." *Newsweek.* February 15, 1988:52.

The Powell Survey (1986):

Powell, G. "What Do Tomorrow's Managers Think about Sexual Intimacy in the Workplace?" *Business Horizons.* 29(4) (July/August 1986) 32–33.

The Quinn Survey (1977):

Quinn, R. "Coping with Cupid: The Formation, Impact, and Management of Romantic Relationships in Organizations." *Administrative Science Quarterly.* 22 (1977):30–45.

Office Romance Survey Results

Sample Characteristics

Demographic industry statistics: N = 100 respondents

Marketing/Sales	10%
Computers/Data Processing	8%
Recruitment/Real Estate/Brokerage	7%
Medical/Legal/Educational	13%
Publishing/Media/Communications	12%
Manufacturing/Chemicals/Shipping	10%
Banking/Accounting/Insurance	19%
Retail/Cosmetics/Fashion	5%
Electrical/Contracting	4%
Other	12%
	100%

Size of company: __28%__ Fortune 500 __48%__ Medium-sized
__24%__ Entrepreneurial

Survey Responses

1. Are you aware of, or have you ever personally been involved in, an office romance in your company or organization?

__76%__ Yes __24%__ No

2. In your opinion, how commonplace are office romances in your company?

    26% Very common

    37% Beginning to happen more and more

    37% Not at all common

3. Does your company have a *formal* policy on office romance, as distinguished from a policy on sexual harassment?

    12% Yes

    88% No, not yet

4. Is there an *informal* norm or policy in your company culture regarding office romance?

If so, how would you describe it?

    32% Romance is discouraged.

    68% Romance is neither discouraged nor encouraged.

5. If an informal norm or policy exists, is it applied differently according to level?

    18% Romance is discouraged, especially between boss-subordinates, but not discouraged among peers.

    5% Romance is discouraged among members of the same department, but not discouraged among members in different departments.

    77% Difficult to say; depends on the individual situation.

6. How would you describe your company culture?

    50% Action-oriented, creative, innovative

    50% Reactive, conservative, traditional

7. How would you describe your departmental culture?

    55% Action-oriented, creative, innovative

    45% Reactive, conservative, traditional

8. In your opinion, what are the perceived *risks* for those who participate in an office romance? (Responses may not total to 100 due to multiples.)

    63% Careers could be threatened.

    65% Professional relationships could be ruined.

    55% Work performance may decline.

    55% Coworkers may lose respect.

    71% I don't believe there are any risks if the couple acts professionally.

9. In general, what *benefits* can be achieved from an office romance in the work environment? (Responses may not total to 100 due to multiples.)

34%	Improved morale because "love is in the air"
26%	People easier to deal with when they're in love
27%	Improved communication, teamwork, and cooperation among depts.
34%	Increased creativity and innovation
53%	I don't believe there are any benefits.

10. Do the risks and benefits depend upon gender?

55%	Risks are greater for women.
10%	Benefits are greater for men.
35%	Risks and benefits are applied equally regardless of gender.

11. Do the risks and benefits depend upon level?

63%	Risks are greater for higher level managers in the company.
6%	Benefits are greater for lower level employees.
31%	Risks and benefits do not depend on level in the company.

Survey Case Data (N = 94)

12. Think of an office romance that you may have observed in a work environment. What levels did the participants represent?

30%	Peers at the same level in different departments
23%	Peers at the same level in the same or closely related dept.
24%	Boss-subordinate relationship across levels
21%	Boss-subordinate relationship in the same department
29%	No information

13. How visible were the participants regarding their romance?

20%	Very visible; everyone knew about the romance
40%	Somewhat visible; some people knew but others did not
36%	Not at all; the couple thought no one knew, but we did
4%	No information

14. What happened to the participants as they pursued their romance (Responses may not equal 100% due to multiples.)

     41%   They were easier to get along with.

     10%   They were more difficult to get along with.

     29%   They were more productive in their jobs.

     23%   They were less productive in their jobs.

     28%   Coworkers lost respect for them because of the romance.

     36%   Coworkers resented the romance because they showed favoritism to each other.

15. What actions by management were taken, if any?

     64%   No action at all; management turned a blind eye.

     10%   Management forced a transfer or dismissal of one party.

     10%   Management issued reprimands and warnings.

     25%   One party willingly transferred or left the company.

16. Please add whatever additional comments you would like to offer on this controversial subject. *Thank you for your participation!*

APPENDIX E:

Legal Issues

Companies vary in their attitudes toward office romance. Some have policies, others rely on informal norms in their corporate cultures. But legally, what can and cannot a company do?

According to the 1988 Bureau of National Affairs report, a review of current law and the most significant court rulings reveal that:

1. *Employers may prohibit dating in their work environment.* But few do so. Employers must demonstrate that dating and romantic relationships interfere with company morale; risk creating favoritism or the appearance of it in hiring, assignment, and promotion decisions; and may result in reduced work productivity. Several employee challenges to dating bans have also been upheld, so this may be in question in future years.

2. Thus far, *no court has found that discrimination based on a dating relationship is equivalent to discrimination based on marital status.* However, some courts recognize that dating relationships spur the same arguments employers use to justify rules prohibiting married couples—harm to employee morale, favoritism, and reduced productivity. But these same courts have ruled that marital status discrimination laws only protect and further the sanctity of marriage, and do not apply to dating.

3. *Romantic relationship prohibitions on public workers may infringe on their right to privacy and therefore be subject to court decision on employees' constitutional claims under a strict scrutiny standard.* Rules prohibiting dating among employees probably will be upheld, although three current U.S. Supreme Court justices have opposed them.

4. *Where an employee submits to the sexual advances of a supervisor and is granted a promotion or some other employment benefit because of that submission, another employee who is harmed by the favoritism has a right of action under Title VII of the Civil Rights Act of 1964,* which bars discrimination on the basis of sex. However, it is not clear whether such a right of action exists if the favored employee has entered into the sexual relationship willingly and without coercion.

Please be aware that legal doctrine on this matter varies from state to state. Sample cases from recent court rulings that appeared in the Bureau of National Affairs 1988 report are:

ROMANCE AND EMPLOYMENT AT WILL

Rulon-Miller v. IBM, Calif Ct App, 1984, 117LRRM 3309
A now-famous case between Gina Rulon-Miller and IBM. Ms. Rulon-Miller was fired from IBM because she was dating an employee of a competitor. She brought suit, and the court upheld a $200,000 jury award in favor of Rulon-Miller due to the covenant of good faith and fair-dealing practices in the state of California.

Crozier vs. UPS, Calif Ct App, 1983, 115 LRRM 3535
Crozier, a manager, was discharged for dating a non-manager, in violation of UPS policy prohibiting fraternization. Because morale had been disrupted and the plaintiff had promoted the women he had been dating, the court argued there was good cause for dismissal. The UPS decision was upheld.

MARITAL STATUS DISCRIMINATION

C. *Thorrez Industries v. Mich Dept of Civil Rights,* Mich Ct App, 1979, 24 FEP Cases 113
A female employee brought suit under the state's fair employment practices law, which prohibits discrimination on the basis of marital status. She alleged that she had been discharged as a result of her affair

with another employee; he was not fired. Because the male employee was valuable to the firm because of key skills, the owner discharged the plaintiff. The court ruled that the employer chose to discharge the female employee not because of her sex but because she was less skilled and trained and upheld the employer's decision.

Manhattan Pizza Hut v. New York State Human Rights Appeal Board, NY Ct App, 1980, 51 N.Y. 2nd 506, 415 N.E. 2d 950, 434 N.Y.S. 42d 961
The state's highest court found that New York's anti-discrimination law referred only to an individual's status—whether married, separated, divorced, widowed, or single—and was not intended to forbid employment discrimination based on the marital relationship, only on marital status. The state law would not prohibit employers from discriminating against employees who were married to supervisors.

RIGHTS TO PRIVACY

Rodgers vs. IBM, DC WPa, 1980, 115 LRRM 4608
The U.S. District Court in Western Pennsylvania found that a manager's right to privacy had not been infringed upon when he was discharged following complaints from coworkers about his personal relationship with a subordinate.

Hollenbaugh vs. Carnegie, DC WPa, 1977, 436 F.Supp 1328, aff'g, CA 3, 1978, 578 F.2nd 1374, cert den., US SupCt, 1978, 439 U.S. 1052
A claim alleging violation of the right to privacy under the First, Fourth, Ninth, and Fourteenth Amendments to the U.S. Constitution was rejected in an action brought by two library employees fired for engaging in "open adultery." Since evidence showed that members of the community were aware of and objected to the librarians' living arrangements, the Supreme Court of the United States found that the discharge was not arbitrary, unreasonable, or capricious, and therefore did not violate their equal protection rights nor rights of privacy.

TITLE VII CASES

Kersul v. Skulls Angels, Inc., DC SNY, 1985, 42 FEP Cases 987
The U.S. District Court held that an employee had stated a claim under Title VII by alleging that she was denied favorable benefits and terms and conditions of employment because her supervisor favored another employee with whom he had a sexual relationship.

King v. Palmer, CA DC, 1985, 39 FEP Cases 877
A nurse brought suit under Title VII after she failed to obtain a promotion to a supervisory position, allegedly because the individual who received the promotion had a sexual relationship with her supervisor. The court ruled in favor of the defendant, saying that the woman had failed to submit direct proof that the sexual relationship had been consummated. But the District of Columbia Court reversed the decision, ruling that direct proof was not necessary.

For a more complete legal case list, please refer to the Bureau of National Affairs Special Report, *Corporate Affairs: Nepotism, Office Romance, and Sexual Harassment*, 1988, published by the Bureau at 1231 25th Street, NW, Washington, D.C., 20037.

CREDITS

pp. 4, 172—These survey results are reprinted by permission of *News Health* magazine. Copyright © 1987 Rodale Press, Inc. All rights reserved.

pp. 14, 31–33—These quotes are reprinted, by permission of the publisher, from "Managing Attraction and Intimacy at Work" by Marcy Crary, *Organizational Dynamics*, Spring 1986. Copyright © 1986 by American Management Association, New York. All rights reserved.

p. 51—The quote from "Managing Sexual Attraction in the Workplace," by Kaleel Jamison, is from *Personnel Administrator*, copyright © 1983, the American Society for Personnel Administration, Alexandria, Va.

p. 52—This quote and other material from this article reprinted, by permission of the publisher, from "Why There's Romancing at the Office," by Anderson and Hunsaker from *Personnel*, February 1985. Copyright © 1985 by American Management Association, New York. The rights reserved.

pp. 98–99, 145—The quotes on these pages are reprinted by permission of the *Harvard Business Review*. Excerpts from "Managers and Lovers" by Eliza G. C. Collins, September/October 1983. Copyright © 1983 by the President and Fellows of Harvard College; all rights reserved.

p. 106—The material attributed to professors Deal and Kennedy is adapted from *Corporate Cultures*, copyright © 1982, Addison-Wesley Publishing Co., Inc., Reading, Massachusetts. Used with permission.

287

pp. 120–121—The quote on these pages is from Morrison, White, and Van Velsor, *Breaking the Glass Ceiling*, copyright © 1987, Addison-Wesley Publishing Co., Inc., Reading, Massachusetts. Reprinted with permission.

p. 123–124—This quote is from *Men and Women of the Corporation*, Rosabeth Moss Kanter copyright 1977, Basic Books, New York.

p. 125—The quote here, an excerpt from "Power Failure in Management Circuits" by Rosabeth Moss Kanter, is reprinted by permission of the *Harvard Business Review* (July/August 1979). Copyright © 1979 by the President and Fellows of Harvard College; all rights reserved.

pp. 73, 124–125—The quotes given on these pages are from *Powerplay: What Really Happened at Bendix*, by Mary Cunningham. Copyright © 1984, Simon and Schuster, New York.

pp. 131, 231—The quotes on these pages and the material in Appendix E are from *Corporate Affairs: Nepotism, Office Romance and Sexual Harassment* (A BNA Special Report). Copyright © 1988 by the Bureau of National Affairs, Inc., Washington, D.C. Reprinted by permission.

pp. 147, 149—The quotes on these pages are from *Games Mother Never Taught You*, by Betty Lehan Harragan, copyright © 1977, Rawson Associates, New York.

pp. 153–154—The quote on these pages is from Clawson and Kram, "Managing Cross-Gender Mentoring," in *Business Horizons*, May–June 1984, pp. 22–32.

p. 184—The quote here is reprinted from "Coping with Cupid: The Formation, Impact, and Management of Romantic Relationships in Organizations," by Robert E. Quinn, published in *Administrative Sciences Quarterly*, vol. 22, #1. Copyright © 1977 Administrative Science Quarterly. The references on page 24 are adapted from the same source.

pp. 191 and 206–207—The data on page 191 and the quote on pages 206–207 are from "Extramarital Sexual Crisis: Common Themes and Therapy Implications," in the *Journal of Sexual and Marital Therapy*, Copyright © Winter 1984, pp. 239–254.

p. 191—The reference to 70 percent of women married five years or less having participated in an adulterous affair is taken from *Women in Love: A Cultural Revolution in Progress*, by Shere Hite, Alfred A. Knopf, copyright © 1987.

p. 221—The material on the stages of relationships is adapted from *How to Make Love All the Time*, by Barbara DeAngelis, copyright © 1987, Rawson Associates, New York.

pp. 207–208—The quotes on these pages are from *Intimate Partners: Patterns in Love and Marriage*, copyright © 1987, Alfred A. Knopf.

p. 247—The quote on this page is from an article in *Redbook*, copyright © 1978, Mary Catherine Bateson and Rhoda Metraux.

INDEX

Printed in the United States
By Bookmasters